To PETER

CCSP Self-Study
CCSP CSI
Exam Certification Guide

Ido Dubrawsky
Paul Grey, CCIE No. 10470

Cisco Press

800 East 96th Street
Indianapolis, IN 46240 USA

CCSP Self-Study
CCSP CSI Exam Certification Guide

Ido Dubrawsky
Paul Grey

Copyright© 2004 Cisco Systems, Inc.

Published by:
Cisco Press
800 East 96th Street
Indianapolis, IN 46240 USA

Printed in the United States of America 1 2 3 4 5 6 7 8 9 0

First Printing December 2003

Library of Congress Cataloging-in-Publication Number: 2003101711

ISBN: 1-58720-089-9

Warning and Disclaimer

This book is designed to provide information about the Cisco CSI exam. Every effort has been made to make this book as complete and as accurate as possible, but no warranty or fitness is implied.

The information is provided on an "as is" basis. The authors, Cisco Press, and Cisco Systems, Inc., shall have neither liability nor responsibility to any person or entity with respect to any loss or damages arising from the information contained in this book or from the use of the discs or programs that may accompany it.

The opinions expressed in this book belong to the authors and are not necessarily those of Cisco Systems, Inc.

Trademark Acknowledgments

All terms mentioned in this book that are known to be trademarks or service marks have been appropriately capitalized. Cisco Press or Cisco Systems, Inc., cannot attest to the accuracy of this information. Use of a term in this book should not be regarded as affecting the validity of any trademark or service mark.

Corporate and Government Sales

Cisco Press offers excellent discounts on this book when ordered in quantity for bulk purchases or special sales. For more information, please contact: **U.S. Corporate and Government Sales**   1-800-382-3419   corpsales@pearsontechgroup.com.

For sales outside of the U.S. please contact: **International Sales**   1-317-581-3793   international@pearsontechgroup.com.

Feedback Information

At Cisco Press, our goal is to create in-depth technical books of the highest quality and value. Each book is crafted with care and precision, undergoing rigorous development that involves the unique expertise of members from the professional technical community.

Readers' feedback is a natural continuation of this process. If you have any comments regarding how we could improve the quality of this book, or otherwise alter it to better suit your needs, you can contact us through e-mail at feedback@ciscopress.com. Please make sure to include the book title and ISBN in your message.

We greatly appreciate your assistance.

Publisher: John Wait

Editor-in-Chief: John Kane

Executive Editor: Brett Bartow

Production Manager: Patrick Kanouse

Acquisitions Editor: Michelle Grandin

Development Editors: Dayna Isley, Betsey Henkels

Copy Editor: Bill McManus

Team Coordinator: Tammi Barnett

Book and Cover Designer: Louisa Adair

Composition: Interactive Composition Corporation

Indexer: Brad Herriman

Cisco Press Program Manager: Sonia Torres Chavez

Cisco Representative: Anthony Wolfenden

Manager, Marketing Communications, Cisco Systems: Scott Miller

Cisco Marketing Program Manager: Edie Quiroz

Technical Editors: Greg Abelar, Steve Hanna, Michael Overstreet

CD-ROM Reviewer: Jamey Brooks

CISCO SYSTEMS

Corporate Headquarters
Cisco Systems, Inc.
170 West Tasman Drive
San Jose, CA 95134-1706
USA
http://www.cisco.com
Tel: 408 526-4000
      800 553-NETS (6387)
Fax: 408 526-4100

European Headquarters
Cisco Systems Europe
11 Rue Camille Desmoulins
92782 Issy-les-Moulineaux
Cedex 9
France
http://www-europe.cisco.com
Tel: 33 1 58 04 60 00
Fax: 33 1 58 04 61 00

Americas Headquarters
Cisco Systems, Inc.
170 West Tasman Drive
San Jose, CA 95134-1706
USA
http://www.cisco.com
Tel: 408 526-7660
Fax: 408 527-0883

Asia Pacific Headquarters
Cisco Systems Australia, Pty.,
Ltd
Level 17, 99 Walker Street
North Sydney
NSW 2059 Australia
http://www.cisco.com
Tel: +61 2 8448 7100
Fax: +61 2 9957 4350

Cisco Systems has more than 200 offices in the following countries. Addresses, phone numbers, and fax numbers are listed on the Cisco Web site at www.cisco.com/go/offices

Argentina • Australia • Austria • Belgium • Brazil • Bulgaria • Canada • Chile • China • Colombia • Costa Rica • Croatia • Czech Republic • Denmark • Dubai, UAE • Finland • France • Germany • Greece • Hong Kong Hungary • India • Indonesia • Ireland • Israel • Italy • Japan • Korea • Luxembourg • Malaysia • Mexico The Netherlands • New Zealand • Norway • Peru • Philippines • Poland • Portugal • Puerto Rico • Romania Russia • Saudi Arabia • Scotland • Singapore • Slovakia • Slovenia • South Africa • Spain • Sweden Switzerland • Taiwan • Thailand • Turkey • Ukraine • United Kingdom • United States • Venezuela • Vietnam Zimbabwe

About the Authors

Ido Dubrawsky is a network security architect with the Cisco Systems, Inc., SAFE Architecture Team. He is the primary author of the SAFE Layer 2 Application Note, the SAFE in Action white paper "SAFE SQL Slammer Worm Attack Mitigation," and the white paper "SAFE: IDS Deployment, Tuning, and Logging in Depth." Prior to his work in SAFE, Ido was a member of the Cisco Secure Consulting Service, providing network security assessment and consulting services to customers worldwide. Ido has contributed to numerous books and written extensively on network security and system administration topics. Ido has been working as a system and network administrator for ten years and has focused on network security for the past five years. He holds bachelor's and master's degrees in aerospace engineering from the University of Texas at Austin. He currently resides in Silver Spring, Maryland, with his wife and children.

Paul Grey, CCIE No. 10470, is a senior network architect for Boxing Orange Limited, a leading UK security specialist company, where he provides consultative, design, and implementation services using Cisco products. Paul also holds the CCNP, CCDP, and CCSP certifications and has more than 15 years of experience in the field of designing and implementing networking solutions. He has primarily focused on security solutions over the past 18 months and is currently pursuing his CCIE Security certification. Paul holds a bachelor's in chemistry and physiology from the University of Sheffield.

About the Technical Reviewers

Greg Abelar is a seven year veteran of Cisco Systems, Inc. Greg helped train and assemble the world-class Cisco Technical Assistance Center Security Organization. He is a sought-after speaker on the subject of security architecture. In addition he founded, project managed, and contributed content to the CCIE Security Written Exam.

Steven Hanna is an education specialist at Cisco Systems, Inc., where he designs and develops training on Cisco network security products. Steven has more than eight years of experience in the education field, having been an earth science teacher, a technical instructor, an instructor mentor, and a course developer. Having more than 11 years of experience in the IT field in general, Steven has worked as a network engineer or in an educational role for Productivity Point International, Apple Computer, MCI, Schlumberger Oilfield Services, 3M, and Tivoli Systems, among others. He graduated from the University of Texas at Austin with degrees in geology, political science, and education. He currently holds certifications from the state of Texas, the federal government, Novell, Microsoft, Legato, Tivoli, and Cisco.

Michael Overstreet is the technical team lead for the Security Posture Assessment (SPA) Team at Cisco Systems, Inc. He has more than 10 years experience in networking and network administration, with seven of those years spent in network security. He has worked at Cisco Systems for five years in various roles within the SPA Team. Michael holds a bachelor's degree in computer science from Christopher Newport University.

Dedications

From Ido Dubrawsky:

I wish to thank my beloved wife, Diana, for putting up with all of the late nights and time lost together working on this project—she is truly an Eishet Chayil to me. I would also like to thank my three wonderful children, Isaac, Hadas, and Rinat, for being as good and as understanding as they are when daddy can't spend as much time as they would like playing with them and being with them.

I also wish to thank my parents, Chagai and Nechama Dubrawsky, as well as my sister, Malka, and my brother Amos. Each of you has taught me a different lesson on the importance of hard work and family and has given me the support I needed to finish this project.

From Paul Grey:

This book is dedicated to my loving wife, Carmel, for her never-ending support and belief in me. I would not be where I am today without you and thank you for putting up with the late nights and neglect whilst working on this project and over the past years whilst pursuing my career.

Finally, I must not forget the frequent distractions from my two dogs, Petra and Scotty; they always seemed to know when I needed a quick break from the book.

Acknowledgments

Ido Dubrawsky: Paul Grey, for being a wonderful co-author with me on this project. If you hadn't signed on to this Paul, I certainly wasn't going to do it alone!

Michelle Grandin, acquisitions editor, who must have been biting her nails until the last day hoping I would get all of the chapters done on time. Also, thanks for finding me my co-author. Sorry for the added stress and thanks for sticking with me.

David Phillips, for hiring me at Cisco Systems, Inc., and letting me work with an exceptionally talented bunch of guys in the Cisco Secure Consulting Service.

Brian Ford, for making me laugh and for being a good friend when I needed to rant and rave.

Jason Halpern, for putting up with delays on the Layer 2 white paper while we moved from Austin to Silver Spring and for helping to open my eyes to a much wider picture than what I had been seeing by asking me to work in the SAFE architecture group.

To Greg Abelar, my friend and co-SAFE architect, for being willing to edit this manuscript. Also, thanks to Steve Hanna and Michael Overstreet for providing additional eyes to go over this material.

David Lesnoy, for being a great friend and a good listener when I needed to get away from this project.

Paul Grey: Ido Dubrawsky, for being a great co-author on this project. Even though we are on opposite sides of the world, I hope this partnership will develop into a long-lasting friendship.

Michelle Grandin, acquisitions editor, for her assistance in getting me started on this project, her guidance, and the gentle reminders of the deadlines.

Dayna Isley and Betsey Henkels, the development editors, for persevering in making this project a success. Thanks for sorting out all of the issues.

Andrew Mason, for his encouragement in pursuing this project and listening to my daily ranting and ravings.

Sean Convery and Bernie Trudel, authors of the original "SAFE Enterprise" white paper, and Sean Convery and Roland Saville, authors of the "SAFE: Extending the Security Blueprint to Small, Midsize, and Remote-User Networks" white paper.

All the technical editors—Greg Abelar, Steve Hanna, and Michael Overstreet—who contributed to the technical direction of this book, thanks to you all.

Finally, thanks goes to the rest of the Cisco Press team for bringing this book to fruition.

Contents at a Glance

Contents

Icons Used in This Book

Cisco Systems uses the following standard icons to represent different networking devices. You will encounter several of these icons within this book.

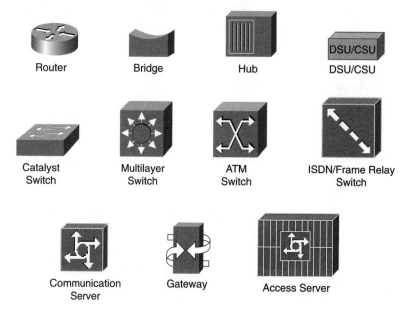

Router	Bridge	Hub	DSU/CSU
Catalyst Switch	Multilayer Switch	ATM Switch	ISDN/Frame Relay Switch
Communication Server	Gateway	Access Server	

Command Syntax Conventions

The conventions used to present command syntax in this book are the same conventions used in the *Cisco IOS Command Reference*, as follows:

- Vertical bars (|) separate alternative, mutually exclusive elements.

- Square brackets [ ] indicate optional elements.

- Braces { } indicate a required choice.

- Braces within brackets [{ }] indicate a required choice within an optional element.

- **Boldface** indicates commands and keywords that are entered literally as shown. In actual configuration examples and output (not general command syntax), boldface indicates commands that are manually input by the user (such as a **show** command).

- *Italics* indicate arguments for which you supply actual values.

Features of This Book

- **"Do I Know This Already?" Quiz**—Each chapter begins with a quiz that helps you determine the amount of time you need to spend studying that chapter. The first table in each chapter outlines the major topics discussed and the "Do I Know This Already?" quiz questions that correspond to those topics. After completing the quiz, use this table to help determine which topics of the chapter you need to focus on most.

- **Foundation Topics**—This is the core section of each chapter that explains the protocols, concepts, and configuration for the topics in the chapter.

- **Foundation Summary**—Near the end of each chapter, a summary collects the most important lists and tables from the chapter. The "Foundation Summary" section is designed to help you review the key concepts in the chapter if you score well on the "Do I Know This Already?" quiz, and these sections are excellent tools for last-minute review.

- **Q&A**—These end-of-the-chapter questions focus on recall, covering topics in the "Foundation Topics" section by using several types of questions. Because the "Do I Know This Already?" quiz questions can help increase your recall as well, you may find that some are restated in the "Q&A" sections. The Q&A is also an excellent tool for final review when your exam date is approaching.

- **CD-ROM-based practice exam**—The companion CD-ROM contains a large number of questions that you can answer by using the simulated exam feature or by using the topical review feature. This is the best tool for helping you prepare for the test-taking process.

Foreword

CCSP CSI Exam Certification Guide is a complete study tool for the CCSP CSI exam, enabling you to assess your knowledge, identify areas to concentrate your study, and master key concepts to help you succeed on the exams and in your daily job. The book is filled with features that help you master the skills to implement appropriate technologies to build secure networks based on the Cisco Systems SAFE Blueprint. This book was developed in cooperation with the Cisco Internet Learning Solutions Group. Cisco Press books are the only self-study books authorized by Cisco for CCSP exam preparation.

Cisco and Cisco Press present this material in text-based format to provide another learning vehicle for our customers and the broader user community in general. Although a publication does not duplicate the instructor-led or e-learning environment, we acknowledge that not everyone responds in the same way to the same delivery mechanism. It is our intent that presenting this material via a Cisco Press publication will enhance the transfer of knowledge to a broad audience of networking professionals.

Cisco Press will present study guides on existing and future exams through these Exam Certification Guides to help achieve Cisco Internet Learning Solutions Group's principal objectives: to educate the Cisco community of networking professionals and to enable that community to build and maintain reliable, scalable networks. The Cisco career certifications and classes that support these certifications are directed at meeting these objectives through a disciplined approach to progressive learning. To succeed on the Cisco career certifications exams, as well as in your daily job as a Cisco-certified professional, we recommend a blended learning solution that combines instructor-led, e-learning, and self-study training with hands-on experience. Cisco Systems has created an authorized Cisco Learning Partner program to provide you with the most highly qualified instruction and invaluable hands-on experience in lab and simulation environments. To learn more about Cisco Learning Partner programs available in your area, please go to www.cisco.com/go/authorizedtraining.

The books Cisco Press creates in partnership with Cisco Systems will meet the same standards for content quality demanded of our courses and certifications. It is our intent that you will find this and subsequent Cisco Press certification and training publications of value as you build your networking knowledge base.

Thomas M. Kelly
Vice-President, Internet Learning Solutions Group
Cisco Systems, Inc.
October 2003

Introduction

All About the Cisco Certified Security Professional Certification

The Cisco Certified Security Professional (CCSP) certification is the newest midlevel certification from Cisco Systems. This certification is on a par with CCNP and CCDP. The aim of this certification is to provide professional-level recognition to network engineers in the design and implementation of Cisco secure networks. This certification provides validation of knowledge and skills in key areas of security, including firewalls, intrusion detection, VPNs, identity, and security management.

To achieve the CCSP certification you must pass a set of five exams. Each exam covers a different topic in securing networks with Cisco equipment. These topics include

- Configuring perimeter routers

- Configuring Cisco routers with the Firewall Feature Set

- Securing Cisco routers, firewalls, and VPNs

- Configuring authentication, authorization, and accounting (AAA) on Cisco devices

- Deploying and implementing Cisco intrusion detection systems (IDSs)

- Configuring and monitoring Cisco routers, firewalls, VPN concentrators, and IDSs

- Configure site-to-site and remote-access VPNs using Cisco routers, firewalls, and VPN concentrators

This is not an exhaustive list of topics for the exams. For more detailed information about each specific exam and the topics covered by that exam, consult that exam's web page at Cisco.com.

Exams Required for Certification

Successful completion of a group of exams is required to achieve the CCSP certification. The exams generally match the topics covered in the official Cisco courses. Table I-1 summarizes CCSP exam-to-course mappings.

CCSP certifications are valid for three years like the CCNP and the CCDP. Re-certification is required to keep the certification valid for every three-year period after that.

Table I-1 *Exam-to-Course Mappings*

Certification	Course	Exam Number	Exam Name
CCNA	Introduction to Cisco Networking Technologies (INTRO) and Interconnecting Cisco Network Devices (ICND)	640-801 (or both exams 640-811 and 642-821)	CCNA Exam
CCSP	Securing Cisco IOS Networks	642-501	Securing Cisco IOS Networks (SECUR)
	Cisco Secure PIX Firewall Advanced	642-521	Cisco Secure PIX Firewall Advanced (CSPFA)
	Cisco Secure Intrusion Detection System	642-531	Cisco Secure Intrusion Detection System (CSIDS)
	Cisco Secure VPN	642-511	Cisco Secure VPN (CSVPN)
	Cisco SAFE Implementation	642-541	Cisco SAFE Implementation (CSI)

Other Certifications

Cisco has a wide variety of certifications beyond the CCSP. These certifications are outlined in Table I-2. For additional information regarding any Cisco certifications, consult the website at Cisco.com and clicking on **Learning & Events>Career Certifications and Paths**.

Table I-2 *Additional Cisco Certifications*

Certification	Purpose, Prerequisites
CCNA	Demonstrates a basic level of knowledge of networking and Cisco device configuration
CCDA	Demonstrates a basic level of knowledge in the design and implementation of networks using Cisco equipment
CCNP	Indicates an advanced level of knowledge with networks and network protocols
CCDP	Indicates an advanced level of knowledge of network design using LAN, WAN, and remote access systems
CCIP	Advanced certification focusing on individuals working at service providers who have a detailed understanding of networking technologies such as IP routing, IP QoS, BGP, and MPLS
CCIE—Service Provider	Expert level certification covering IP and IP routing, optical, DSL, dial, cable, wireless, WAN switching, content networking, and IP telephony

Table I-2 *Additional Cisco Certifications (Continued)*

Certification	Purpose, Prerequisites
CCIE—Routing and Switching	Expert-level certification focusing on IP, IP routing, non-IP desktop protocols such as IPX and SNA, and bridge- and switch-related technologies
CCIE—Voice	Focuses solely on those technologies and applications that comprise a Cisco Enterprise VoIP solution
CCIE—Security	Expert-level certification covering IP and IP routing as well as specific security technologies and Cisco implementations of those technologies

The remainder of this introduction covers how to use this book to prepare for the Cisco CSI Implementation exam.

CSI Exam Blueprint

The CSI exam focuses on the "SAFE: Extending the Security Blueprint to Small, Midsize, and Remote-User Networks" blueprint (SAFE SMR for short), published in 2001. This blueprint covers designing and securing small and medium-sized networks and providing secure network access to remote users, such as mobile workers and telecommuters.

The CSI course provides the knowledge and skills needed to implement and use the principles and axioms presented in the SAFE SMR white paper. The course primarily focuses on the labs. These labs allow students to build complete end-to-end security solutions using the SAFE SMR white paper as the blueprint. The following devices are covered in the course as well as their configuration and functionality with regard to the SAFE SMR white paper:

- Cisco IOS routers
- PIX Firewalls
- VPN Concentrators
- Cisco IDS Sensors
- Cisco HIDS
- Cisco VPN Client (Software and Hardware)

The CSI exam covers a variety of topics related to the course and the SAFE SMR white paper. Table I-3 lists these topics along with the applicable chapter in which information on each topic can be found in this guide. Note that because security vulnerabilities and preventative measures continue apace, Cisco Systems reserves the right to change the exam objectives without notice. Although you may refer to the list of exam objectives listed in Table I-3, always check on the Cisco Systems website to verify the actual list of objectives to be sure you are prepared before taking an exam. You can view the current exam objectives on any current Cisco certification exam by visiting their website at Cisco.com and clicking **Learning & Events>Career Certifications and Paths**.

Table I-3 *CSI Exam Objectives*

Objective	Chapter Covering the Objective
Security Fundamentals	
Need for Network Security	5
Network Attack Taxonomy	6–9
Network Security Policy	5
Management Protocols and Functions	10
Architectural Overview	
Design Fundamentals	2, 4
SAFE Axioms	3
Security Wheel	5
Cisco Security Portfolio	
Secure Connectivity—Virtual Private Network Solutions	12
Secure Connectivity—The 3000 Concentrator Series	12
Secure Connectivity—Cisco VPN-Optimized Routers	12
Perimeter Security Firewalls—Cisco PIX and Cisco IOS Firewall	12
Intrusion Protection—IDS and Cisco Secure Scanner	11
Identity—Access Control Solutions	12
Security Management—VMS and CSPM	12
Cisco AVVID	12
SAFE Small Network Design	
Small Network Corporate Internet Module	13
Small Network Campus Module	13
Implementation—ISP Router	14
Implementation—Cisco IOS Firewall Features and Configuration	14
Implementation—PIX Firewall	14

Table I-3 *CSI Exam Objectives (Continued)*

Objective	Chapter Covering the Objective
SAFE Medium-Sized Network Design	
Medium-Sized Network Corporate Internet Module	15
Medium-Sized Network Corporate Internet Module Design Guidelines	15
Medium-Sized Network Campus Module	15
Medium-Sized Network Campus Module Design Guidelines	15
Medium-Sized Network WAN Module	15
Implementation—ISP Router	16
Implementation—Edge Router	16
Implementation—Cisco IOS Firewall	16
Implementation—PIX Firewall	16
Implementation—NIDS	16
Implementation—HIDS	16
Implementation—VPN Concentrator	16
Implementation—Layer 3 Switch	16
SAFE Remote-User Network Implementation	
Key Devices	17
Threat Mitigation	17
Software Access Option	17
Remote-Site Firewall Option	17
Hardware VPN Client Option	17
Remote-Site Router Option	17

Recommended Training for CCSP

The recommended training path for the CCSP certification is as follows:

- **Securing Cisco IOS Networks (SECUR)**—Covers router security, AAA, basic threat mitigation, Cisco IOS Firewall CBAC, authentication proxy, and IDS implementation, as well as configuring IPSec on Cisco IOS routers.

- **Cisco Secure VPN (CSVPN)**—Covers VPNs and IPSec technologies, configuring the Cisco VPN 3000 concentrator and the Cisco VPN 3002 hardware client, and configuring the Cisco VPN 3000 concentrator for LAN-to-LAN IPSec tunnels using preshared keys, digital certificates, and NAT.

- **Cisco Secure PIX Firewall Advanced (CSPFA)**—Covers the PIX Firewall family, PIX configuration, access control lists (ACLs), translations, object grouping, IPSec connections, and firewall management.

- **Cisco Secure Intrusion Detection System (CSIDS)**—Covers IDS configuration, alarms and signatures, signature and IP blocking configuration, Cisco IDS architecture and maintenance, and enterprise IDS management.

- **Cisco SAFE Implementation (CSI)**—Covers the design of networks based on the SAFE SMR white paper.

Figure I-1 illustrates the training track for CCSP as of April 2003.

This Book's Audience

This book is written for the network engineer who already has a strong background in network operations. It is assumed that the reader has some background in network security and understands such concepts as network scans, exploitation, and defense. Security operations personnel will also find this book useful in understanding the Cisco SAFE design for small, midsize, and remote-user networks.

How to Use This Book to Pass the Exam

One way to use this book is to read it from cover to cover. Although that may be helpful to many people, it also may not be very time efficient, especially if you already know some of the material covered by this book.

One effective method is to take the "Do I Know This Already?" quiz at the beginning of each chapter. You can determine how to proceed with the material in the chapter based on your score on the quiz. If you get a high score, you might simply review the "Foundation Summary" section of that chapter. Otherwise, you should review the entire chapter. These are simply guidelines to help you effectively manage your time while preparing for this exam.

This book is broken into six parts that cover each of the CSI exam topics.

Figure I-1 *CCSP Training/Exam Track*

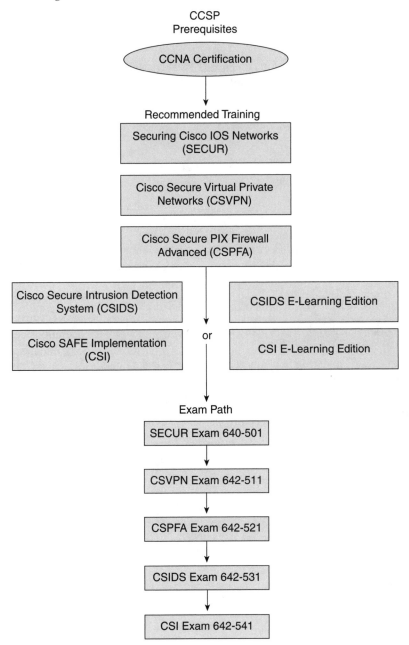

Part I, "Cisco SAFE Overview," includes Chapters 1 to 4:

- Chapter 1, "What Is SAFE?" introduces the SAFE network architecture blueprints and the purpose of each.

- Chapter 2, "SAFE Design Fundamentals," introduces some of the basic design principles that are used to develop the SAFE small, medium-sized, and remote-user network designs and the classifications of security threats.

- Chapter 3, "SAFE Design Concepts," reviews the five axioms described in the SAFE blueprints.

- Chapter 4, "Understanding SAFE Network Modules," describes the Campus, Corporate Internet, and WAN modules.

Part II, "Understanding Security Risks and Mitigation Techniques," includes Chapters 5 to 10:

- Chapter 5, "Defining a Security Policy," explains the need for a security policy and the goals and components it should contain. This chapter also describes the Security Wheel concept.

- Chapter 6, "Classifying Rudimentary Network Attacks," covers many common attacks, including reconnaissance attacks, unauthorized access, DoS attacks, application layer attacks, and trust exploitation attacks.

- Chapter 7, "Classifying Sophisticated Network Attacks," builds on Chapter 6 by covering more advanced attacks, including IP spoofing attacks, traffic sniffing, password attacks, man-in-the-middle attacks, port redirection, and virus and Trojan-horse applications.

- Chapter 8, "Mitigating Rudimentary Network Attacks," includes methods to protect your network against the attacks discussed in Chapter 6.

- Chapter 9, "Mitigating Sophisticated Network Attacks," describes methods to protect your network against the attacks described in Chapter 7.

- Chapter 10, "Network Management," describes in-band and out-of-band network management as well as network management protocols, including Telnet, SSH, SSL, syslog, SNMP, TFTP, and NTP.

Part III, "Cisco Security Portfolio," includes Chapters 11 and 12:

- Chapter 11, "Cisco Perimeter Security Products," concentrates on the perimeter security and intrusion detection options offered by Cisco.

- Chapter 12, "Cisco Network Core Security Products," describes Cisco products for securing network connectivity, securing identity, and managing security and then describes Cisco AVVID.

Part IV, "Designing and Implementing SAFE Networks," includes Chapters 13 to 17:

■ Chapter 13, "Designing Small SAFE Networks," describes the components of a SAFE small network design and shows examples of the Campus module and Corporate Internet module in a small network.

■ Chapter 14, "Implementing Small SAFE Networks," uses the design recommendations discussed in Chapter 13 as a basis for examining the specific configuration requirements for each component of the small network.

■ Chapter 15, "Designing Medium-Sized SAFE Networks," examines the specific security design requirements of the SAFE medium-sized network, including design guidelines and alternatives for each module.

■ Chapter 16, "Implementing Medium-Sized SAFE Networks," builds on Chapter 15 by describing the configuration requirements for achieving the desired functionality in your medium-sized network.

■ Chapter 17, "Designing Remote SAFE Networks," examines the security design requirements of a remote-user network.

Part V, "Scenarios," includes Chapter 18:

■ Chapter 18, "Scenarios for Final Preparation," combines the topics discussed throughout the book into six scenarios. This chapter emphasizes an overall understanding of the SAFE design philosophy, associated security threats, threat mitigation, the Cisco Secure product portfolio, and the implementation of these products used in the small, midsize, and remote-user network designs.

Part VI, "Appendixes," includes the following:

■ Appendix A, "Answers to the 'Do I Know This Already?' Quizzes and Q&A Sections," provides the answers to the quizzes that appear in each chapter.

■ Appendix B, "General Configuration Guidelines for Cisco Router and Switch Security," summarizes general recommendations that you should consider adopting on all Cisco routers and switches to tighten the security of these devices.

The following sections provide answers to common questions related to the CSI exam.

Are the Prerequisites Required to Pass the Exam?

Attaining the CCNA certification is not a requirement to pass this exam. It is theoretically possible to pass this exam without first taking the CCNA exam; however, it would be extremely difficult to pass this exam without having a CCNA *equivalent* level of knowledge. Much of this exam is dependent on familiarization with Cisco equipment features and configuring those features. The CCNA exam tests the student's level of knowledge and familiarization of the Cisco IOS command line as well as basic concepts in networking. *Note that although it is not required that you first take the CCNA exam before taking any of the CCSP exams, you will not receive the CCSP certification until you have obtained the CCNA certification.*

I've Completed All Prerequisites for the CCSP Except Taking CSI—Now What?

Once you have taken all of the CCSP exams except for the CSI exam, you need only prepare for this exam and take it. Successfully completing the other CCSP exams will help you significantly with this exam, because it may ask questions about some of the Cisco security equipment that you have already been tested on in the other exams. Taking the other CCSP exams before approaching the CSI exam may well be one of the better study methods for passing the CSI exam.

I Have Not Taken All the Prerequisites—Will This Book Still Help Me to Pass?

That is a hard question to answer. It all depends on your level of knowledge, familiarity, and comfort with Cisco security products. This book is designed to help you prepare to take the CSI exam; however, it is not a guarantee that if you work through this book you will pass the exam. That is still very much dependent on you and your experience.

Exam Registration

The CSI exam is a computer-based exam, with multiple-choice, fill-in-the-blank, list-in-order, and simulation-based questions. You can take the exam at any Pearson VUE (http://www.pearsonvue.com) or Prometric (http://www.2test.com) testing center. Your testing center can tell you the exact length of the exam. Be aware that when you register for the exam, you might be told to allow a certain amount of time to take the exam that is longer than the testing time indicated by the testing software when you begin. This is because VUE and Prometric want you to allow for some time to get settled and take the tutorial about the testing engine.

Book Content Updates

Because Cisco Systems will occasionally update exam objectives without notice, Cisco Press may post additional preparatory content on the web page associated with this book at http://www .ciscopress.com/1587200899. It's a good idea to check the website a couple of weeks before taking your exam, to review any updated content that may be posted online. We also recommend that you periodically check back to this page on the Cisco Press website to view any errata or supporting book files that my be available.

The *CCSP CSI Exam Certification Guide* is designed to help you attain CCSP certification by successfully preparing you for the CSI exam. In addition to the exam topics covered, this book provides several scenarios to help guide you through some of the concepts inherent in SAFE so that you understand how implementing those concepts can lead you to design and implement a more secure network. Additionally, this book provides a CD-ROM with example test questions to help you practice taking the exam. It is up to you, however, to use this guide as you see appropriate in your preparation for the CSI exam. Good luck.

Part I covers the following Cisco CSI exam topics:

- Design Fundamentals
- SAFE Axioms

Part I: Cisco SAFE Overview

This chapter covers the following topics:

- SAFE: A Security Blueprint for Enterprise Networks

- SAFE: Extending the Security Blueprint to Small, Midsize, and Remote-User Networks

- SAFE VPN: IPSec Virtual Private Networks in Depth

- SAFE: Wireless LAN Security in Depth–Version 2

- SAFE: IP Telephony Security in Depth

- Additional SAFE White Papers

- Looking Toward the Future

What Is SAFE?

SAFE is a network architecture blueprint developed by engineers at Cisco Systems. SAFE is intended to be a flexible and dynamic blueprint for security and virtual private networks (VPNs) that is based on the Cisco Architecture for Voice, Video, and Integrated Data (AVVID). The intention is to enable businesses to successfully and securely take advantage of available e-business economies and to compete in the emerging Internet economy with assurance. While the SAFE architecture lab was built on a "greenfield" modular approach, the benefits of implementing SAFE can be realized even if the architecture is not deployed in its entirety according to the white paper, "SAFE: Extending the Security Blueprint to Small, Midsize, and Remote-User Networks."

The original SAFE blueprint, introduced by Cisco in 2000 in the white paper "SAFE: A Security Blueprint for Enterprise Networks," applied only to enterprise networks. Cisco has continued to expand and develop the SAFE blueprint, as published in various white papers, to encompass other network architectures such as small, medium-sized, and remote-user networks; IP telephony networks; wireless networks; and IPSec-based VPNs.

SAFE also includes application notes that cover specific technologies in greater detail. SAFE "in-action" white papers cover how the SAFE blueprint and architecture can effectively mitigate attacks, based on experience from prior real-life events such as the Code-Red, Nimda, SQL Slammer, RPC DCOM, and W32/Blaster worms.

SAFE tries to closely emulate the functional requirements of today's networks. It is first and foremost a security architecture. However, this does not mean that SAFE is a rigid architecture. Quite the contrary, SAFE is both resilient and scalable, using a modular design as the basic underlying architecture for the network. The following sections provide brief overviews of the major SAFE white papers that have been published to date, which include the following:

- SAFE: A Security Blueprint for Enterprise Networks

- SAFE: Extending the Security Blueprint to Small, Midsize, and Remote-User Networks

- SAFE VPN: IPSec Virtual Private Networks in Depth

- SAFE: Wireless LAN Security in Depth–Version 2

- SAFE: IP Telephony Security in Depth

Later in the chapter, you also learn more about the SAFE white papers that target specific security threats. To read the SAFE white papers, visit the SAFE website at http://www.cisco.com/go/safe.

SAFE: A Security Blueprint for Enterprise Networks

The original SAFE white paper, "SAFE: A Security Blueprint for Enterprise Networks" (hereafter referred to as "SAFE Enterprise"), describes the blueprint for an enterprise network. This blueprint, shown in Figure 1-1, was designed from the bottom up to incorporate security throughout the network. This blueprint divides the network into various modules based on the common function of the devices. (Chapter 4, "Understanding SAFE Network Modules," describes each module in more detail.) The focus of the design is the concept of "separation of duties and trust." Where there are differing levels of trust, the devices for that function (for example, VPN or remote access) are segregated and isolated in their own module to help mitigate any possible vulnerabilities and attacks that may occur through those devices. The following axioms (discussed in more detail in Chapter 3, "SAFE Design Concepts") were used in driving the design of this blueprint:

- Routers are targets.

- Switches are targets.

Figure 1-1 *SAFE Enterprise Blueprint*

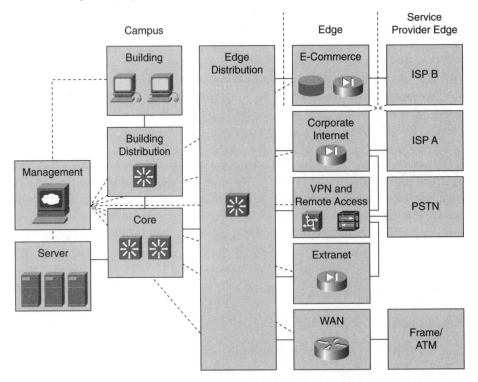

- Networks are targets.

- Hosts are targets.

- Applications are targets.

The SAFE Enterprise white paper introduced the new concept that network designers should follow security-oriented objectives when designing a network. These design objectives, listed next, are based on the concept of "defense-in-depth," which is described in greater detail in Chapter 2, "SAFE Design Fundamentals":

- Security and attack mitigation based on policy

- Security implementation throughout the infrastructure

- Secure management and reporting

- Authentication and authorization of users and administrators to critical network resources

- Intrusion detection for critical resources and subnets

- Support for emerging network applications

SAFE: Extending the Security Blueprint to Small, Midsize, and Remote-User Networks

The white paper "SAFE: Extending the Security Blueprint to Small, Midsize, and Remote-User Networks" extends the principles discussed in the SAFE Enterprise white paper and sizes them appropriately for smaller networks. These smaller networks include branches of larger enterprise networks as well as standalone and small to medium-sized network deployments. The design also covers the telecommuter and the mobile worker.

The SAFE small network blueprint is shown in Figure 1-2. Here the emphasis is the application of the blueprint to a small, business network. The redundancy in device functionality inherent in the SAFE Enterprise white paper blueprint is removed to achieve cost-effective deployment of security throughout the network.

The SAFE midsize network blueprint is shown in Figure 1-3. In this blueprint, the complexity of the Corporate Internet Module is significantly greater than in the small network blueprint because of the additional demands of remote access through the use of VPNs. Additionally, this blueprint includes network intrusion detection systems (NIDSs) as part of the overall security strategy.

Figure 1-2   *SAFE Small Network*

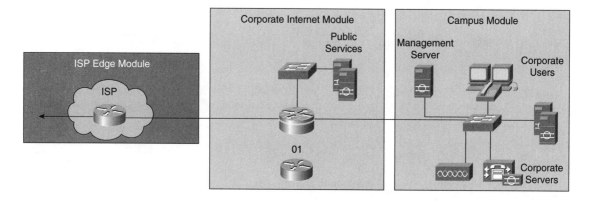

Figure 1-3   *SAFE Midsize Network*

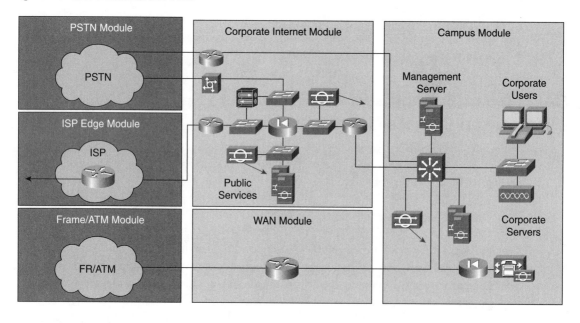

Finally, in the SAFE remote-user network blueprint, shown in Figure 1-4, the focus is on the flexibility of the designs. The objectives of SAFE can be met through more than one implementation method.

Figure 1-4 *SAFE Remote-User Network*

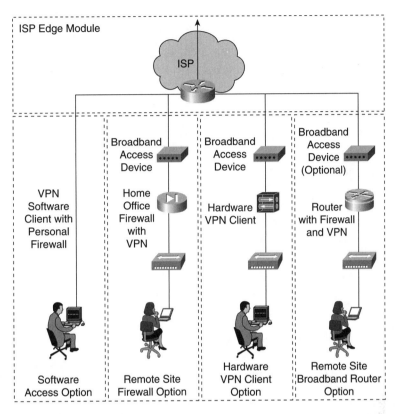

SAFE VPN: IPSec Virtual Private Networks in Depth

The "SAFE VPN: IPSec Virtual Private Networks in Depth" white paper discusses in detail the design and security of IPSec VPNs, including specific design considerations and best-practice recommendations for enterprise IPSec VPN deployment. This white paper considers VPN design at various levels, from the remote-user network design all the way up to a distributed large network VPN design. The design objectives used in the SAFE VPN white paper include

- The need for secure connectivity

- Reliability, performance, and scalability of the design

- Options for high availability

- Authentication of users and devices in the VPN

- Secure management of the VPN and devices attached

- Security and attack mitigation before and after IPSec tunnels

SAFE: Wireless LAN Security in Depth–Version 2

The "SAFE: Wireless LAN Security in Depth–Version 2" white paper discusses wireless LAN (WLAN) implementations, with a focus on the overall security of the design. Among the best practices this white paper recommends is to consider network design elements, such as mobility and quality of service (QoS). This white paper describes the following design objectives, listed in order of priority:

- Security and attack mitigation based on policy

- Authentication and authorization of users to wired network resources

- Wireless data confidentiality

- User differentiation

- Access point management

- Authentication of users to network resources

- Options for high availability (large enterprise only)

This document begins with an overview of the architecture and then details four wireless network designs. These designs are for large, medium-sized, small, and remote-user WLANs. This white paper also introduces six new axioms into SAFE:

- Wireless networks are targets.

- Wireless networks are weapons.

- 802.11 is insecure.

- Security extensions are required.

- Network availability impacts wireless.

- User differentiation occurs in wireless LANs.

SAFE: IP Telephony Security in Depth

The "SAFE: IP Telephony Security in Depth" white paper covers best-practice information for designing and implementing secure IP telephony networks. Like the other two SAFE "in Depth" white papers previously discussed, this white paper focuses on one technology and details how to best secure that technology within the overall context of SAFE. Similar to the SAFE Wireless white paper, "SAFE: IP Telephony Security in Depth" covers several deployment models for IP telephony, ranging from a large network deployment to a small network deployment.

The base premise of the white paper is that the IP telephony deployment must provide secure, ubiquitous IP telephony services to the locations and users that require it, while maintaining as many of the characteristics of traditional telephony as possible. This white paper adds 10 more axioms to the overall list of SAFE axioms:

- Voice networks are targets.

- Data and voice segmentation is key.

- Telephony devices don't support confidentiality.

- IP phones provide access to the data-voice segments.

- PC-based IP phones require open access.

- PC-based IP phones are especially susceptible to attacks.

- Controlling the voice-to-data segment interaction is key.

- Establishing identity is key.

- Rogue devices pose serious threats.

- Secure and monitor all voice servers and segments.

Additional SAFE White Papers

Aside from the main SAFE white papers described previously in this chapter, the Cisco SAFE architecture design group has written additional white papers that cover several topics:

- **"SAFE L2 Application Note"**—Discusses Layer 2 network attacks, their impact, and how to mitigate them

- **"SAFE SQL Slammer Worm Attack Mitigation"**—Covers the recent Microsoft SQL Slammer worm and various methods to mitigate its impact on a network

- **"SAFE Nimda Attack Mitigation"**—Covers the Nimda worm of September/October 2001 and how to mitigate its effects and propagation through the SAFE concepts

- **"SAFE Code-Red Attack Mitigation"**—Covers the July 2001 Code-Red/Code-Redv2 worms and how to mitigate their effects and propagation through the use of SAFE concepts

- **"SAFE RPC DCOM/Blaster Attack Mitigation"**—Covers the August 2003 RCP DCOM/Blaster worm and how to mitigate its effects and propagation through the use of SAFE concepts

Looking Toward the Future

SAFE is a continuously growing and evolving blueprint. As new technologies are emerging and being deployed, the Cisco SAFE Architecture Group is researching how to incorporate these technologies within the SAFE blueprint. Additionally, new "in Depth" white papers are being researched and written to provide system and network administrators with the knowledge needed to effectively secure their networks.

This chapter covers the following topics:

- SAFE Design Philosophy

- Security Threats

CHAPTER 2

SAFE Design Fundamentals

This chapter introduces some of the fundamental design concepts used to develop the "SAFE: Extending the Security Blueprint to Small, Midsize, and Remote-User Network Networks" blueprint designs. One of the most fundamental aspects of the SAFE design is that security and attack mitigation are based on policy. Other objectives that contribute to the overall design include secure management and reporting, a security infrastructure that is implemented throughout the entire design, intrusion detection, user authentication, and, above all, cost effectiveness. These concepts are discussed in greater detail throughout this chapter.

"Do I Know This Already?" Quiz

The purpose of the "Do I Know This Already?" quiz is to help you decide if you really need to read the entire chapter. If you already intend to read the entire chapter, you do not necessarily need to answer these questions now.

The 12-question quiz, derived from the major sections in the "Foundation Topics" portion of the chapter, helps you determine how to spend your limited study time.

Table 2-1 outlines the major topics discussed in this chapter and the "Do I Know This Already?" quiz questions that correspond to those topics.

Table 2-1 *"Do I Know This Already?" Foundation Topics Section-to-Question Mapping*

Foundations Topics Section	Questions Covered in This Section
SAFE Design Philosophy	1–8
Security Threats	9–12

CAUTION   The goal of self-assessment is to gauge your mastery of the topics in this chapter. If you do not know the answer to a question or are only partially sure of the answer, you should mark this question wrong for purposes of the self-assessment. Giving yourself credit for an answer you correctly guess skews your self-assessment results and might provide you with a false sense of security.

1. The SAFE blueprint calls for the deployment of security throughout the network. What is the term used to describe this concept?

   a. Inclusive defense

   b. Defensive coverage

   c. Defense in depth

   d. Exhaustive security

   e. Total security

2. What term is used to describe a network that is solely for management traffic and is separate from the main network that is carrying user traffic?

   a. Management network

   b. In-band network

   c. Secure network

   d. Out-of-band network

   e. Control network

3. What is user authentication based on?

   a. The proper credentials to access a system

   b. The right to access a system

   c. The need to access a system

   d. The desire to access a system

   e. All of the above

4. What does authorization ensure?

   a. That the user can communicate with the device

   b. That the user is allowed to send traffic through the device

   c. That the user can access the system

   d. That the user has sufficient privileges to execute a command or a process

   e. That the user can exit the system

5. What is critical to maximizing the success of network intrusion detection?

    a. Processor speed

    b. Deployment

    c. Brand of IDS

    d. Type of IDS

    e. All of the above

6. According to the security policy, which of the following does the network administrator need to implement?

    a. Suggestions

    b. Procedures

    c. Rules

    d. Axioms

    e. Guidelines

7. Which of the following are considered "IDS attack mitigation"?

    a. Patches

    b. Blocking/shunning

    c. Route changes

    d. TCP resets

    e. All of the above

8. Authorization allows for what kind of control in determining accountability in the network?

    a. High-level

    b. None

    c. Granular

    d. Low

    e. Defined

9. What is a determined, technically competent attack against a network called?

    a. Hacking attempt

    b. Break-in

    c. Intrusion

    d. Structured threat

    e. Unstructured threat

10. What is a "script kiddie" most likely considered?

    a. Structured threat

    b. Determined hacker

    c. Unstructured threat

    d. Skilled attacker

    e. None of the above

11. Which of the following can be considered an internal threat?

    a. Disgruntled employee

    b. Former employee

    c. Contractor

    d. Consultant

    e. All of the above

12. What is the primary focus of internal attackers?

    a. Access to the Internet

    b. Cracking into other desktop systems

    c. Privilege escalation

    d. Denial of service attacks

    e. Deleting data

The answers to the "Do I Know This Already?" quiz are found in Appendix A, "Answers to the 'Do I Know This Already?' Quizzes and Q&A Sections." The suggested choices for your next step are as follows:

- **10 or less overall score**—Read the entire chapter. This includes the "Foundation Topics" and "Foundation Summary" sections, and the "Q&A" section.

- **11 or more overall score**—If you want more review on these topics, skip to the "Foundation Summary" section and then go to the "Q&A" section. Otherwise, move to the next chapter.

Foundation Topics

SAFE Design Philosophy

This chapter focuses on the design philosophy behind the SAFE blueprints. The heart of SAFE is the inclusion of security throughout the network and within the end systems themselves. To that end, the original SAFE Enterprise document used several design objectives to meet that criteria. This is SAFE's design philosophy.

The embodiment of this design philosophy can be summed up in the six design objectives SAFE is based upon:

- Security and attack mitigation based on policy

- Security implementation throughout the infrastructure

- Secure management and reporting

- Authentication and authorization of users and administrators to critical network resources

- Intrusion detection for critical resources and subnets

- Support for emerging networked applications

- Cost-effective deployment

Each of these design objectives is described, in turn, in more depth in the sections that follow.

Security and Attack Mitigation Based on Policy

At the heart of any network security effort is the policy. The network security policy drives the decisions that determine whether an action or an event is considered a threat. A good security policy enables the network administrators or security personnel to deploy security systems and software throughout the infrastructure. This includes providing to the administrative personnel the capacity to deploy intrusion detection systems (IDSs), antivirus software, and other technologies in order to mitigate both existing threats and potential threats. The focus is on the security of the network and the data that exists on the servers in the network.

The security policy also defines how attack mitigation will occur. This can be through the implementation of shunning or blocking by firewalls and routers of attacks coming in from the Internet and from the internal network or through the use of TCP resets. If a Cisco IDS sensor identifies an attack on a network LAN, it can terminate the connection by sending TCP reset packets to both ends of the connection. By sending TCP reset packets, the IDS is effectively able to immediately close the connection between the source and target systems.

A security policy is a set of rules that defines the security goals of the organization. The policy is typically a high-level document that provides the authority for the network administration staff to enforce the rules governing the network. A formal definition of a security policy is provided by RFC 2196: "A security policy is a formal statement of the rules by which people who are given access to an organization's technology and information assets must abide. (Fraser, Barbara, RFC 2196, p. 6.)"

The security policy defines the procedures to use and the suggested guidelines for security personnel and network administrators. Without this concept of basing security and attack mitigation on a policy, the overall effort of securing a network becomes a haphazard patchwork of initiatives that are more likely to leave the network vulnerable to attack.

Security Implementation Throughout the Infrastructure

The SAFE blueprint calls for security to be implemented throughout the network. This means from the edge router all the way down to the end system. The implementation of security is done through a "defense-in-depth" approach. If an attacker bypasses one layer, he still faces other layers before he reaches critical network resources. This layered defense approach maximizes the security around critical resources such as servers, databases, and applications while minimizing the impact on network functionality and usability.

Secure Management and Reporting

All management of network devices and end systems is conducted in a secure manner. This requires that network devices ideally be managed through an out-of-band (OOB) network. Ideally this network is where access to the console interface of the network devices is located. An OOB network is completely separate from the network that carries the normal enterprise traffic. If an OOB network cannot be constructed or used for management, then the next best solution is to use encryption to secure communication between the network devices and the management system. This encryption is part of such management protocols as Secure Sockets Layer (SSL), Simple Network Management Protocol v3 (SNMPv3), or Secure Shell Protocol (SSH).

Authentication and Authorization for Access to Critical Resources

There are two primary methods of access control: authentication and authorization. Authentication is the process by which a user or a device proves the validity of their identification to an authoritative source. This source can be the login process on a host, the access device of a network, an application such as a database or web server, or one of a wide range of other systems on a network. Authorization is the process by which a user provides the credentials that prove that she has sufficient permission to execute a command or a process on a system or network device.

Critical network resources such as routers, firewalls, switches, IDSs, and applications all require authentication before access is granted. Authentication ensures that the user or administrator has the necessary credentials to access a device or system. Additional authorization is required to perform various actions on network devices and servers.

Users and administrators must authenticate before they are granted access to a device or a server. Authentication can be in the form of a single-factor authentication system, such as a password, or a two-factor authentication system, such as a public key or smart card.

Authorization ensures that the user or administrator has sufficient privileges to execute a command or a process. Authorization enables you to determine who is accountable for any particular action and to define more clearly the role of users and administrators.

Intrusion Detection for Critical Resources and Subnets

Intrusion detection has emerged as one of the critical network technologies that are necessary to properly secure a network. The following are the two general categories of IDSs, which are discussed in the next sections:

- Host-based IDS (HIDS)

- Network IDS (NIDS)

Host-Based IDS

A HIDS is software that is installed and runs on end systems such as servers, desktops, and laptops. The function of a HIDS is to provide a last line of defense if the NIDS misses an attack, which can occur if either the NIDS's signature database is out of date or the attacker is able to employ an evasion technique to hide the attack from the NIDS. HIDSs monitor the host and attempt to detect illegal actions, such as the replacement of a critical file or the execution of an illegal instruction in computer memory. As such, HIDSs have quickly become an important part in the success of IDSs in general.

Network IDS

A NIDS works by monitoring network traffic for patterns of attack. When the NIDS detects an attack, it may simply raise an alarm on a management console, execute a block by inserting a new rule into a router's or firewall's access control list (ACL), or execute some other method to terminate the connection.

The function of the NIDS is broken into two main categories:

- Misuse detection (also known as a signature-based IDS)

- Anomaly detection

A signature-based IDS identifies attacks by comparing network traffic to a database that contains signatures of exploits used to attack systems. An anomaly-based IDS uses profiles of network traffic to determine what is considered "normal." Anything that falls outside that profile is considered to be anomalous and indicative of a potential attack. Most NIDSs deployed in networks today are a hybrid system combining aspects of misuse detection and anomaly detection.

Deployment is critical to maximizing the success of an IDS. It is insufficient to place an IDS device in the middle of a network and expect that it will be able to identify and respond to all possible attacks. As networks have grown tremendously over the past few years, the amount of traffic traversing the network wire has also increased. Consequently, the IDS needs to be properly placed at strategic locations throughout the network to maximize its effectiveness and flexibility in protecting critical network resources.

Consider the network shown in Figure 2-1. The NIDSs are placed at intranet junction points such as the remote access systems and the extranet connections to business partners. Additionally, HIDSs have been deployed on critical servers throughout the network. The HIDS is a failsafe device should an attack go undetected by the NIDS. A HIDS is also used where a NIDS may be inappropriate because of, for example, an insufficient number of devices on the network, a low threat level, or a prohibitive cost factor.

Figure 2-1 *Intrusion Detection for Critical Resources*

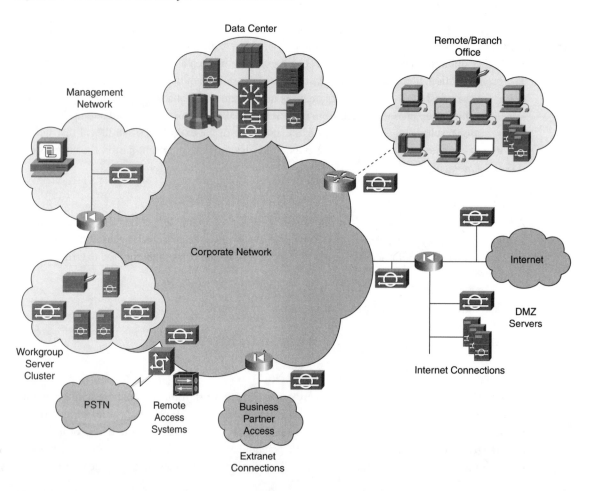

Support for Emerging Networked Applications

Technology evolves through the need for newer, better, and faster applications. These applications are more dependent than ever on the network for their proper use and operation. In the past, applications were monolithic in nature and relied on the fact that users accessed the application from within the same system the application was installed on. Today's distributed applications require a secure network to ensure secure communication between the application and the user. SAFE accommodates these emerging applications through the flexibility of the design. The deployment of new applications does not require a significant re-engineering of the network security state; rather, minor modifications can be made to provide access to these applications. This flexibility also helps to ensure that the overall security state of the network is maintained if a vulnerability in the application is discovered.

Cost-Effective Deployment

While security is an integral component of today's network architecture, it must be deployed and integrated in a cost-effective manner. The high price of equipment and implementation can become an impediment. The blueprint "SAFE: Extending the Security Blueprint to Small, Midsize, and Remote-User Networks" integrates functionality within various network devices, lowering the cost of security deployment. As in any given architecture, choosing whether to use a network device's integrated functionality as a specialized appliance must be determined based on the particular needs of the network design. However, using the firewall feature set on a router rather than a dedicated firewall appliance or using the intrusion detection capabilities in a router rather than a dedicated IDS appliance can result in substantial cost savings. This does not indicate that such integrated functionality is appropriate wherever a specialized appliance is called for because some situations require the depth of functionality that only specialized appliances provide.

Security Threats

Networks are subjected to a wide variety of attacks. These attacks include privilege escalation, access attempts, and many others. All of these attacks are defined as network threats and can be categorized according to two classifications:

- Structured versus unstructured

- Internal versus external

Using these classifications is helpful to better understand the threats themselves and how to deal with them.

Structured Threats

Structured threats are created by attackers who typically are highly motivated and technically competent. Such attackers may act alone or in small groups to understand, develop, and use sophisticated hacking techniques to bypass all security measures to penetrate unsuspecting enterprises. These groups or individuals may be involved with major fraud and theft cases reported to law enforcement agencies. Occasionally such attackers are hired by organized crime, industry competitors, or state-sponsored intelligence-collection organizations. Structured threat attackers may also fall into a relatively new categorization known as *hacktivists*, hackers who are motivated by seeking out a venue to express their political point of view. Structured threats represent the greatest danger to an organization or enterprise.

Unstructured Threats

Unstructured threats consist primarily of random attackers using various common tools, such as malicious shell scripts, password crackers, credit card number generators, and dialer daemons. Although attackers in this category may have malicious intent, many are more interested in the intellectual challenge of cracking safeguards than creating havoc. The attacks perpetrated by the attackers who fall under this category tend to be unfocused and relatively unsophisticated. If the security of the network is too strong for them to gain access, they may fall back to using a denial of service (DoS) as a last resort at saving face. Rarely are the individuals who fall into this category anything more than what is commonly termed a *script kiddie*. These types of attempts represent the bulk of Internet-based attacks.

Internal Threats

Internal threats are typically from disgruntled former or current employees. Internal threats can be structured or unstructured in nature. Structured internal threats represent an extreme danger to enterprise networks because the attacker already has access to the network. The focus of their efforts often is in the elevation of their privilege level from that of a user to an administrator. Although internal threats may seem more ominous than threats from external sources, security measures are available for mitigating the threats and responding when attacks occur.

External Threats

External threats consist of structured and unstructured threats originating from an external source. These threats can have malicious and destructive intent, such as denial of service (DoS), data theft, or distributed denial of service (DDoS), or can simply be errors that generate unexpected network behavior, such as the misconfiguration of the enterprise's Domain Name System (DNS), which results in all e-mail being delayed or returned to the sender.

Foundation Summary

The "Foundation Summary" section of each chapter lists the most important facts from the chapter. Although this section does not list every fact from the chapter that will be on your CSI exam, a well-prepared CSI candidate should at a minimum know all the details in each "Foundation Summary" section before taking the exam.

The heart of SAFE is the inclusion of security throughout the network and within the end systems themselves. To that end, the original SAFE Enterprise document used several design objectives to meet that criteria. This is SAFE's design philosophy.

The embodiment of this design philosophy can be summed up in the six design objectives SAFE is based upon

- Security and attack mitigation based on policy

- Security implementation throughout the infrastructure

- Secure management and reporting

- Authentication and authorization of users and administrators to critical network resources

- Intrusion detection for critical resources and subnets

- Support for emerging networked applications

The following points outline the purpose and the need for a security policy:

- Allows network administrators and security personnel to deploy security systems and software throughout the infrastructure

- Defines how attack mitigation will occur

- Defines the role of firewalls and routers in attack mitigation

- Defines the role of the IDS in attack mitigation

The SAFE blueprint calls for the secure management of network device and end systems. This can be achieved in one of two ways:

- Using an OOB management network

- Using encrypted protocols such as SSH, HTTPS, and SNMPv3

There are two primary methods of access control:

■ *Authentication* ensures the user or administrator has the necessary credentials to access a device or system.

■ *Authorization* ensures that the user or administrator has sufficient privileges to execute a command or a process.

Intrusion detection has emerged as one of the critical network technologies necessary to properly secure a network. There are two general categories of IDSs:

■ A HIDS is software installed and running on end systems such as servers, desktops, and laptops. The function of a HIDS is to provide a last line of defense should an attack be missed by the network IDS.

■ A NIDS works by monitoring network traffic for patterns of attack and then responding accordingly.

Deployment is critical to maximizing the success of the IDS. Properly placing the IDS at strategic locations throughout the network maximizes its effectiveness and helps ensure that an attack will not go undetected.

All network attacks can be categorized according to the following classifications:

■ Structured threats are created by attackers who are more highly motivated and technically competent.

■ Unstructured threats primarily consist of random attackers using various common tools, such as malicious shell scripts, password crackers, credit card number generators, and dialer daemons.

■ Internal threats are typically from disgruntled former or current employees. Internal threats can be structured or unstructured in nature.

■ External threats consist of structured and unstructured threats originating from an external source.

Q&A

As mentioned in the introduction, "All About the Cisco Certified Security Professional Certification," you have two choices for review questions. The questions that follow next give you a bigger challenge than the exam itself by using an open-ended question format. By reviewing now with this more difficult question format, you can exercise your memory better and prove your conceptual and factual knowledge of this chapter. The answers to these questions are found in Appendix A.

For more practice with exam-like question formats, including questions using a router simulator and multiple choice questions, use the exam engine on the CD-ROM.

1. What does a good network security policy allow?

2. What does the network security policy define?

3. How does a "defense-in-depth" approach work in network security?

4. What is an OOB network used for in SAFE?

5. What can be used in place of an OOB network?

6. What is authentication?

7. What is authorization?

8. How does a NIDS work?

9. How does a HIDS work?

10. Why is deployment critical to the success of the IDS?

11. How is SAFE able to accommodate emerging network applications?

12. What are the four types of threats faced by a network?

13. What are internal threats?

14. What are external threats?

15. What are structured threats?

16. What are unstructured threats?

This chapter covers the following topics:

- SAFE Architecture Overview

- Examining SAFE Design Fundamentals

- Understanding SAFE Axioms

CHAPTER 3

SAFE Design Concepts

This chapter introduces the fundamental concepts used in the SAFE design blueprint. These concepts represent the basis upon which decisions were made in developing the blueprint. These concepts are not restricted to use in the SAFE blueprint alone. Their application in most network designs will yield significant improvements in the overall security of the network architecture.

"Do I Know This Already?" Quiz

The purpose of the "Do I Know This Already?" quiz is to help you decide if you really need to read the entire chapter. If you already intend to read the entire chapter, you do not necessarily need to answer these questions now.

The 10-question quiz, derived from the major sections in the "Foundation Topics" portion of the chapter, helps you determine how to spend your limited study time.

Table 3-1 outlines the major topics discussed in this chapter and the "Do I Know This Already?" quiz questions that correspond to those topics.

Table 3-1   *"Do I Know This Already?" Foundation Topics Section-to-Question Mapping*

Foundations Topics Section	Questions Covered in This Section
SAFE Architectural Overview	1
Examining SAFE Design Fundamentals	2 and 3
Understanding SAFE Axioms	4–10

CAUTION   The goal of self-assessment is to gauge your mastery of the topics in this chapter. If you do not know the answer to a question or are only partially sure of the answer, you should mark this question wrong for purposes of the self-assessment. Giving yourself credit for an answer you correctly guess skews your self-assessment results and might provide you with a false sense of security.

1. SAFE can best be described as which of the following types of architectures?

   a. High availability

   b. Redundant

   c. Security

   d. Performance

   e. Design

2. Which of the following is a benefit of using modular architecture in the network design?

   a. Modules are smaller and more manageable.

   b. Modules improve communication between various segments of the network.

   c. Modular architecture provides for an easier, more cost-effective method to secure each new service as needed as well as to integrate that service into the overall security architecture of the network.

   d. There is no real benefit to modular architecture in network design.

3. What is the SAFE design philosophy?

   a. Ensure security through hardened networks.

   b. Ensure security through obscurity.

   c. Minimize network services and harden systems to prevent a successful attack.

   d. Use flexible and manageable approaches to network design.

   e. There is no overall SAFE design philosophy.

4. Which of the following is not a SAFE axiom?

   a. Routers are targets.

   b. Networks are targets.

   c. Applications are targets.

   d. Hosts are targets.

   e. Network data is a target.

5. The SAFE blueprint recommends which of the following?

   a. Lock down Telnet access to routers.

   b. Use VLAN 1 for switch management.

   c. Update hosts to the latest patch level regardless of the consequences.

   d. Use authentication in routing protocols and in VTP.

   e. Set all user ports on switches to trunking mode.

6. Which of the following two items describe hosts according to SAFE?

   a. Hosts are considered some of the more secure elements on a network.

   b. Hosts represent the greatest security concerns for administrators.

   c. Locking down hosts is fairly simple to do.

   d. Hosts don't really represent targets on a network.

   e. Hosts are the most visible targets.

7. Which of the following are IDS response methods available in Cisco IDS?

   a. TCP reset

   b. ICMP error response

   c. UDP reset

   d. Shunning

   e. Connection interception

8. Which of the following is true?

   a. Out-of-band management networks utilize encrypted protocols such as SSH and SSL to protect management traffic on the production network.

   b. In-band management traffic does not cross the production network.

   c. Out-of-band management networks provide the highest level of security by separating management traffic to its own network.

   d. Secure, in-band management protocols include Telnet, SSH, TFTP, and SSL.

9. What is the primary goal of a DDoS attack?

    a. Knock a web server offline

    b. Gain access to a system

    c. Consume all bandwidth leading to a network, thereby making the target unreachable

    d. Redirect traffic to another site

10. Which of the following network ranges are not private addresses?

    a. 10.100.100.0/24

    b. 128.83.15.0/24

    c. 66.92.141.0/8

    d. 192.16.0.0/16

    e. 172.30.45.0/16

The answers to the "Do I Know This Already?" quiz are found in Appendix A, "Answers to the 'Do I Know This Already?' Quizzes and Q&A Sections." The suggested choices for your next step are as follows:

- **8 or less overall score**—Read the entire chapter. This includes the "Foundation Topics" and "Foundation Summary" sections, and the Q&A section.

- **9 or 10 overall score**—If you want more review on these topics, skip to the "Foundation Summary" section and then go to the "Q&A" section. Otherwise, move to the next chapter.

Foundation Topics

SAFE Architecture Overview

The SAFE architecture is designed to emulate, as closely as possible, the functional requirements of today's networks. SAFE is first and foremost a security architecture that is designed to prevent most attacks from affecting network resources. Attacks that succeed in penetrating the first line of defense or those that originate from inside the network must be quickly and accurately detected and contained to minimize their impact. A network can be secure and still provide the critical functionality that users expect. Network security and functionality are *not* mutually exclusive.

The process of choosing between the integrated functionality of a network device versus a specialized appliance continues throughout the network design process. Whereas integrated functionality is certainly a very attractive prospect because it can be implemented on existing equipment, appliances provide significantly greater depth of functionality when the requirements are advanced and greater performance is required. When designing the reference implementations of the SAFE networks, if the design requirements did not dictate a specific choice, the designers opted to use the integrated functionality of a network device rather than an appliance, to reduce the complexity and the cost of the overall design.

The architecture covered by the CSI exam is based on the blueprint "SAFE: Extending the Security Blueprint to Small, Midsize, and Remote-User Networks" (also known as "SAFE SMR"). This blueprint does not consider redundancy and resiliency as factors but does consider cost-effective security deployment as a factor.

Examining SAFE Design Fundamentals

Because an organization's network tends to evolve gradually as the organization's IT requirements increase, many organizations do not have an overall design concept or philosophy in place that guides network growth, the result of which is that networks become less secure and more difficult to manage and troubleshoot as they grow. The SAFE design philosophy is modular, and modularity enhances the flexibility, manageability, and security of a network. This approach has two significant advantages:

- The security relationship between the modules can be addressed.

- The design permits the designers to phase in security on a per-module basis rather than attempt to implement security throughout the entire network architecture in a single phase.

The SAFE blueprints are reference architectures only that are based on a "greenfield" approach. This approach provides for the design and development of the network from scratch rather than from a pre-existing architecture already in place. It is not always possible, nor is it expected, for network engineers who choose to implement the SAFE architecture to match the design in the blueprint verbatim. Most production networks cannot be easily dissected into the distinct modules that are described in the blueprints. SAFE does, however, provide design templates that network engineers can use to enhance security on their networks.

The following underlying fundamentals that guided the design of the SAFE blueprint are stated in every SAFE white paper:

- Security and attack mitigation based on policy

- Security implementation throughout the infrastructure

- Cost-effective deployment

- Secure management and reporting

- Authentication and authorization of users and administrators to critical network resources

- Intrusion detection for critical resources and subnets

The SAFE blueprints use modules to address the distinct security requirements of each network area. This allows for rapid, consistent deployment of security throughout the enterprise without the need to redesign the network each time a new service is added. The module templates in SAFE provide for an easier, more cost-effective method to secure each new service as needed and to integrate that service into the overall security architecture of the network. Additionally, each module in SAFE is designed to provide security in cases of failure of the security devices that feed into the module. The concept of "defense in depth" is implemented on both the inbound and outbound data paths of each module.

The unique feature of the SAFE blueprint is that it is the first to recommend and explain exactly where and why security solutions should be included. The SAFE blueprint is designed to provide maximum performance while maintaining network security and integrity.

Understanding SAFE Axioms

The SAFE axioms outlined in the white papers available on the Cisco Systems SAFE website (http://www.cisco.com/go/safe) provide several best common practices (BCPs). The following are the five axioms, which are described in the sections that follow:

- Routers are targets.

- Switches are targets.

- Networks are targets.

■ Hosts are targets.

■ Applications are targets.

Routers Are Targets

Three functions of routers are discussed in this section. First, routers are devices that announce network addresses through routing protocols. Second, routers filter the functionality of network traffic. Third, routers connect one network to another, a function that has made routers an increasingly popular target for intruders. Because they are so often targets, hardening them is critical. Router security postures can be improved by implementing the following best practices:

■ **Lock down Telnet access to routers**—This can be accomplished through the following means:

— Restrict the protocols that are used to connect to the router for administration.

— Use access control lists (ACLs) to restrict which IP addresses can connect to the router.

— Require a password for login.

— Ensure that sessions time out when they are no longer being used.

— Consider SSH or HTTS as options that are more secure than Telnet.

■ **Lock down SNMP access to routers**—This can be accomplished through the following means:

— Use SNMP version 2 at a minimum.

— Choose community string names with the same care as passwords.

— Require authentication.

— Restrict the IP addresses that can connect to the SNMP port on the router.

■ **Use TACACS+ to control access to the router**—Using an authentication, authorization, and accounting (AAA) system allows for the collection of information about user logins, user logouts, HTTP accesses, privilege-level changes, commands executed, and similar events. AAA log entries are sent to authentication servers by using the TACACS+ or RADIUS protocol and are recorded locally by those servers, typically in disk files. TACACS+ passwords are not transmitted in clear text, so the threat of password sniffing to steal passwords is mitigated.

■ **Turn off unneeded services**—This includes the TCP and UDP small services (chargen, discard, and echo) and the finger service. If the Network Time Protocol (NTP) is not needed, consider disabling it. If the Cisco Discovery Protocol (CDP) is not required for network management, disable it as well.

■ **For routing protocols, consider using an authentication method to ensure that the routing updates are valid**—Use message digest authentication instead of plaintext password authentication.

For a more complete document on improving the security of Cisco routers, refer to this website: http://www.cisco.com/warp/public/707/21.html.

Switches Are Targets

Like their router counterparts, switches are increasingly coming under attack by intruders. These attacks are targeting both OSI Layer 2 and Layer 3 switches. Many of the attacks to switches are unique to the function that they perform in a network. These attacks include VLAN hopping—in which an attacker in one VLAN gains access to a host in another VLAN that is not normally accessible from the attacker's VLAN—and MAC address spoofing. The common best practices for routers, which were listed previously, also apply to switches, as do the following switch-specific best practices:

- **Always use a dedicated VLAN ID for all trunk ports**—This prevents VLAN-hopping attacks.

- **Avoid using VLAN 1 for management**—VLAN 1 is the native VLAN on all Cisco switches. Any switch ports that are not assigned to a unique VLAN are automatically assigned to VLAN 1.

- **Set all user ports to nontrunking mode**—Along with using a dedicated VLAN ID for all trunk ports, this setting is necessary to prevent VLAN-hopping attacks.

- **Deploy port security for user ports**—When possible, configure each port to associate a limited number of MAC addresses (approximately two to three). This deployment mitigates MAC flooding and other network attacks.

- **Have a plan for the ARP security issues in your network**   —Enable Spanning Tree Protocol attack mitigation (BPDU Guard, Root Guard). This helps mitigate the possibility of an attacker spoofing a root bridge in the network topology and successfully executing a man-in-the-middle attack.

- **Enable Spanning Tree Protocol attack mitigation**—This is accomplished through *BPDU Guard* and *Root Guard.*

- **Use private VLANs**—When appropriate, this allows for the further division of Layer 2 networks.

- **Use CDP only where appropriate**—CDP is a proprietary protocol that aids in managing Cisco devices. However, the information available in CDP can provide an attacker with desired information. Limiting the use of CDP to areas of the network that are considered sufficiently secure is considered a best practice.

- **Disable all unused ports and put them in an unused VLAN**—This prevents network intruders from plugging into unused ports and communicating with the rest of the network.

- **Use VTP passwords**—VLAN Trunking Protocol (VTP) is used to propagate VLAN configuration information from a server switch to client switches. Requiring VTP authentication in VTP advertisements reduces the likelihood that the VTP advertisements are spoofed by an attacker.

- **Use Layer 2 port authentication such as 802.1x**—802.1x provides for the authentication of clients that attempt to connect to a network.

For more information on improving the security of Layer 2 switches, refer to the "SAFE Enterprise Layer 2 Addendum" Application Note on Cisco.com.

Hosts Are Targets

Hosts are the most frequently targeted aspects of a network. They represent the most visible target to an attacker and the biggest security problem for an administrator. Attackers see hosts as the most valuable target because of the applications that are run on them, the data that is stored on them, and the fact that they can be used as launch points to other destinations. Because hosts are highly visible and consist of numerous different combinations of hardware platforms, operating systems, and applications (each with its own set of patches and updates), hosts represent the lowest-hanging fruit on a network and are the target of choice for an attacker.

Hosts, therefore, represent the most successfully attacked elements on a network. For example, consider a typical web server on an enterprise network. The web server application may be from one vendor, the operating system from another, and the hardware from a third. Additionally, the web server may be running some freely available CGI programs or a commercial application that interfaces with the web server, such as a SQL database. All of these various components of the host may contain multiple vulnerabilities, some more severe than others. This is not to say that using operating system software and application software from one manufacturer is more secure; in some cases, quite the contrary has proven to be true. However, the lesson is that the more complex a system is, the greater the possibility of a failure.

When securing hosts, pay considerable attention to the system components. Keep systems up to date with the latest patch revision levels. Be sure to test the updates on test systems before you apply the patches to systems in a production environment. Patches can create unexpected conflicts between software components and result in a DoS by preventing the application or system from properly operating.

In addition, when securing hosts, turn off any "unnecessary services"—services that are not required for the proper functioning and management of the system. For example, many UNIX systems come with "small" services turned on by default, which include echo, chargen, and discard. These services represent a potential target of a DoS attack. If the host is not an FTP server, disable the FTP service and, if possible, remove the FTP software package.

Other potential avenues of attack are the use of default accounts and poor user passwords. Accounts on production systems should be limited to only those users who need to access the system for management purposes or to affect maintenance on the software.

The key to successfully improving the security of a system is to lower the number of possible avenues of attack to a minimum. Additionally, you should consider the use of host-based intrusion prevention software on critical systems, to further improve the security posture of the system. Improving the overall security posture of the system does not necessarily mean that the system will become impenetrable; it will, however, certainly make an attack much harder.

Networks Are Targets

Network attacks are the most difficult to defend against because they typically take advantage of an intrinsic property of the network itself. This category of attacks includes Layer 2 attacks, distributed denial of service (DDoS) attacks, and network sniffers.

The Layer 2 attacks can be mitigated through the use of the best practices previously listed in the sections "Routers Are Targets" and "Switches Are Targets." The impact of sniffing can be mitigated through the implementation of a switched network and through the use of the same set of best practices.

DDoS attacks are much more difficult to protect against, however. Typically, the goal of a DDoS attack is to shut down an entire network rather than one particular host. The primary method of a DDoS network attack is to consume all of the bandwidth going to and from the network. A side effect of a DDoS attack might be that a target system on the network crashes.

Cooperation between the end customer and its ISP is the only effective way to mitigate many of the effects of a DDoS attack. The ISP can provide rate limitations on the outbound interface of the router that is providing the ISP link to the customer so that undesired traffic can be dropped when it exceeds a prespecified amount of the total bandwidth in the link.

Common forms of DDoS attacks include ICMP floods, TCP SYN floods, and UDP floods. One defense that administrators can devise to protect their systems is to follow filtering guidelines as specified in RFC 1918 and RFC 2827. RFC 1918 specifies the network address ranges that are reserved for private use, and RFC 2827 describes egress filtering for networks. When implemented on the ISP side of a WAN link, filtering helps prevent packets with source addresses within the ranges covered in RFC 1918, as well as other spoofed traffic, from reaching the customer end of the uplink. At the customer end, following the filtering guidelines discussed in these two RFCs helps prevent attackers from launching DDoS attacks using spoofed IP addresses by blocking them at the customer edge router. Although this strategy does not prevent DDoS attacks from happening, it does prevent the attacker from masking the source address of the attacking hosts.

NOTE Consider the following example to understand the impact that a DDoS attack can have on a network. A typical enterprise organization has a DS1 (1.544 Mbps) link to its ISP. This provides access not only for the enterprise to the Internet but also for the enterprise's customers to the corporate web server and to the FTP server for downloading patches.

An attacker with 100 systems under his control begins a DDoS attack against the enterprise web server. Assume that each system under his control sits on a variety of DSL and ISDN links so that the average bandwidth for these 100 systems is 256 kbps. If all 100 of the systems are used in a coordinated attack against the web server and each fills up its link to the Internet with traffic, the total aggregate traffic generated is 25.6 Mbps:

100 systems * 256 kbps/system (avg) = 25.6 Mbps

This is easily 16 times greater than the size of the target enterprise's link to the Internet. Even if only half of the systems were able to flood at their full link capacity, the Internet link for the enterprise would still be

50 systems * 256 kbps/system + 50 systems * 128 kbps/system = 19.2 Mbps

Applications Are Targets

Applications are also targets because, like host operating systems, they are susceptible to coding errors. The extent of the damage caused by application coding errors can vary from a minor "HTTP 404 File Not Found" error to something considerably worse such as a buffer overflow that provides direct interactive access to a host. Applications need to be kept up to date as much as possible. Furthermore, public domain applications and custom-developed applications should be audited to ensure that potential vulnerabilities are not introduced to the system with the installation of the software. These audits should consider the following factors:

■ Analysis of the calls that the application makes to other applications and to the operating system itself

■ The application privilege level

■ The level of trust the application has for the surrounding systems

■ The method of transport the application uses to transmit data across the network

This level of auditing is necessary to resolve potentially known vulnerabilities that would reduce the security posture of the system and the network as a whole.

Intrusion Detection Systems

Intrusion detection systems (IDSs) fall into two primary categories: network IDS (NIDSs) and host-based IDS (HIDSs). NIDSs provide an overall view of activity on a network and the capability to alert upon discovery of an attack. HIDSs excel in providing after-the-fact analysis of an attack on a host, and, with newer host-based intrusion prevention systems (IPSs), they are able to prevent an attack from succeeding by intercepting OS and application calls on the host.

All IDS require some level of adjustment, or tuning, to eliminate false positives. False positives are alarms that are triggered by activity that is benign in nature. Once the IDS has been tuned appropriately, additional mitigation techniques can then be implemented. There are two primary mitigation techniques in the Cisco IDS offerings:

■ Shunning

■ TCP resets

Shunning uses ACLs on routers and firewalls to block offending traffic from a source IP address. You must take great care when applying this technique because a skilled attacker may use spoofed packets in the attack to cause the IDS to add filters to the router or firewall that block legitimate traffic. To reduce this problem, it is recommended that you use shunning only against TCP traffic, because it is more difficult to spoof than UDP traffic. Additionally, use short shun times—just long enough to provide the network administrator with sufficient time to determine a more permanent course of action. Shunning is recommended on the internal network, however, for several reasons, including the assumption that effective RFC 2827 filtering is being used on the internal network and the fact that internal networks tend not to have the same level of stateful filtering as edge connections.

The second mitigation technique, TCP resets, is available only against TCP-based connections and provides for the termination of the attack by sending TCP reset packets to both the attacking and the attacked hosts. Switched environments pose some additional challenges to TCP reset, but these can be overcome by using a Switched Port Analyzer (SPAN) or mirror port.

Secure Management and Reporting

Reporting is a design fundamental that addresses the requirement to log suspicious network activity. Additionally, it is also very important to actually read the log entries or summarize them if possible. Without log review, it is not possible to develop a complete picture of a potential security event.

Another item addressed by this topic includes management of the various network devices in the blueprint. Unlike the SAFE Enterprise blueprint, which utilizes an out-of-band network management method whereby all management traffic traverses a network infrastructure that is separate and distinct from the production network, the SAFE SMR blueprint utilizes an in-band network management scheme. To ensure the confidentiality and integrity of the management traffic, in-band management schemes require the use of encrypted protocols such as SSH, SSL, and IPSec where possible.

For management of devices outside of a firewall, there are several considerations to take into account:

- What management protocol does the device support?

- Should the management channel be active at all times?

- Is this management channel necessary?

Answering these three questions provides sufficient analysis in weighing the risks of management traffic outside of the firewall.

Syslog is the most common, supported method of reporting events on network devices. Synchronizing the time on network devices through the use of NTP further enhances the capability to correlate events from multiple devices.

Change management also represents a vital link in an overall comprehensive security policy. It is important that any changes done to network infrastructure devices be recorded and that known, good configurations be archived through the use of FTP or TFTP.

Foundation Summary

The "Foundation Summary" section of each chapter lists the most important facts from the chapter. Although this section does not list every fact from the chapter that will be on your CCSP exam, a well-prepared CCSP candidate should at a minimum know all the details in each "Foundation Summary" section before taking the exam.

The five primary axioms of SAFE are listed next along with recommendations for how to mitigate some of the attacks against them:

■ **Routers are targets.**

— Lock down Telnet access to routers.

— Lock down SNMP access to routers.

— Control access to routers through the use of TACACS+.

— Turn off unneeded services.

— For routing protocols, consider using an authentication method to ensure that the routing updates are valid.

■ **Switches are targets.**

— Always use a dedicated VLAN ID for all trunk ports.

— Avoid using VLAN 1 for management.

— Set all user ports to nontrunking mode.

— Deploy port security where possible for user ports.

— Devise a plan for the ARP security issues in your network. Enable Spanning Tree Protocol attack mitigation.

— Use private VLANs where appropriate.

— Use CDP only where appropriate.

— Disable all unused ports and put them in an unused VLAN.

— Use VTP.

— Use Layer 2 port authentication such as 802.1x.

- **Networks are targets.**

  — Employ RFC 1918 and RFC 2827 filtering to reduce the impact of DDoS attacks that employ IP address spoofing.

  — Communicate with the ISP to ensure that it applies traffic rate limits and QoS features on the outbound link of its router.

- **Hosts are targets.**

  — Keep systems up to date with patches and updates.

  — Turn off unnecessary services.

  — Ensure users use passwords that can't be guessed, by periodically testing them.

  — Minimize access to the system by limiting user accounts to only those who need to access a given system.

  — Install host-based intrusion prevention software.

- **Applications are targets.**

  — Analyze the calls that an application makes to other applications and to the operating system itself.

  — Analyze the application privilege level.

  — Identify the level of trust the application has for the surrounding systems.

  — Analyze the method of transport the application uses to transmit data across the network.

  — Install host-based intrusion prevention software.

Q&A

As mentioned in the introduction, "All About the Cisco Certified Security Professional Certification," you have two choices for review questions. The questions that follow next give you a bigger challenge than the exam itself by using an open-ended question format. By reviewing now with this more difficult question format, you can exercise your memory better and prove your conceptual and factual knowledge of this chapter. The answers to these questions are found in Appendix A.

For more practice with exam-like question formats, including questions using a router simulator and multiple choice questions, use the exam engine on the CD-ROM.

1. What are some of the benefits of using a dedicated appliance for security rather than the same integrated functionality in another device?

2. What are the two significant advantages to SAFE's use of modules in the blueprint?

3. What is the primary method that a DDoS attack uses to achieve its effects?

4. Why do hosts represent the greatest risk on a network?

5. Is it important to lock down Telnet, web, or SNMP access to devices, and if so, why?

6. What is the role of VTP in a network? What could an attacker do with VTP? How can attacks using VTP be made less likely to succeed?

7. What is 802.1x? How can it be used to improve the security of a network?

8. What are the four factors a software audit should consider when determining the security of an application?

This chapter covers the following topics:

- SAFE Modules Overview

- Understanding the Campus Module

- Understanding the Corporate Internet Module

- Understanding the WAN Module

CHAPTER 4

Understanding SAFE Network Modules

This chapter introduces the module construct of the "SAFE: Extending the Security Blueprint to Small, Midsize, and Remote-User Networks" blueprint. In general, a network that is based on the SAFE design principles tries to follow a modular concept when dividing out network functions. It is not required that the design adhere strictly to the SAFE blueprint; however, it is important to realize that the security benefits of SAFE are derived from these blueprints and can be realized only if the network design meets the blueprint recommendations.

"Do I Know This Already?" Quiz

The purpose of the "Do I Know This Already?" quiz is to help you decide if you really need to read the entire chapter. If you already intend to read the entire chapter, you do not necessarily need to answer these questions now.

The 11-question quiz, derived from the major sections in the "Foundation Topics" portion of the chapter, helps you determine how to spend your limited study time.

Table 4-1 outlines the major topics discussed in this chapter and the "Do I Know This Already?" quiz questions that correspond to those topics.

Table 4-1 *"Do I Know This Already?" Foundation Topics Section-to-Question Mapping*

Foundations Topics Section	Questions Covered in This Section
SAFE Modules Overview	1
Understanding the Campus Module	2–5
Understanding the Corporate Internet Module	6–9
Understanding the WAN Module	10–11

CAUTION The goal of self-assessment is to gauge your mastery of the topics in this chapter. If you do not know the answer to a question or are only partially sure of the answer, you should mark this question wrong for purposes of the self-assessment. Giving yourself credit for an answer you correctly guess skews your self-assessment results and might provide you with a false sense of security.

1. Which of the following module(s) is not part of the "SAFE: Extending the Security Blueprint to Small, Midsize, and Remote-User Networks" blueprint?

   a. Campus module

   b. E-Commerce module

   c. Corporate Internet module

   d. WAN module

   e. Management module

2. Which of the following functions is *not* provided by the Layer 3 switch in the medium-sized network Campus module?

   a. Routing and switching of production and management traffic

   b. Distribution layer services such as routing, quality of service (QoS), and access control

   c. Connectivity for the corporate and management servers

   d. Firewall protections between VLANs

   e. Traffic filtering between subnets

3. What does RFC 2827 cover in terms of network security?

   a. RFC 2827 describes the address ranges for private networks.

   b. RFC 2827 provides for the routing of VLAN traffic across a distribution switch.

   c. RFC 2827 describes filtering to help reduce the risk of attack through source address spoofing.

   d. RFC 2827 describes the process of setting up a connection between two systems using TCP.

   e. RFC 2827 defines OSPF version 2.

4. What is the function of private VLANs in the SAFE blueprint and where are they implemented?

   a. Private VLANs are used to help mitigate the risk associated with the exploitation of trust relationships, and they are implemented at the Layer 3 core switch.

   b. Private VLANs are used to help mitigate the risk associated with VLAN hopping attacks, and they are implemented at the Layer 2 core switch.

   c. Private VLANs are used to help mitigate the risk associated with VLAN hopping attacks, and they are implemented at the Layer 3 core switch.

   d. Private VLANs are used to help mitigate the risk associated with the exploitation of trust relationships, and they are implemented at the Layer 2 distribution switches.

5. What is the purpose of the NIDS in the medium-sized Campus module?

   a. To detect attacks originating from *outside* the Campus module that may result from a workstation compromised by an unauthorized dial-in modem or attacks from viruses, worms, or disgruntled employees.

   b. To detect attacks originating from *within* the Campus module that may result from a workstation compromised by an unauthorized dial-in modem or attacks from viruses, worms, or disgruntled employees.

   c. To detect attacks originating from *within* the Campus module that may result from a workstation compromised by an attacker gaining access through the Internet.

   d. To detect attacks originating from *outside* the Campus module that may result from a workstation compromised by an attacker gaining access through the Internet.

   e. The medium-sized network Campus module does not include a network intrusion detection appliance.

6. The ISP router is considered to be owned and managed by which of the following?

   a. Owned by the ISP and managed by the ISP

   b. Owned by the ISP and managed by the customer

   c. Owned by the customer and managed by the ISP

   d. Owned by the customer and managed by the customer

7. What is the primary purpose of the private VLANs in the medium-sized network Corporate Internet module?

   a. To provide traffic segmentation for remote systems that are terminating their IPSec tunnels on the VPN concentrator

   b. To mitigate trust exploitation attacks

   c. To improve bandwidth outside of the firewall in the module

   d. To facilitate the use of an IDS in the module

   e. None of the above

8. Which of the following key devices are not present in the small network Corporate Internet module?

   a. Firewall

   b. VPN concentrator

   c. NIDS appliance

   d. Dial-in access server

   e. Layer 2 switch

9. Where is the NIDS appliance(s) deployed in the medium-sized network Corporate Internet module blueprint?

    a. In the public services segment

    b. External to the firewall behind the edge router

    c. Behind the firewall's internal interface

    d. On the VPN/remote-access segment of the firewall before the VPN concentrator

    e. In front of the dial-in access server

10. Which of the following are factors in determining whether a WAN module is needed?

    a. When there is an unjustifiable cost factor of migrating to IPSec VPNs

    b. Whenever management feels that WANs are justified

    c. When QoS requirements cannot be met through the use of IPSec VPNs

    d. When private networks are needed for security reasons

    e. When existing legacy WAN connections exist

11. Which of the following describe how ACLs are applied in the WAN module?

    a. Inbound ACLs restrict the traffic that is permitted into the medium-sized network Campus module from the remote locations.

    b. Inbound ACLs restrict the traffic that is permitted to reach the remote networks.

    c. Outbound ACLs determine what traffic is permitted into the medium-sized network Campus module from the remote locations.

    d. Outbound ACLs determine what traffic from the medium-sized network Campus module is permitted to reach the remote networks.

The answers to the "Do I Know This Already?" quiz are found in Appendix A, "Answers to the 'Do I Know This Already?' Quizzes and Q&A Sections." The suggested choices for your next step are as follows:

■ **9 or less overall score**—Read the entire chapter. This includes the "Foundation Topics" and "Foundation Summary" sections, and the "Q&A" section.

■ **10 or 11 overall score**—If you want more review on these topics, skip to the "Foundation Summary" section and then go to the "Q&A" section. Otherwise, move to the next chapter.

Foundation Topics

SAFE Modules Overview

The "SAFE: Extending the Security Blueprint to Small, Midsize, and Remote-User Networks" (SAFE SMR) blueprint was written approximately one year after the successful release of "SAFE: A Security Blueprint for Enterprise Networks" (SAFE Enterprise). The SAFE SMR blueprint provides best practice information about designing and securing networks that are of a smaller scale than that described in the original SAFE Enterprise white paper. SAFE SMR uses the same principles as the original SAFE Enterprise white paper and scales them appropriately for smaller networks. These smaller networks can be branches of larger, enterprise networks or standalone small to medium-sized deployments. SAFE SMR also covers other deployment designs, such as telecommuters and mobile workers.

The general design of the SAFE SMR includes two core modules:

- The Campus module

- The Corporate Internet module

The small and medium-sized network designs both use these two modules. The medium-sized network design goes further to cover additional WAN modules that are not included in the small network design.

Understanding the Campus Module

The Campus module contains the end-user workstations and the corporate intranet servers and management servers. This module also contains the Layer 2 and Layer 3 devices that provide the underlying network infrastructure. In the medium-sized and small networks covered in the SAFE SMR design, the Campus module is a combination of the various modules that comprise the campus segment in the SAFE Enterprise white paper. This combination is done to reflect the smaller scale of the design in the small and medium-sized network designs and to reduce the overall cost. Also, this design does not include redundancy, which further reduces costs.

Figures 4-1 and 4-2 show the SAFE medium-sized and small network Campus module designs, respectively. In the medium-sized network design, the Layer 3 switch provides connectivity for the Layer 2 switches as well as VLAN segmentation and inter-VLAN routing. All servers, including the corporate intranet servers and the management server, connect directly into the Layer 3 switch. Additionally, the network intrusion detection system (NIDS) management interface connects into this switch.

In the SAFE small network Campus module design, shown in Figure 4-2, the host-based IDS (HIDS) provides for protection on the various servers within the module. The Layer 3 switch that is available in the medium-sized network design is replaced with a Layer 2 switch. Typically, in networks of this size, no VLANs are configured; however, if VLANs are desired, then inter-VLAN routing can be provided by the edge router or firewall in the Corporate Internet module (discussed in the section "Understanding the Corporate Internet Module," later in this chapter).

Figure 4-1 *SAFE Medium-Sized Network Campus Module*

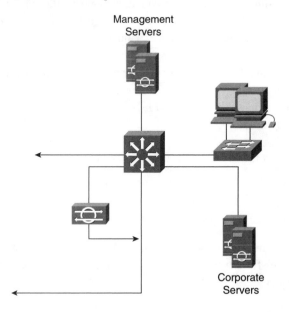

Figure 4-2 *SAFE Small Network Campus Module*

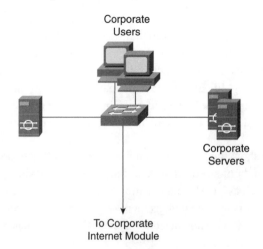

Key Campus Module Devices

There are significant differences between the Campus module design for the small network and that for the medium-sized network, summarized in Table 4-2. The key devices in the small network Campus module are the Layer 2 switches. In the medium-sized network, there are several key devices, including Layer 2 and Layer 3 switches and an IDS. The functions of these devices along with management hosts are described in the following sections.

Table 4-2 *Key Devices in the Campus Module*

Key Devices	Functions	Medium-Sized Network	Small Network
Layer 2 switch	Includes private VLAN support and provides network access to the end devices	X	X
Corporate servers	Provide DNS, e-mail, file, and print services to end devices	X	X
User workstations	Provide data and network services to users	X	X
Management hosts	Provide management for network devices; typically use SNMP	X	X
Layer 3 switch	Provides distribution services to the Layer 2 switches and routes production and management traffic within the Campus module	X	
NIDS management host	Provides alarm aggregation and analysis for all NIDS appliances throughout the Campus and Corporate Internet modules	X	
Syslog host	Aggregates firewall, router, and NIDS logs	X	
Access control server	Provides authentication services to network devices such as network access servers (NASs)	X	
OTP server	Provides for authorization of one-time password (OTP) authentication relayed from the access control server	X	
Sysadmin host	Provides for configuration, software, and content changes on network devices	X	
NIDS appliance	Provides for deep packet inspection of traffic traversing various segments of the network	X	

Layer 2 Switch

The Layer 2 switch provides end-user workstation connectivity to small and medium-sized networks. Private VLANs are implemented on these switches to help reduce the risk of trust exploitation attacks.

Layer 3 Switch

The Layer 3 switch provides several functions to the medium-sized network Campus module, including the following:

- Routing and switching of production and management traffic

- Distribution layer services such as routing, QoS, and access control

- Connectivity for the corporate and management servers

- Traffic filtering between subnets

The Layer 3 switch provides separate segments for the corporate servers, the management servers, and the corporate users and provides connectivity to the WAN and Corporate Internet modules. These segments are provided through the deployment of VLANs.

A Layer 3 switch also provides for an additional line of defense against internal attacks through the use of access control lists (ACLs). You can use internal ACLs to protect one department's servers from access by users in another department. Additionally, the use of network ingress filtering (described in RFC 2827) on the corporate user and corporate intranet server VLANs helps reduce the risk of attack through internal source address spoofing.

Private VLANs can be used within each VLAN to mitigate attacks through trust exploitation. Additional protection of the management servers is provided through extensive Layer 3 and Layer 4 ACLs at the interface connecting the management segment VLAN. These ACLs restrict connectivity between the management servers and the devices under their control. Only those IP addresses being managed and only those protocols necessary to conduct management are permitted. Additionally, only established connections are permitted back through the ACLs.

NIDS Appliance

Intrusion detection within the medium-sized network Campus module is provided by a single NIDS appliance. The port to which this appliance is connected on the Layer 3 switch is configured to mirror all network traffic from all VLANs that require monitoring. This appliance provides detection and analysis of both attacks that originate from *within* the Campus module and external attacks that get past the firewall. These attacks could result from a compromised workstation with an unauthorized dial-in modem, disgruntled employees, viruses and worms, or an internal workstation that has been compromised by an outside user.

Management Hosts

The NIDS appliances and the HIDSs installed on the corporate servers are all managed through the IDS management host. This host provides for alarm aggregation and analysis for all IDS devices throughout the Campus module and the Corporate Internet module.

Other management hosts in the medium-sized network design include the following:

■ A syslog host for aggregation of firewall, router, and NIDS logs

■ An access control server for authentication services to network devices, such as NASs

■ An OTP server for authorization of OTP authentication relayed from the access control server

■ A sysadmin host for configuration, software, and content changes on network devices

Alternative Campus Module Designs

If the medium-sized network is small enough, you can eliminate the Layer 2 switches and connect all end-user workstation directly into the core switch. Private VLANs are still implemented to reduce the risk of attacks due to trust exploitation. If desired, you can replace the NIDS appliance with an IDS module in the core switch, which then provides for higher traffic throughput into the IDS system.

In the small network, the lack of a Layer 3 switch places additional emphasis on host and application security. Also, private VLANs are configured on the Layer 2 switch to mitigate the risk of trust exploitation attacks. HIDSs are installed on the corporate servers and management systems to protect those servers from attack.

Understanding the Corporate Internet Module

The Corporate Internet module provides internal users with access to the Internet. It also provides public services such as DNS, FTP, e-mail, and web services to external users. In both medium-sized and small networks, VPN traffic from remote users and remote sites terminates in this module. Additionally, dial-in connections from remote users also terminate here. Unlike its counterpart in the SAFE Enterprise blueprint, the SAFE SMR Corporate Internet module is not designed to handle e-commerce traffic or applications.

Figure 4-3 shows the design of the SAFE medium-sized network Corporate Internet module, and Figure 4-4 shows the SAFE small network Corporate Internet module. The SAFE medium-sized network Corporate Internet module provides for a public services segment where web, mail, and other publicly accessible servers are located. Additionally, this design provides for remote access both through a connection to the Public Switched Telephone Network (PSTN) and through IPSec

VPNs that terminate in the VPN/dial-in segment. The firewall is at the center of the design and controls access to the various segments.

The SAFE small network design shown in Figure 4-4 provides for a firewall, or a router with firewall capabilities, as the primary security device. All publicly accessible servers are located on a DMZ segment off of this device.

Figure 4-3 *SAFE Medium-Sized Network Corporate Internet Module*

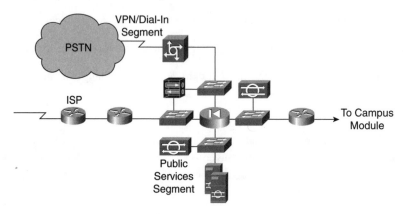

Figure 4-4 *SAFE Small Network Corporate Internet Module*

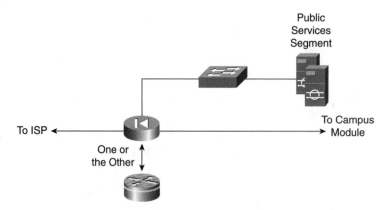

Key Corporate Internet Module Devices

There are several key devices in the Corporate Internet module that are common between the medium-sized network design and the small network design. The key devices in both the small and medium-sized network designs are summarized in Table 4-3. This table also indicates in which network these devices can be found.

Table 4-3 *Key Devices in Corporate Internet Module*

Key Devices	Functions	Medium-Sized Network	Small Network
Hosts for small and medium-sized networks	DNS Server: Provides authoritative external DNS resolution; relays internal requests to the Internet. FTP Server: Provides public interface for file exchange between Internet users and the corporate network; can be combined with the HTTP server to reduce cost. HTTP Server: Provides public information about the enterprise or the organization; can be combined with the FTP server to reduce cost. SMTP Server: Provides e-mail service for the enterprise by relaying internal e-mail bound for external addresses; can inspect content as well.	X	X
Firewall	Provides network-level protection of resources through stateful filtering of traffic. Can provide remote IPSec tunnel termination for users and remote sites. Also provides differentiated access for remote-access users.	X	X
ISP router	Provides connectivity from the ISP to the network.	X	
Dial-in server	Authenticates remote dial-in users and terminates their dial-up connection.	X	
Layer 2 switches	Provides for Layer 2 connectivity within the Corporate Internet module. Can also provide support for private VLANs.	X	
Internal router	Provides routing within the module.	X	
NIDS appliance	Provides for deep packet inspection of traffic traversing various segments of the network.	X	
Edge router	Provides for connectivity to the Internet and rudimentary filtering through ACLs.	X	X
VPN concentrator	Authenticates remote users and terminates their IPSec tunnels.	X	

Hosts for Small and Medium-Sized Networks

Additional hosts in both the medium-sized and small network Corporate Internet module designs include the following systems:

- A DNS server to provide for authoritative external name resolution and to relay internal network requests to the Internet

- An FTP server to provide for file exchange between Internet users and the corporate network

- An HTTP server to provide public information about the enterprise or the organization

- An SMTP server to provide for e-mail service both inbound and outbound; could also provide for e-mail content inspection

Each system requires that HIDS software be installed to help detect and mitigate attacks and the possible exploitation of these systems. These systems represent the endpoint devices that provide significant services to the Internet presence of the corporation.

Firewall

The firewall provides additional filtering capabilities in both designs. The firewall in the small network blueprint provides for one additional demilitarized zone (DMZ) segment, whereas the firewall in the medium-sized network blueprint provides for multiple DMZ segments.

In the medium-sized network design, the firewall provides for a public services segment and a VPN/dial-in segment. Publicly available servers, such as web, e-mail, and FTP servers, reside in the public services segment. Inbound filtering is used to limit the traffic that reaches the public servers. Outbound filtering reduces the possibility that a compromised public server can be used for further exploitation of the network. To achieve this goal, specific filters are in place to prevent any unauthorized connections that originate in the public services segment from being generated. Private VLANs can be used in the segment to prevent an attacker who successfully compromises a server from exploiting other servers in the public services segment. Other services that the firewall provides include SMTP command filtering and termination of site-to-site VPNs.

The VPN/dial-in segment of the firewall is used to filter inbound traffic from the dial-in access server and the VPN concentrator. Private VLANs can be provided in this segment to prevent an attacker who compromises either a VPN connection or a dial-in connection from affecting other connections that terminate on the devices in this segment.

In the small network blueprint, the firewall provides for much of the functionality that is provided in a medium-sized network. However, only one additional segment is available, the public services segment. The firewall also provides for SMTP command filtering, as in the medium-sized network design, and provides a termination point for remote sites, preshared keys, and VPN tunnels. The remote users authenticate to the access control server in the Campus module.

Many firewall appliances and firewall software packages provide for rudimentary NIDS capabilities; however, those capabilities, if used, can result in a degradation of the firewall's performance.

ISP Router

The ISP router is found in the medium-sized network design only and its primary purpose is to provide connectivity to a provider network. ACLs provide for address filtering in accordance with RFC 1918 and RFC 2827 in both directions of traffic. Additionally, egress traffic from the ISP provides for rate limitations on nonessential traffic from the ISP network to the enterprise to reduce the effects of denial of service (DoS) and distributed denial of service (DDoS) attacks.

Edge Router

The edge router provides various functionalities in both the medium-sized and the small network design. In both networks, this device should be configured to drop most fragmented packets.

In the medium-sized network blueprint, the edge router provides the point of demarcation between the medium-sized network and the ISP network. Basic traffic filters provide for address filtering in accordance with RFC 1918 and RFC 2827. Additionally, only expected IP traffic is permitted through. For example, IPSec and IKE traffic that is destined for the VPN concentrator or the firewall is permitted through.

In the small network design, the edge router provides for address filtering in both directions in accordance with RFC 1918 and RFC 2827. Additionally, nonessential traffic that exceeds prespecified thresholds is rate limited to reduce the impact of DDoS attacks. Agreements between the enterprise and the ISP that provide for additional traffic-rate limiting help push the DDoS mitigation further upstream of this router.

Dial-In Server

Dial-in user connections in medium-sized networks are terminated at the NAS. Authentication is provided by the access control server using the three-way Challenge Handshake Authentication Protocol (CHAP). Once a user has been authenticated, she is assigned an IP address from a predefined pool.

Layer 2 Switches

The Layer 2 switches in the medium-sized network blueprint provide for connectivity between devices in the Corporate Internet module. Several switches are implemented rather than a single switch with multiple VLANs, to reduce the impact of device misconfiguration. Each segment in the module has a switch to provide for device connectivity. These switches are configured with private VLANs to reduce the potential of device compromise through trust exploitation.

Internal Router

The primary function of the internal router in the medium-sized network blueprint is to provide for Layer 3 separation and routing between the Campus module and the Corporate Internet module. The device functions solely as a router without any filtering capabilities and provides a final point of demarcation between the routed intranet and the external network. Most firewalls do not participate in any routing protocols; therefore, it is important to provide a point of routing within the Corporate Internet module that does not rely on the rest of the network.

NIDS Appliance

The public services segment of the medium-sized network's firewall includes a NIDS appliance. This device is configured in a restrictive stance because signatures that are matched here have already passed through the firewall. Each of the servers in the public services segment has HIDS software installed. The function of the HIDS is to monitor for any illegal activity on the host at the OS and application levels. Finally, the external SMTP server provides for mail content filtering services to prevent viruses or Trojan-horse applications from reaching the end users on the internal network.

In addition to the IDS in the public services segment, a NIDS appliance is deployed between the firewall's private interface and the internal router. This NIDS is also set to a restrictive stance; however, unlike the NIDS in the public services segment, this NIDS is capable of initiating a countermeasure against detected activity. This response can be through TCP resets or ACL shuns. Attacks encountered at this NIDS may indicate that a public services host has been compromised and that the attacker is using that host as a platform to gain further entry into the internal network. This segment permits only traffic that is in response to initiated flows, this is from select ports on the public services segment or that is from the remote-access segment.

VPN Concentrator

The remote-access VPN concentrator provides secure connectivity to the medium-sized network for remote users. Authentication is provided by the access control server, which queries the OTP server to verify user credentials. IPSec policy is pushed from the concentrator to the client and prevents split tunneling, whereby the client maintains both a live connection to the external Internet and the secure connection to the medium-sized network. This policy forces the client to route all traffic through the medium-sized network, including traffic that is ultimately destined for the Internet. Encryption is provided through use of the 3DES algorithm and data integrity is provided through use of the Secure Hash Algorithm/Hash-Based Message Authentication Code (SHA/HMAC).

In the medium-sized network blueprint, the VPN terminates outside the firewall, at the VPN concentrator. This enables the firewall to filter remote-user traffic, which it wouldn't be able to do if the VPN device were placed behind the firewall, because VPN traffic is encrypted until it reaches the VPN concentrator. This deployment also allows the IDS on the inside of the firewall's private interface to inspect traffic from remote VPN users.

In the small network, remote-access VPN termination occurs at the edge router/firewall.

Alternative Medium-Sized Network Corporate Internet Module Designs

The medium-sized network blueprint provides for alternative placements of devices within the designs. For example, in the medium-sized network, you can implement a stateful firewall on the edge router. This has the added benefit of providing greater defense in depth to this module. Also, you can insert another NIDS just outside the firewall. This NIDS provides for important alarm information that normally is not seen because of the firewall. The NIDS device can also provide validation of the inbound ACLs on the edge router.

> **CAUTION**   When deciding whether or not to place a NIDS outside the firewall, be sure to consider the large volume of alarms that may be generated. If a NIDS is placed outside the firewall, it is recommended that the NIDS be configured to alarm at a lower severity than alarms generated by the NIDS behind the firewall's private interface. Also, it may be wise to have this NIDS' alarms log to a separate management server so that the legitimate alarms receive the appropriate attention.

Another possible alternative in the medium-sized network blueprint is to eliminate the internal router in the Corporate Internet module and integrate its functions into the Layer 3 switch of the Campus module. The drawback to this alternative is that this requires the Corporate Internet module to rely on the Campus module for Layer 3 routing.

Another alternative is to provide additional content filtering beyond that provided by the mail server. This could take the form of a proxy system that provides URL filtering in the public services segment to filter the types of web pages that employees can access, or it could take a different form such as URL inspection on a firewall device.

Alternatives to the small network blueprint are geared toward either separating network device functions or increasing capacity. In either case, the small network quickly begins to look like the medium-sized network design.

Understanding the WAN Module

The WAN module in the medium-sized network blueprint is included only when connections to remote locations are desired or needed over a private network and QoS requirements cannot be met through the use of IPSec VPNs. Another factor in determining whether a WAN module is needed is the cost of migrating to IPSec VPNs when existing legacy WAN connections exist. The key device in the WAN module is the router, which provides connectivity to the remote locations.

Security in this module is provided through the use of ACLs and additional Cisco IOS security features. Inbound ACLs restrict what traffic is permitted into the medium-sized network Campus module from the remote locations, and outbound ACLs determine what traffic from the medium-sized Campus module is permitted to reach the remote networks. Some of the additional Cisco IOS security features include the firewall feature set, which provides firewall capabilities within the router, inline IDS capabilities, TCP SYN flood attack mitigation, and IPSec VPN tunnel termination.

Foundation Summary

The "Foundation Summary" section of each chapter lists the most important facts from the chapter. Although this section does not list every fact from the chapter that will be on your CCSP exam, a well-prepared CCSP candidate should at a minimum know all the details in each "Foundation Summary" section before taking the exam.

The Cisco SAFE Implementation exam uses the SAFE SMR blueprint as the basis of the network design in the exam. The medium-sized network consists of three primary modules:

- The Corporate Internet module

- The Campus module

- The WAN module

Table 4-4 summarizes the various modules in both the medium-sized and small network blueprints.

Table 4-4 *SAFE SMR Modules*

Module Name	Medium-Sized Network Blueprint	Small Network Blueprint
Campus module	X	X
Corporate Internet module	X	X
WAN module	X	

The SAFE small network blueprint consists of only two modules:

- The Corporate Internet module

- The Campus module

Table 4-5 shows the key devices that are used in the Campus module for both small and medium-sized networks.

Table 4-5   *Key Devices in the Campus Module*

Key Devices	Functions	Medium-Sized Network	Small Network
Layer 2 switch	Includes private VLAN support and provides network access to the end devices	X	X
Corporate servers	Provide DNS, e-mail, file, and print services to end devices	X	X
User workstations	Provide data and network services to users	X	X
Management hosts	Provide management for network devices; typically use SNMP	X	X
Layer 3 switch	Provides distribution services to the Layer 2 switches and routes production and management traffic within the Campus module	X	
NIDS management host	Provides alarm aggregation and analysis for all NIDS appliances throughout the Campus and Corporate Internet modules	X	
Syslog host	Aggregates firewall, router, and NIDS logs	X	
Access control server	Provides authentication services to network devices such as NASs	X	
OTP server	Provides for authorization of OTP authentication relayed from the access control server	X	
Sysadmin host	Provides for configuration, software, and content changes on network devices	X	
NIDS appliance	Provides for deep packet inspection of traffic traversing various segments of the network	X	

Table 4-6 lists the key devices that are used in the Corporate Internet module in small and medium-sized networks.

Table 4-6 *Key Devices in Corporate Internet Module*

Key Devices	Functions	Medium-Sized Network	Small Network
Hosts for small and medium-sized networks	DNS Server: Provides authoritative external DNS resolution; relays internal requests to the Internet. FTP Server: Provides public interface for file exchange between Internet users and the corporate network; can be combined with the HTTP server to reduce cost. HTTP Server: Provides public information about the enterprise or the organization; can be combined with the FTP server to reduce cost. SMTP Server: Provides e-mail service for the enterprise by relaying internal e-mail bound for external addresses; can inspect content as well.	X	X
Firewall	Provides network-level protection of resources through stateful filtering of traffic. Can provide remote IPSec tunnel termination for users and remote sites. Also provides differentiated access for remote-access users.	X	X
ISP router	Provides connectivity from the ISP to the network.	X	
Dial-in server	Authenticates remote dial-in users and terminates their dial-up connection.	X	
Layer 2 switches	Provides for Layer 2 connectivity within the Corporate Internet module. Can also provide support for private VLANs.	X	
Internal router	Provides routing within the module.	X	
NIDS appliance	Provides for deep packet inspection of traffic traversing various segments of the network.	X	

continues

Table 4-6 *Key Devices in Corporate Internet Module (Continued)*

Key Devices	Functions	Medium-Sized Network	Small Network
Edge router	Provides for connectivity to the Internet and rudimentary filtering through ACLs.	X	X
VPN concentrator	Authenticates remote users and terminates their IPSec tunnels.	X	

The public services segment houses the publicly accessible servers, which provide such services as FTP, DNS, SMTP, and web services, and should be protected using host intrusion detection.

The NIDS appliances are deployed in two locations, allowing for traffic inspection and analysis in two critical junctions of the blueprint:

- In the public services segment

- In the internal segment between the firewall's private interface and the internal router

Q&A

As mentioned in the introduction, "All About the Cisco Certified Security Professional Certification," you have two choices for review questions. The questions that follow next give you a bigger challenge than the exam itself by using an open-ended question format. By reviewing now with this more difficult question format, you can exercise your memory better and prove your conceptual and factual knowledge of this chapter. The answers to these questions are found in Appendix A.

For more practice with exam-like question formats, including questions using a router simulator and multiple choice questions, use the exam engine on the CD-ROM.

1. What is the purpose of the ISP router in the SAFE medium-sized network blueprint? What features does this device provide for traffic control?

2. What management devices are found in the Campus module of the SAFE medium-sized network blueprint?

3. What are the functions provided by the Layer 3 switch in the medium-sized network Campus module?

4. What is the primary function of the Layer 2 switches in the Campus and Corporate Internet modules of the SAFE design?

5. What is the function of the internal router in the Corporate Internet module of the SAFE medium-sized network blueprint?

6. Where are the NIDS appliances located in the Corporate Internet module of the SAFE medium-sized network blueprint?

7. What are the key network devices in the Corporate Internet module of the SAFE small network blueprint and what are their functions?

8. The firewall in the SAFE medium-sized network blueprint divides the Corporate Internet module into four segments. What are they?

9. What are some of the precautions to take when placing a NIDS appliance outside of the firewall in the Corporate Internet module of the SAFE medium-sized network blueprint?

10. What authentication protocol is recommended at the NAS of the Corporate Internet module in the SAFE medium-sized network blueprint?

Part II covers the following Cisco CSI exam topics:

- Need for Network Security

- Network Security Policy

- Security Wheel

- Network Attack Taxonomy

- Management Protocols and Functions

Part II: Understanding Security Risks and Mitigation Techniques

This chapter covers the following topics:

- The Need for Network Security

- Security Policy Characteristics, Goals, and Components

- The Security Wheel

CHAPTER 5

Defining a Security Policy

The first step in implementing security in a networked environment is to determine how that security will be defined and enforced. A security policy provides the overall framework for the network security implementation and provides the rationale and the motive for the guidelines and procedures that will be used. The security policy is the blueprint, or constitution, that describes in broad terms how security will be conducted in the network. Without a security policy, efforts to implement and enforce security in a networked environment can be haphazard and uncoordinated.

"Do I Know This Already?" Quiz

The purpose of the "Do I Know This Already?" quiz is to help you decide if you really need to read the entire chapter. If you already intend to read the entire chapter, you do not necessarily need to answer these questions now.

The 11-question quiz, derived from the major sections in the "Foundation Topics" portion of the chapter, helps you determine how to spend your limited study time.

Table 5-1 outlines the major topics discussed in this chapter and the "Do I Know This Already?" quiz questions that correspond to those topics.

Table 5-1 *"Do I Know This Already?" Foundation Topics Section-to-Question Mapping*

Foundations Topics Section	Questions Covered in This Section
The Need for Network Security	1–3
Security Policy Characteristics, Goals, and Components	4–9
The Security Wheel	10–11

CAUTION The goal of self-assessment is to gauge your mastery of the topics in this chapter. If you do not know the answer to a question or are only partially sure of the answer, you should mark this question wrong for purposes of the self-assessment. Giving yourself credit for an answer you correctly guess skews your self-assessment results and might provide you with a false sense of security.

1.   Why is network security becoming increasingly important?

    a.   Information is more important today than it has been in the past.

    b.   Vendors do not provide sufficient security in their products.

    c.   Attackers are posing an increasing threat to the capabilities of businesses to function efficiently and securely.

    d.   Network attacks are launched not only from external sources but also increasingly from within the network.

    e.   b and c are correct.

    f.   c and d are correct.

2.   What are the two primary reasons for the increasing threat to network systems?

    a.   Network administrators are not diligent in securing their networks.

    b.   The Internet is ubiquitous.

    c.   Vendors are not diligent in eliminating software bugs.

    d.   Easy-to-use operating systems and development environments have become pervasive.

    e.   b and d are correct.

    f.   a and c are correct.

3.   Within the scope of network security, what does CIA stand for?

    a.   Common information assurance

    b.   Confidentiality, identification, and assurance

    c.   Core Internet attacks

    d.   Confidentiality, integrity, and availability

4.   What does a network security policy do?

    a.   Describes the procedures to secure a network

    b.   Defines the framework used to protect the assets connected to a network

    c.   Provides legal and financial guidance to secure a network

    d.   Describes a network's level of security

5. What is the main goal of a network security policy?

  a. To ensure that system users, staff, and managers are informed of their responsibilities for protecting corporate technology and information assets

  b. To secure the network so that attackers cannot gain access

  c. To provide a framework that is used to protect computers on a network and ensure that users authenticate their identity

  d. To provide legal protection to the IT staff

6. What three characteristics should a network security policy have?

  a. It should be implementable, capable of defining roles, and enforceable

  b. It should be administrative, managerial, and understandable

  c. It should be definable, restrictive, and enforceable

  d. It should be implementable, understandable, and enforceable

7. What are the two types of network security policies?

  a. Administrative

  b. Restrictive

  c. Managerial

  d. Permissive

8. What are some of the elements of a network security policy?

  a. Acceptable-use policy

  b. Download policy

  c. Encryption policy

  d. Extranet policy

  e. All of the above

9. What is a risk assessment?

  a. A process of determining the vulnerabilities on a network

  b. The reduction of the level of risk in a network

  c. The ability to verify that risk exists

  d. A verification that no risk exists in the network

  e. A method that allows the level of risk inherent in a system to be quantified

10. What is the Security Wheel?

    a. It defines network security as a *continuous* process that is built around the corporate security policy.

    b. It is a system whereby once the network is secured according to the outline of the security policy, the network is considered secure.

    c. It defines the method that is used to secure a network.

    d. None of the above.

11. Which of the following are phases of the Security Wheel? Select all that apply.

    a. Security policy implementation

    b. Testing

    c. Monitoring and detection

    d. Improvement

    e. Analysis

    f. All of the above

The answers to the "Do I Know This Already?" quiz are found in Appendix A, "Answers to the 'Do I Know This Already?' Quizzes and Q&A Sections." The suggested choices for your next step are as follows:

■ **9 or less overall score**—Read the entire chapter. This includes the "Foundation Topics" and "Foundation Summary" sections, and the "Q&A" section.

■ **10 or more overall score**—If you want more review on these topics, skip to the "Foundation Summary" section and then go to the "Q&A" section. Otherwise, move to the next chapter.

Foundation Topics

The Need for Network Security

With the recent unparalleled growth of the Internet has come a greater degree of exposure to personal information, government secrets, and confidential data as well as corporate information assets. Network systems are at a greater degree of exposure to attack than ever before. Attackers are posing an increasing threat to the capabilities of businesses to function efficiently and securely. Attackers are no longer only individuals external to the network who are solely interested in gaining access to the network to either deface a web page or disrupt operations. Increasingly, attackers are individuals within the network.

There are many reasons for the increasing threat to networks. One reason is the ubiquity of the Internet. As more and more companies and households go on line, the number of vulnerable systems available to an attacker grows at an incredible pace. Furthermore, this same ubiquity of the Internet facilitates the exchange of knowledge and experience on a global scale. In the past, networks were designed to provide connectivity only to known parties, such as business partners and authorized clients, and the closed network was not necessarily connected to the public Internet. This is no longer the case. Today's open networks require connectivity to the Internet for e-commerce and telecommuting needs.

Additionally, more and more companies are realizing the benefits of conducting business across the Internet. Whether these benefits are through an e-commerce website or in applications such as e-learning and customer service, the need for security on increasingly open networks has become a fundamental aspect of business in today's economy.

Another reason for the increasing threat to networks is the pervasiveness of easy-to-use operating systems and development environments. More and more sites containing information and, in some cases, malicious code are readily available to would-be attackers. This has significantly reduced the required level of knowledge and experience to successfully attack a network.

New regulations are coming into effect in the United States with such legislation as the Health Insurance Portability and Accountability Act (HIPAA), the Gramm-Leach-Bliley Act (GLBA), and the Sarbanes-Oxley Public Company Accounting Reform and Investor Protection Act. HIPAA, enacted in 1996, was brought about as an effort at healthcare reform during the Clinton administration. This law requires the Department of Health and Human Services (HHS) to develop standards and guidelines that will provide for the standardization of the electronic data interchange of specified administrative and financial transactions. Additionally, HHS also must develop standards and guidelines to protect the security and confidentiality of patient health information.

GLBA, enacted in 1999, specifies requirements that are similar to HIPAA but applicable to financial institutions with regard to customer information. Finally, the Sarbanes-Oxley Act of 2002 specifies that corporate officers and corporate boards can be held accountable for the security of their systems and their networks. The security of the corporate network ties directly into the protection of investments covered by this new law.

Security Policy Characteristics, Goals, and Components

A security policy defines the framework that is used to protect the assets that are connected to a network. RFC 2196, "Site Security Handbook," defines a security policy as ". . .a formal statement of the rules by which people who are given access to an organization's technology and information assets must abide."

Without a security policy, the availability of a network can be compromised. By defining the basis with which the information assets and the systems connected to the network are used and protected, the security policy helps to reduce the risk of systematic security failure within the network.

A policy is a document or set of documents that defines the specific requirements or rules that must be met to reach a particular goal. In many instances, a security policy is a collection of shorter documents that are point-specific; that is, each covers a specific topic. In the case of IT and network security, such policies can include an acceptable-encryption policy that defines the requirements for the use of encryption within an organization. More commonly, security policies include an acceptable-use policy that might cover the rules and regulations for appropriate use of the computing facilities. In every case, the policy considers only one topic and addresses the uses of that topic within the context of the overall security of the network.

The main goal of a security policy is to ensure that system users, staff, and managers are informed of their responsibilities for protecting corporate technology and information assets. The security policy should specify the mechanisms through which these responsibilities can be met while also providing a baseline from which to acquire, configure, and audit computer systems and networks for compliance with the policy.

There are two general types of network security policies:

■ **Permissive**—Based on the assumption "everything that is not expressly prohibited is permitted."

■ **Restrictive**—Based on the assumption "everything that is not expressly permitted is prohibited."

A permissive security policy is the equivalent of an access control list with the **permit ip any any** command as the last statement. A restrictive security policy is better than a permissive policy because it allows the administrators and managers to more easily define the proper use of the network and its assets.

Security Policy Components

A successful security policy can be subdivided into smaller subpolicies, each of which covers a specific topic related to the overall security of the network. The breadth and scope of each subpolicy can vary according to the needs of administrators and managers. Each subpolicy can be referenced as a standalone document as well as function as part of an overall security policy. Section 2.2 of the "Site Security Handbook" lists several elements of an overall security policy, including:

- Computer technology purchasing guidelines that specify required, or preferred, security features. These should supplement existing purchasing policies and guidelines.

- A privacy policy that defines reasonable expectations of privacy regarding such issues as monitoring of e-mail, logging of keystrokes, and accessing users' files.

- An access policy that defines access rights and privileges to protect assets from loss or disclosure by specifying acceptable-use guidelines for users, operations staff, and management. It should provide guidelines for external connections, data communications, connecting devices to a network, and adding new software to systems. It should also specify any required notification messages (for example, connect messages should provide warnings about authorized usage and line monitoring and not simply say "Welcome").

- An accountability policy that defines the responsibilities of users, operations staff, and management. It should specify an audit capability and provide incident-handling guidelines (that is, what to do and who to contact if a possible intrusion is detected).

- An authentication policy that establishes trust through an effective password policy and by setting guidelines for remote-location authentication and the use of authentication devices (for example, one-time passwords and the devices that generate them).

- An availability statement that sets users' expectations for the availability of resources. It should address redundancy and recovery issues and specify operating hours and maintenance downtime periods. It should also include contact information for reporting system and network failures.

- An IT system and network maintenance policy that describes how both internal and external maintenance people are allowed to handle and access technology. One important topic to be addressed is whether remote maintenance is allowed and how such access is controlled. Another area for consideration is outsourcing and how it is managed.

- A violations-reporting policy that indicates which types of violations (for example, privacy and security, internal, and external) must be reported and to whom the reports are made. Providing a nonthreatening atmosphere and the possibility of anonymous reporting results in a greater probability that a violation will be reported if it is detected.

- Supporting information that provides users, staff, and management with contact information for each type of policy violation; guidelines on how to handle outside queries about a security incident, or information that may be considered confidential or proprietary; and cross-references to security procedures and related information, such as company policies and governmental laws and regulations.

It is possible to further subdivide the preceding policies to provide a greater degree of granularity on specific topics. The SysAdmin, Audit, Network, Security (SANS) Institute defines 27 possible policies, some of which focus on very specific topics. Among the 27 SANS Institute polices are the following:

- **Acceptable-encryption policy**—Defines requirements such as cipher type, key length, and appropriate use of encryption algorithms for the communication channels used within the organization, such as host-to-host connections and e-mail.

- **Acceptable-use policy**—Defines the boundaries of acceptable use of corporate resources (whether they be physical equipment or network services) as well as the responsibilities of the user in protecting corporate assets and equipment. Additionally, an acceptable-use policy may specify the boundaries of acceptable behavior of users on the corporate network.

- **Antivirus policy**—Defines guidelines for effectively protecting the organization's network from the threat and the effects of computer viruses and worms.

- **Extranet policy**—Defines the requirements that third-party organizations must meet to connect to the corporate network. These requirements should include the necessary security obligations that the third party must comply with. Although this policy should also require the signing of a third-party connection agreement in order to access the organization's networks, it need not include the specific wording of such an agreement.

- **Information-sensitivity policy**—Defines classification levels for the organization's information. Classification should be based on the sensitivity of the information. This policy should also provide for the mechanisms to secure that information.

- **Remote-access policy**—Defines the methods that authorized users can use to access the network from an offsite or remote location. This policy ties into the VPN policy described later in this list and covers additional topics such as dial-in access and security.

- **Internal-lab security policy**—Defines the security requirements for internal labs, such as development labs and quality assurance (QA) labs. This policy covers how confidential information and technology (typically considered intellectual property, such as source code) is to be protected. In addition, this policy should provide guidelines that define how to prevent the activities of the lab from endangering production facilities on the network.

- **Internet DMZ equipment policy**—Provides the standards and the guidelines to be used to secure systems located outside the organization's firewalls. These systems typically exist in areas between the corporate firewalls and the edge devices such as routers. These areas are considered "dirty" or "semitrusted."

- **Password-protection policy**—Provides definitions for the composition and characteristics of passwords and how they are to be stored and protected.

- **Audit policy**—Defines the requirements and the standards through which network security audits are performed. This document is also used as a source of authority for the network security staff to conduct audits, investigate any incidents, and monitor user and system activity. It also defines the requirements for conforming to stated security policies.

- **VPN security policy**—Defines the requirements for remote access to the organization's networks using VPN technology. The document defines which VPN technologies are appropriate (such as IPSec, PPTP, and L2TP) and the range of internal networks visible to users of the VPN.

- **Wireless networking and communication policy**—Defines the standards and requirements to connect to the corporate network using a wireless technology, such as 802.11 or Bluetooth.

This is by no means an exhaustive list of all the possible policies that can be part of an overall security policy. The references at the end of this chapter provide a good starting point with which to develop a sound security policy.

Characteristics of a Good Security Policy

There are three primary characteristics of a good security policy:

- Most important, the policy *must* be enforceable and it *must* apply to everyone.

- The policy *must* be capable of being implemented through system administration procedures and through the publication of acceptable-use guidelines or other appropriate methods.

- The policy *must* clearly define the areas of responsibility and the roles of users, administrators, and management.

Failure to meet these three requirements seriously weakens the effectiveness of a security policy and calls into question its role in defining the overall security of the network.

Security Policy Goals

Without an overall design, network security can become a hodge-podge of rules and guidelines that can easily contradict each other. Any and all security-related decisions that are made affect the security level of the network as well as its functionality and ease of use. Good decisions regarding security cannot be made without first defining the overall goals and a roadmap to attain those goals. Without this roadmap, using security tools is meaningless, because it is impossible to determine what to check for and what restrictions should be imposed.

Security goals are determined mainly by working through the following key trade-offs:

- **Services offered versus security provided**—Each network service offered, such as Telnet, Simple Mail Transfer Protocol (SMTP), and the web, carries a security risk. In some cases these risks are outweighed by the benefits that the service provides.

- **Ease of use versus security**—Providing users with a system that is easy to use and that requires little or no training is very convenient. However, the reality is that such systems sometimes also bring with them significant security risks. Requiring security usually results in a loss of convenience.

- **Cost of security versus risk of loss**—Security has a variety of costs: expenses for personnel, equipment, and software; decreased ease of use; and decreased performance. However, the costs of security systems must be weighed against the potential cost of the loss of confidential information, loss of privacy, and loss of service. A risk assessment is essential to understand the cost-benefit trade-offs of implementing a security policy.

Some motivating factors for the establishment of a security policy include:

- **Security posture baseline**—Without knowing the current state of the security on the network, it is impossible to determine how to improve it.

- **Security implementation framework**—A security policy provides a roadmap for implementing and improving network security.

- **Defining appropriate behavior**—A security policy can provide guidelines for proper behavior on the corporate network and consequences for inappropriate behavior.

- **Identification of the necessary tools and procedures**—The security policy can help to define which tools and procedures are needed to implement the desired security on the network.

- **Defining roles and communicating consensus**—The security policy defines roles for users, managers, and administrators and helps to communicate consensus among decision makers.

- **Incident-handling framework**—The policy needs to provide the definition of an incident-handling process and procedures for disaster recovery.

A key motivating factor in creating and implementing a security policy is to ensure that the organization realizes the benefits of the cost and effort spent on security. Risk assessment or analysis is used as a guide toward this end. A security risk assessment identifies the risk to an organization of its current security posture. Assessing risk involves determining two basic elements:

- Which assets need to be protected

- What the threats are to those assets

For each asset, the basic aim is to assure *confidentiality, integrity, and availability (CIA)*. Threats to assets can be further defined by identifying the following threat elements:

- Consequences of the threat if nothing is done

- How often the threat may occur

- A measure of the likelihood that the threat will occur

Once the risks associated with various threats have been identified, they can be ranked according to their severity and impact to the enterprise.

Risk Assessment

Risk assessment is a method that enables an organization to quantify the level of risk inherent in a system. For computer networks, it is a way to identify, analyze, and determine how to control and minimize losses that may be associated with events on the network. Although there is no possible way to ever reduce the level of risk to zero (that would entail ceasing network operations), a risk assessment enables network managers and security personnel to identify risks in the network and their location and methods to eliminate or reduce their impact on network operations.

Asset Identification

The first step in a risk assessment is to identify the assets that need to be protected. Without this first step, there is no logical way to proceed to define the threats. Assets include both tangible and intangible property. Examples of tangible property include computer hardware, network equipment, and phone systems. Intangible property includes intellectual property and data. The following list of asset categories is paraphrased from Charles Pfleeger's 1996 book *Security in Computing*:

- Hardware items such as computers, printers, routers, switches, firewalls, and other devices that exist physically on the network

- Software such as operating systems, programs (both commercial and home grown), and utilities

- Information stored both on line and off line in any format as well as audit log information and all network security logs

- Users, administrators, and managers

- Documentation of programs, hardware, and corporate policies

- Supplies such as magnetic media, forms, and office supplies

Threat Identification

After the assets are identified, threats to those assets can be identified. When you are conducting a risk assessment or analysis, it is necessary to consider the nature of the threats. Some of the more common threats mentioned in RFC 2196 include

- Unauthorized access to resources and information

- Unintentional or unauthorized disclosure of information

- Denial of service (DoS)

While this is certainly not a comprehensive list, it does provide a starting point for security personnel to identify threats to corporate assets.

The Security Wheel

The implementation of a security policy typically involves four steps:

Step 1   Develop the security policy.

Step 2   Implement the security products called for by the security policy.

Step 3   Inspect the policy periodically.

Step 4   Handle incidents as they occur.

This process does not provide for the continual adaptation of the security policy to changes in the network environment. The Security Wheel concept treats network security as a *continuous* process that is built around the corporate security policy. This process is divided into four stages:

1. Securing the network.

2. Monitoring the network.

3. Testing the security of the network.

4. Improving the security of the network.

During the first phase of the Security Wheel, security solutions are implemented. This process involves deploying firewalls, VPN devices, intrusion detection systems (IDSs), and authentication systems and patching any systems that require a patch. These systems are deployed to stop or prevent unauthorized access or activities.

The second phase in the Security Wheel involves monitoring the network to detect violations of the security policy. Monitoring includes system auditing and real-time intrusion detection. This step is designed to validate the security implementation that is conducted in the first stage.

The testing phase of the Security Wheel involves validating the effectiveness of the security policy implementation. Validation is done through system auditing and vulnerability scanning.

In the fourth phase of the Security Wheel, the information gathered during the monitoring and testing phases is used to improve the security implementation of the network. At this phase, adjustments can be made to the security policy as vulnerabilities (both new and old) and risks are identified.

The fourth phase feeds back into the first and the process begins anew. Figure 5-1 illustrates the Security Wheel concept.

Figure 5-1 *The Security Wheel*

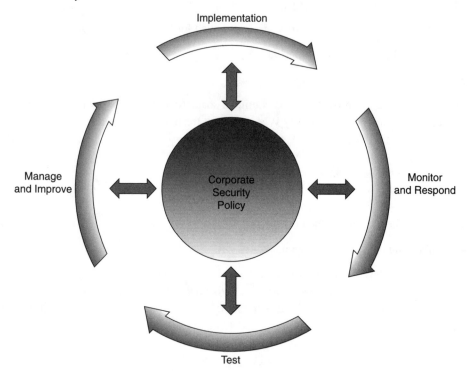

Foundation Summary

The "Foundation Summary" section of each chapter lists the most important facts from the chapter. Although this section does not list every fact from the chapter that will be on your CSI exam, a well-prepared CSI candidate should at a minimum know all the details in each "Foundation Summary" section before taking the exam.

There are two primary reasons for the increasing threat to networks:

- The ubiquity of the Internet

- The pervasiveness of easy-to-use operating systems and development environments

A security policy defines the framework that is used to protect the assets that are connected to a network. The main goal of a security policy is to ensure that system users, staff, and managers are informed of their responsibilities for protecting corporate technology and information assets.

The two general types of network security policies are

- Permissive policies

- Restrictive policies

To be effective, a security policy must

- Be enforceable and apply to everyone

- Be capable of being implemented through system administration procedures and through the publication of acceptable-use guidelines or other appropriate methods

- Clearly define the areas of responsibility and the roles of users, administrators, and management

The key trade-offs to consider when establishing the security goals of a security policy include the following:

- The risks of offering some services versus the overall level of security provided

- The ease of use of the network versus the desired security level

- The cost of implementing the desired security versus the potential cost of losing confidential information, privacy, or service

The two basic elements that are determined during a security risk assessment are the following:

- Which assets need to be protected. The basic aim for each asset is to ensure the CIA of the asset.

- What the threats are to those assets.

Threats can be further defined through three elements:

- The consequences of the threat if nothing is done

- How often the threat may occur

- The measure of the likelihood that the threat will occur

Risk assessment is a method that enables an organization to quantify the level of risk that is inherent in a system. The first step in risk assessment is to identify assets such as hardware, software, and intellectual property. The second step is to identify the threats to the assets. These threats include unauthorized access to resources and information, unintentional or unauthorized disclosure of information, and DoS.

A successful security policy can be subdivided into smaller policies, each covering a specific topic related to the overall security of the network. Some of these "subpolicies" include the following:

- Acceptable-use policy

- Authentication policy

- Accountability policy

- Access policy

- Privacy policy

- Violations-reporting policy

In the Security Wheel concept, network security is treated as a *continuous* process that is built around the corporate security policy. This process is divided into four phases:

1. Securing the network.

2. Monitoring the network.

3. Testing the security of the network.

4. Improving the security of the network.

Q&A

As mentioned in the introduction, "All About the Cisco Certified Security Professional Certification," you have two choices for review questions. The questions that follow next give you a bigger challenge than the exam itself by using an open-ended question format. By reviewing now with this more difficult question format, you can better exercise your memory and prove your conceptual and factual knowledge of this chapter. Appendix A provides the answers to these questions so that you can verify the topic areas in which you are proficient and those topic areas for which you need to study further.

For more practice with exam-like question formats, including questions using a router simulator and multiple choice questions, use the exam engine on the CD-ROM.

1. What are the three elements of a good security policy?

2. What are some of the more common threats described in RFC 2196?

3. What are the key trade-offs that define the corporate security goals?

4. Within the field of network security, what does CIA stand for?

5. What are some of the physical assets of a network?

6. What is a privacy policy?

7. What is an acceptable-use policy?

8. Describe the four phases of the security wheel.

References

Fraser, B. "Site Security Handbook – RFC 2196." http://www.ietf.org/rfc/rfc2196.txt; September 1997.

Malik, S. *Network Security Principles and Practices*. Indianapolis, Indiana: Cisco Press; 2003.

Pfleeger, C. *Security in Computing*, 2d ed. Englewood Cliffs, New Jersey: Prentice Hall; 1996.

The SANS Institute. "The SANS Security Policy Project." http://www.sans.org/resources/policies; 2002.

This chapter covers the following types of attacks:

- Reconnaissance Attacks

- Denial of Service Attacks

- Unauthorized Access Attacks

- Application Layer Attacks

- Trust Exploitation Attacks

CHAPTER 6

Classifying Rudimentary Network Attacks

This chapter covers a wide range of attacks, including reconnaissance attacks, unauthorized access, denial of service (DoS) attacks, application layer attacks, and trust exploitation attacks. All of these attacks are designed for either one of two purposes: to gain access to a system or network or to deny access to a system or network to legitimate users. To understand how to defend against these attacks, you first must understand how the attacks work. Therefore, each of these attacks is covered in greater detail in the sections that follow. Defense against the attacks described here is covered in Chapter 8, "Mitigating Rudimentary Network Attacks."

"Do I Know This Already?" Quiz

The purpose of the "Do I Know This Already?" quiz is to help you decide if you really need to read the entire chapter. If you already intend to read the entire chapter, you do not necessarily need to answer these questions now.

The 10-question quiz, derived from the major sections in the "Foundation Topics" portion of the chapter, helps you determine how to spend your limited study time.

Table 6-1 outlines the major topics discussed in this chapter and the "Do I Know This Already?" quiz questions that correspond to those topics.

Table 6-1 *"Do I Know This Already?" Foundation Topics Section-to-Question Mapping*

Foundations Topics Section	Questions Covered in This Section
Reconnaissance Attacks	1–2
Denial of Service Attacks	3–4
Unauthorized Access Attacks	5
Application Layer Attacks	6–8
Trust Exploitation Attacks	9–10

> **CAUTION** The goal of self-assessment is to gauge your mastery of the topics in this chapter. If you do not know the answer to a question or are only partially sure of the answer, you should mark this question wrong for purposes of the self-assessment. Giving yourself credit for an answer you correctly guess skews your self-assessment results and might provide you with a false sense of security.

1. Ping is a reliable ICMP echo scan. What is another reliable type of scan that can be used to enumerate hosts on a target network?

   a. ICMP echo-reply scan

   b. ICMP traceroute scan

   c. Blind TCP scan

   d. UDP ping

   e. ICMP timestamp scan

2. What TCP bit must be set to allow packets to pass through a router's access control list?

   a. PSH

   b. URG

   c. DMP

   d. SYN

   e. ACK

3. Which of the following are examples of DDoS attack tools?

   a. SQL Slammer

   b. stacheldracht

   c. trin00

   d. slapper

   e. Li0n

4. DDoS attacks are based on a two-tier model of systems. What are the two types of systems involved in a DDoS attack called?

   a. Client and server

   b. Target and attacker

   c. Zombie and client

   d. Handler and agent

   e. Master and target

5. Unauthorized access attacks can be conducted over what applications?

    a. Telnet

    b. SSH

    c. FTP

    d. HTTPS

    e. All of the above

6. What does an attacker gain by using application layer attacks?

    a. The ability to perform a denial of service

    b. Reconnaissance

    c. Access to a host

    d. Target enumeration

7. Which of the following are application layer attacks?

    a. IIS directory traversal

    b. Ping of death

    c. ICMP flood

    d. land.c

    e. Solaris snmpXdmid buffer overflow

8. Which of the following attacks is related to a buffer overflow?

    a. Buffer underflow

    b. Miss-by-one attack

    c. Format string attack

    d. Fast Data MMU Miss attack

    e. None of the above

9. Which services on UNIX hosts do trust exploitation attacks typically involve?

    a. Telnet

    b. FTP

    c. RSH

    d. R-login

    e. None of the above

10. How do trust exploitation attacks work?

    a. By bypassing all authentication methods on a system

    b. By providing the attacker with a trust token that can be used to gain access to any host on the network

    c. By exploiting the file systems exported by a server

    d. None of the above

The answers to the "Do I Know This Already?" quiz are found in Appendix A, "Answers to the 'Do I Know This Already?' Quizzes and Q&A Sections." The suggested choices for your next step are as follows:

- **8 or less overall score**—Read the entire chapter. This includes the "Foundation Topics" and "Foundation Summary" sections, and the "Q&A" section.

- **9 or more overall score**—If you want more review on these topics, skip to the "Foundation Summary" section and then go to the "Q&A" section. Otherwise, move to the next chapter.

Foundation Topics

Reconnaissance Attacks

Network reconnaissance is the act of gathering information about a network in preparation for a possible attack. This information can be garnered from a wide variety of sources. The sources of information for a reconnaissance attack can include what is called *uncontrollable information*, which is information that the network staff cannot control because it is disseminated to network sweeps and port scans. Some examples of uncontrollable information include the IP address ranges owned by a company, which an attacker can determine through the use of the ARIN, RIPE, or APNIC databases, and domain name ownership information and DNS server IP addresses, which an attacker can determine by querying network registry databases such as Network Solutions or Register.com.

Typically, after an attacker identifies the network ranges for a target, the attacker begins host discovery, which can be accomplished in a variety of ways. One way is to use ICMP ping sweeps or scans of the network ranges. Another way is to use a blind-TCP scan, whereby the attacker uses a tool, such as Nmap, to scan the network ranges using TCP instead of ICMP. This scan can search for common services such as web, mail, and FTP services. Although a blind-TCP scan may not provide a complete picture of all possible hosts that are reachable across the Internet, it does provide a sufficient list of publicly available servers. The blind-TCP scan can remain virtually invisible to network administrators because it searches only the set of ports that are likely to be open. Figure 6-1 shows how a blind-TCP scan works. In most cases, only two parts of the TCP three-way handshake (SYN, SYN-ACK, ACK) are completed. The scanning tool may choose not to complete the three-way handshake or it may send a RESET (RST) packet back to close the target's half-open TCP port.

Figure 6-1 *Blind-TCP Scan*

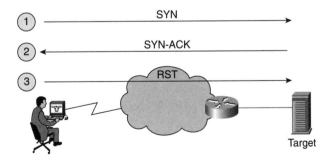

Other methods of host discovery include using TCP scans with unusual flag settings. For example, suppose the attacker suspects that the network administrators have access control lists (ACLs)

deployed on the edge router of the network to filter inbound TCP connections but allow connections that are a part of existing connections to originate from the inside of the network. To work around this obstacle, the attacker may try a TCP ACK scan (a scan in which the ACK bit in the TCP header is set) to pass packets through the router's ACLs. When the packets reach their targets, the proper response (as defined in RFC 793) by a host to an unsolicited TCP ACK packet is either to send a TCP RST packet back to the originator if a service is running on the port in question or to not respond at all if there is no service associated with the port being targeted. Once an attacker has enumerated the hosts on a network, the attacker can move on identify the operating system of the target host as well as enumerating the services available in order to try to compromise that host on one of those services.

Network reconnaissance cannot be entirely prevented. Blocking ICMP echo and echo-reply scans at the edge router stops ping sweeps but does so at the expense of important diagnostic capabilities. Protecting against network reconnaissance involves a more complex combination of remedies such as ICMP filtering, eliminating service banners on hosts, and reducing the number of available service on hosts. These techniques are discussed in more detail in Chapter 8.

Denial of Service Attacks

DoS attacks are not aimed at gaining access to a network or the information on a network but rather at making a service or a network unavailable to legitimate users. DoS attacks fall into two general categories:

- **Nondistributed denial of service**—These attacks are directed against a specific service such as Telnet, FTP, or some other service.

- **Distributed denial of service (DDoS)**—These attacks are directed at a specific host or network with the aim of preventing access to the target by consuming all of the bandwidth to the target.

Nondistributed Denial of Service Attacks

DoS attacks against specific services such as web, FTP, or Telnet services are typically accomplished by acquiring and keeping open all available connections to the service. This approach exploits weaknesses in network architecture and network protocols rather than introducing a software bug. Another method commonly used in DoS attacks is an attack that causes the service to terminate— for example, through a buffer overflow against the BIND named process. DoS attacks include such notables as ICMP ping floods, TCP SYN floods, and the Ping of Death attack.

The TCP SYN flood attack is a DoS attack that is used to open a large number of half-open TCP connections to the target. Half-open TCP connections are ones where the initial SYN packet has been sent to the target, which then responds with the appropriate SYN-ACK packet. The connection remains in a "half-open" state because the final ACK packet from the originating system to the target has not been sent. This leaves the status of the connection in a sort of pending state on the target, which must wait for the TCP connection timer to expire before deleting the connection entry from the TCP state table. During a TCP SYN flood, TCP SYN packets are sent to the target system, which then responds with SYN-ACK packets. The attacker does not send back the necessary ACK packets to the target but keeps sending new SYN packets until the TCP SYN queue on the host becomes filled. Once filled, the target can no longer accept any more TCP connections until some of the TCP SYN connections in the queue age out.

Distributed Denial of Service Attacks

DDoS attacks attempt to inflict damage by flooding the network or the host with useless and undesired traffic. In this type of attack, the attacker gains control of hosts on networks other than the target and installs software on those hosts to control them. Typically, these hosts are considered zombies, slaves, or agents. The hosts that are between the attacker's computer and the agents are known as handlers or masters. The attacker may have developed this additional layer to make it harder to track the DDoS system back to the controlling attacker. The attacker's main host is used to direct the handlers to send traffic that instruct the agents to attack a specific target. By coordinating the agents in a singular attack, the attacker is able to increase the amount of traffic in the overall attack and potentially overwhelm the target. This type of attack is shown in Figure 6-2.

Figure 6-2 *DDoS Attack*

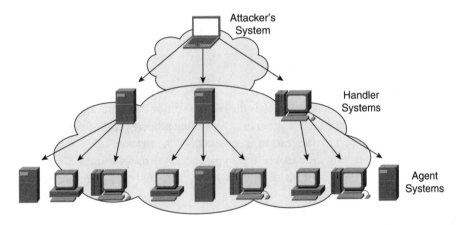

DDoS attacks include stacheldracht, trin00, Tribe Flood Network (TFN), TFN2K, mstream, and shaft.

Unauthorized Access Attacks

Although the category "unauthorized access" is not limited to specific attacks against networks, it does cover the most common type of attack that is executed today. When users, whether legitimate or not, connect to a service port such as SSH or Telnet, they may be greeted with a message stating "Unauthorized Access Is Prohibited." If attackers continue to *attempt* to access the system, their actions are unauthorized. These attacks can occur both outside of and within a network. This attack category does not include an attacker who is connecting to a port to see whether a service is active there; that typically falls into the "reconnaissance" category. Nor does the absence of any warning banner mean that access by anyone is welcome. This category includes any attempt by a person who knowingly tries to access a system to which that person does not have specific access permissions.

Application Layer Attacks

Application layer attacks target specific applications, such as web, FTP, or SMTP services, running on a host. Attackers who successfully exploit a weakness in an application gain access to the host at the same privilege level as the application.

IIS Directory Traversal Vulnerability

One of the most widely known targets of an application layer attack is the Microsoft Internet Information Server (IIS) directory traversal vulnerability or UNICODE attack. An attacker who exploits this vulnerability is capable of searching the directories on the server outside of the web root directory. This allows them to view files that they would normally not have access to. It also allows the attacker to exploit certain commands, such as **tftp**, to further exploit the host. This can all be done through a regular web browser such as Internet Explorer or Netscape. One particular program that was written to use this exploit is called iis-zang, which provides an attacker with a pseudo-command-line interface to the web server. Microsoft provided a patch for this vulnerability in August of 2000 and published Microsoft Security Bulletin MS00-057 regarding this vulnerability.

Buffer Overflow

Another type of application layer attack is the buffer overflow, which is made possible by improper bounds checking of input data in a program. By sending properly crafted data to the program, the attacker is able to redirect the program to execute code of the attacker's choice. This typically results in the creation of a shell for the attacker to then gain access to the system. Buffer overflows can also result in a DoS as in the case of many of the BIND exploits and the Solaris snmpXdmid exploit.

String Attack

String attacks are very similar to buffer overflows. With string attacks, the attacker relies on an improper bounds check in the format of a string to be printed by the program. This type of attack is considerably harder to execute than a standard buffer overflow because of the need to properly inject the attack code into the format statement.

Trust Exploitation Attacks

A trust relationship exists between two systems when each system agrees to accept communication from the other system without explicitly authenticating the connection. Trust is established in a variety of ways. There are Windows trust relationships in which one domain may trust another domain and provide for pass-through authentication. On UNIX systems, there is the r-services trust relationship. The trust involved with r-services differs from Windows trust relationships in that no authentication beyond host name or IP address is needed to establish a communication channel.

The most common way a trust relationship exists in UNIX systems is through the /etc/hosts.equiv file or the .rhosts file in a user's home directory. A connection request is made without any further checking or authentication when the following three conditions are met simultaneously:

- A remote-access request is made using the **rlogin**, **rcp**, **rsh**, or **rdist** facilities.

- The originating machine's name exists in the /etc/hosts.equiv file (or in the requesting user's .rhosts file in the home directory).

- The username of the user making the request exists in the target host's /etc/passwd file.

When these three conditions are met simultaneously, the request is granted by means of the trust relationship, and the request completely bypasses all configured authentication mechanisms on the host.

Another type of trust relationship can occur when two or more systems exist on the same subnet. It is assumed that because the systems reside within the same subnet, they must be *trustable*. One compromised system can easily lead to a compromise of others because of this misguided trust. Another possibility exists when a system on the inside of a firewall explicitly trusts a system on the outside. A compromised external system can then lead to a compromised internal system.

Foundation Summary

The "Foundation Summary" section of each chapter lists the most important facts from the chapter. Although this section does not list every fact from the chapter that will be on the CSI exam, a well-prepared CSI candidate should at a minimum know all the details in each "Foundation Summary" section before taking the exam.

Rudimentary network attacks include the following:

- **Reconnaissance attacks**—Gather information about a network in preparation for another possible attack

- **DoS attacks**—Render a service or a network unavailable to legitimate users

- **Unauthorized access attacks**—Attempts made by a person who knowingly tries to access a system for which that person does not have specific access permissions

- **Application layer attacks**—Exploit specific weaknesses in applications, such as web, FTP, or SMTP services, running on a host

- **Trust exploitation attacks**—Bypass all authentication methods on a system

DoS attacks fall into two general categories:

- **Nondistributed denial of service**—These attacks are directed against a specific service such as Telnet, FTP, or some other service.

- **Distributed denial of service**—These attacks are aimed at a specific host or network with the aim of preventing access to the target by consuming all of the bandwidth to the target.

Q&A

As mentioned in the introduction, "All About the Cisco Certified Security Professional Certification," you have two choices for review questions. The questions that follow next give you a bigger challenge than the exam itself by using an open-ended question format. By reviewing now with this more difficult question format, you can exercise your memory better and prove your conceptual and factual knowledge of this chapter. The answers to these questions are found in Appendix A.

For more practice with exam-like question formats, including questions using a router simulator and multiple choice questions, use the exam engine on the CD-ROM.

1. What are some of the benefits and drawbacks of ICMP scanning?

2. What is the order of events of an attack on a target network?

3. What are trust exploitation attacks?

4. Name some DDoS attacks?

5. What are buffer overflows?

6. What type of attacks are buffer overflows and format string attacks?

7. How does the TCP SYN flood attack work?

8. What is a blind-TCP scan?

9. If a TCP ACK packet is sent to a port where a service is not listening, what is the response defined in RFC 793?

10. If a TCP ACK packet is sent to a port where a service is listening, what is the response defined in RFC 793?

11. What are the two types of systems that are used in a DDoS attack?

This chapter covers the following topics:

- IP Spoofing

- Packet Sniffers

- Password Attacks

- Man-In-The-Middle Attacks

- Port Redirection

- Virus and Trojan-Horse Applications

CHAPTER 7

Classifying Sophisticated Network Attacks

This chapter continues the analysis of various network attacks introduced in Chapter 6, "Classifying Rudimentary Network Attacks." Many of the attacks covered in this chapter typically require that the attacker have software skills that are more advanced than the skills needed to execute the attacks described in Chapter 6. The attacks covered in this chapter include IP spoofing attacks, traffic sniffing, password attacks, man-in-the-middle attacks, port redirection, and virus and Trojan-horse applications.

Some of the attacks covered in this chapter cannot be executed effectively unless the attacker has access to a system on a network. Other attacks, such as IP spoofing, port redirection, and man-in-the-middle attacks, do not require such access but do require additional skill on the part of the attacker in order to be successfully executed. The intent, however, is the same as the attacks covered in the previous chapter: to gain access to a system or network.

"Do I Know This Already?" Quiz

The purpose of the "Do I Know This Already?" quiz is to help you decide if you really need to read the entire chapter. If you already intend to read the entire chapter, you do not necessarily need to answer these questions now.

The 10-question quiz, derived from the major sections in the "Foundation Topics" portion of the chapter, helps you determine how to spend your limited study time.

Table 7-1 outlines the major topics discussed in this chapter and the "Do I Know This Already?" quiz questions that correspond to those topics.

Table 7-1 *"Do I Know This Already?" Foundation Topics Section-to-Question Mapping*

Foundations Topics Section	Questions Covered in This Section
IP Spoofing	1–3
Packet Sniffers	4–5
Password Attacks	6
Man-In-The-Middle Attacks	7
Port Redirection Attacks	8–9
Virus and Trojan-Horse Applications	10

CAUTION The goal of self-assessment is to gauge your mastery of the topics in this chapter. If you do not know the answer to a question or are only partially sure of the answer, you should mark this question wrong for purposes of the self-assessment. Giving yourself credit for an answer you correctly guess skews your self-assessment results and might provide you with a false sense of security.

1. What is the purpose of IP spoofing attacks?

    a. To get packets past a firewall

    b. To gain access to a network resource

    c. To test router access lists

    d. To inject data into a pre-existing communication channel between two systems

    e. None of the above

2. What type of IP spoofing attack occurs if the attacker is not concerned with the responses from the target system?

    a. Bidirectional

    b. Blind

    c. Tangential

    d. Source

    e. Derivational

3. What type of spoofing attack occurs when the attacker controls the routing tables to redirect the response packets back to his IP address?

    a. Bidirectional

    b. Blind

    c. Tangential

    d. Source

    e. Derivational

4. In what mode must a network interface work to receive all packets on the physical network wire and pass those packets up to an application?

    a. Sniffing

    b. Locked

    c. Unlocked

    d. Sensing

    e. Promiscuous

5. Which of the following protocols are susceptible to passive sniffers?

    a. SNMP

    b. SSH

    c. HTTPS

    d. Telnet

    e. HTTP

6. What type of attack is an attacker executing when she connects to a system and tries various account names and common default passwords?

    a. Deduction

    b. Brute-force

    c. Intuitive

    d. Driven

7. For what purpose are man-in-the-middle attacks most commonly used?

    a. To capture sensitive information

    b. To hijack ongoing sessions

    c. To deny service

    d. To corrupt transmitted data

    e. All of the above

8. Port redirection is a specific case of what general category of attack?

    a. IP spoofing

    b. Trust exploitation

    c. Man-in-the-middle

    d. Denial of service

    e. None of the above

9. Which of the following can be used to execute a port redirection attack?

    a. httptunnel

    b. Ethereal

    c. Netcat

    d. strobe

    e. Nmap

10. What is the most common means of propogating viruses and Trojan-horse applications?

    a. E-mail

    b. FTP

    c. scp

    d. The web

    e. NetBIOS shares

The answers to the "Do I Know This Already?" quiz are found in Appendix A, "Answers to the 'Do I Know This Already?' Quizzes and Q&A Sections." The suggested choices for your next step are as follows:

■   **8 or less overall score**—Read the entire chapter. This includes the "Foundation Topics" and "Foundation Summary" sections, and the "Q&A" section.

■   **9 or more overall score**—If you want more review on these topics, skip to the "Foundation Summary" section and then go to the "Q&A" section. Otherwise, move to the next chapter.

Foundation Topics

IP Spoofing

IP spoofing occurs when attackers, whether within a network or outside a network, attempt to gain access to a restricted resource by disguising the IP address of their systems as that of other systems. The system being spoofed by the attacker has access to the restricted resource and the restriction is solely based on the source IP address of the communication.

Typically, IP spoofing is carried out by injecting data into a pre-existing communication channel between two systems to gain unauthorized access to computer systems. If attackers are not interested in the content of the responses from the target system, they can use an IP spoofing attack in a blind or unidirectional fashion in which they assume what the response from the target will be and send their information without any awareness of the response's content. For true bidirectional communication, the attacker must control the routing tables to redirect the packets for the spoofed IP address to the attacker's system.

Packet Sniffers

A packet sniffer is a software application that uses a network adapter card in promiscuous mode. In promiscuous mode, the network adapter card is able to receive all packets on the physical network wire and pass those packets up to an application. Packet sniffers are typically used for network troubleshooting and traffic analysis, but they can also be used to capture sensitive information such as usernames and passwords. Telnet, FTP, SNMP, and SMTP all send their traffic between the client and the server in clear text. This can result in an attacker gaining access to sensitive information by capturing information through a packet sniffer.

If attackers capture usernames and passwords on one system, they can try those same username and password combinations on other systems and potentially gain access. In a worst-case scenario, attackers can gain access to a user account that has administrative privileges. They can then use that account to create a new account with administrative privileges and use it at any time as a back door into a network.

Password Attacks

There are various approaches to attacking a system's passwords. The low-tech approach involves simple brute-force attacks whereby the attacker connects to the system and tries various account names and common default passwords for that account. An attacker who discovers a router on a network and Telnets to the system will try such common default passwords first in the hope that they will provide easy access to the device.

Other avenues of attack against passwords include installed Trojan-horse programs to capture account names and passwords, IP spoofing, and packet sniffers.

Once account information has been captured, the attacker can access the system with the same privilege level as the compromised user. As with packet sniffers, if the account has administrative privileges, the attacker using a password attack can create back doors for future access to the system. Additionally, the attacker can then capture the /etc/passwd and /etc/shadow files from a UNIX host or dump the SAM from a Windows system and use a password attack tool such as L0phtCrack or John the Ripper to crack additional passwords.

A final problem with passwords is that users tend to use the same passwords, however strong, on multiple systems that they connect to. Consequently, an attacker who compromises one account on one system can use that account to gain access to a wide range of systems throughout the network.

Man-In-The-Middle Attacks

Man-in-the-middle attacks cover situations in which the attacker is able to intercept packets that are crossing a network, modify or falsify the information in those packets, and then reinject the modified packets into the network. These attacks can be used to capture sensitive information, hijack ongoing sessions, create DoS occurrences, corrupt transmitted data, or introduce new, typically false, information into network sessions.

An example of a man-in-the-middle attack is shown in Figure 7-1. Here, the attacker intercepts and establishes a communication link with the web server client on the left in step 1. This can be done by spoofing the IP address of the real web server, WWW, in the client's DNS server in Figure 7-1. When the client queries the DNS server for the IP address of the web server, WWW, the DNS server responds with the IP address of the attacker's host. The attacker's host is running a web server with web pages that are identical, or nearly identical, to the web pages on the real web server, WWW. The client connects to the attacker's web server and inputs their information, as shown in step 2. The attacker's host then connects to the real web server, WWW, establishes a connection, and relays the client information to the server in step 3. The response from the server is then relayed back to the client system in steps 4 and 5.

Figure 7-1 *Man-In-The-Middle Attack*

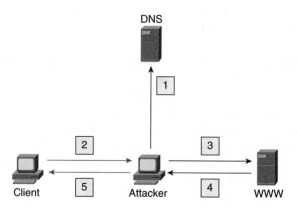

Port Redirection

Port redirection is a specific case of trust exploitation. Essentially, this is a tunneling type of attack. In this case, an attacker uses a compromised host to relay traffic passed through an open port on a firewall or in a router's ACLs that would normally be denied. This is shown in Figure 7-2.

Figure 7-2 *Port Redirection Attack*

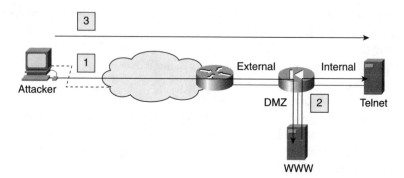

Consider a firewall with three interfaces—internal, external, and a DMZ interface, as shown in Figure 7-1. The hosts on the external interface (those that are in the Internet) can reach the hosts in the DMZ but not those on the internal LAN. The hosts on the internal LAN can reach hosts both in the DMZ and on the outside. The hosts in the DMZ can reach hosts on the outside and hosts on the internal LAN.

A host on the DMZ that is compromised by an attacker may be able to redirect connections directly to the internal LAN. In the example shown in Figure 7-1, an attacker compromises the web server in step 1, and in step 2 sets up a redirection program that takes incoming connections on port 80 and sends the traffic to the Telnet port on a host in the internal network. The attacker then simply connects to the web port on the DMZ host and is automatically connected to the Telnet port on the host in the internal LAN, as shown in step 3. Neither of these connections violates the firewall policy; however, the attacker has achieved a direct connection to the internal network. Examples of software that can provide this capability are Netcat (http://www.atstake.com/research/tools/network_utilities/) and httptunnel (http://www.nocrew.org/software/httptunnel.html).

Virus and Trojan-Horse Applications

Viruses are small pieces of mobile code that attach to other programs or documents and can then infect a computer when the program is executed or the document is opened. Trojan horses are applications that appear to be benign but contain potentially malicious code that can be used to attack the system it is run on.

An example of a Trojan-horse program is one that appears to be a game or some other normal application but when played inserts itself into the system, opens up a port on the host, and sends an e-mail to the attacker that indicates that it has successfully infected the host. The attacker can then connect into the system from the outside and access the system and the network.

Examples of viruses include the Melissa and the "I Love You" viruses, which were Visual Basic scripts attached to e-mail. When the user opened the e-mail, the mail program executed the code found in the scripts, which caused the virus to be mailed to every e-mail address in the user's address book.

Foundation Summary

The "Foundation Summary" section of each chapter lists the most important facts from the chapter. Although this section does not list every fact from the chapter that will be on your CSI exam, a well-prepared CSI candidate should at a minimum know all the details in each "Foundation Summary" section before taking the exam.

Sophisticated network attacks include the following:

- **IP spoofing**—Attackers, whether within a network or outside a network, attempt to gain access to a restricted resource by disguising the IP address of their systems as that of other systems.

- **Packet sniffer**—A software application that uses a network adapter card in promiscuous mode. In promiscuous mode, the network adapter card is able to receive all packets on the physical network wire and pass those packets up to an application.

- **Password attack**—An attacker captures a user's password to access the system with that user's privilege level.

- **Man-in-the-middle attack**—An attacker intercepts packets crossing a network, modifies or falsifies the information in those packets, and then reinjects the modified packets into the network.

- **Port redirection**—A form of trust exploitation in which an attacker uses a compromised host to relay traffic passed through an open port on a firewall or in a router's access lists that would normally be denied.

- **Virus and Trojan-horse applications**—Viruses are small pieces of mobile code that attach to other programs or documents and can then infect a computer when the program is executed or the document is opened. Trojan horses are applications that appear to be benign but contain potentially malicious code that can be used to attack the system it is run on.

Q&A

As mentioned in the introduction, "All About the Cisco Certified Security Professional Certification," you have two choices for review questions. The questions that follow next give you a bigger challenge than the exam itself by using an open-ended question format. By reviewing now with this more difficult question format, you can exercise your memory better and prove your conceptual and factual knowledge of this chapter. The answers to these questions are found in Appendix A.

For more practice with exam-like question formats, including questions using a router simulator and multiple choice questions, use the exam engine on the CD-ROM.

1. What is an IP spoofing attack?

2. How can an attacker receive packets if he is spoofing the IP address of his system to attack the target?

3. How do packet sniffers work?

4. What kind of information can packet sniffers capture?

5. What is a brute-force password attack?

6. Once attackers have cracked an account through password attacks, what can they do?

7. What is a man-in-the-middle attack?

8. What is a port redirection attack?

9. What are two software packages that an attacker can use to execute a port redirection attack?

10. What is a virus?

11. What is a Trojan-horse application?

This chapter covers the following topics:

- Mitigating Reconnaissance Attacks

- Mitigating Denial of Service Attacks

- Protecting Against Unauthorized Access

- Mitigating Application Layer Attacks

- Guarding Against Trust Exploitation

CHAPTER 8

Mitigating Rudimentary Network Attacks

Chapters 6 and 7 covered various attacks that may be launched against a network. This chapter covers the mitigation of the attacks described in Chapter 6, "Classifying Rudimentary Network Attacks": reconnaissance, unauthorized access, denial of service (DoS), application layer, and trust exploitation attacks. The mitigation techniques discussed in this chapter are based on network security best common practices (BCPs) and on SAFE concepts.

Although both this chapter and Chapter 9, "Mitigating Sophisticated Network Attacks," cover a fair amount of detail on mitigating attacks, by no means do the chapters present an exhaustive discussion. Each attack is unique and has its own set of requirements for an effective defense. Nevertheless, this chapter provides a starting point for network administrators to understand how to implement the principles in SAFE to better protect their networks.

"Do I Know This Already?" Quiz

The purpose of the "Do I Know This Already?" quiz is to help you decide if you really need to read the entire chapter. If you already intend to read the entire chapter, you do not necessarily need to answer these questions now.

The 10-question quiz, derived from the major sections in "Foundation Topics" portion of the chapter, helps you determine how to spend your limited study time.

Table 8-1 outlines the major topics discussed in this chapter and the "Do I Know This Already?" quiz questions that correspond to those topics.

Table 8-1 *"Do I Know This Already?" Foundation Topics Section-to-Question Mapping*

Foundations Topics Section	Questions Covered in This Section
Mitigating Reconnaissance Attacks	1–3
Mitigating Denial of Service Attacks	4–6
Protecting Against Unauthorized Access	7
Mitigating Application Layer Attacks	8–9
Guarding Against Trust Exploitation	10

CAUTION The goal of self-assessment is to gauge your mastery of the topics in this chapter. If you do not know the answer to a question or are only partially sure of the answer, you should mark this question wrong for purposes of the self-assessment. Giving yourself credit for an answer you correctly guess skews your self-assessment results and might provide you with a false sense of security.

1. Which of the following are sources from which an attacker can determine information about a target network?

   a. DNS

   b. ARIN/RIPC/APNIC records

   c. whois information

   d. Phone book

   e. All of the above

2. What does "network posture visibility reduction" mean?

   a. Lower the number of all the servers in the network

   b. Reduce the number of users that can access the network

   c. Eliminate essential services from servers in the public-facing segment to a minimum

   d. Reduce the number of services in the public-facing segment of the network to a minimum

   e. None of the above

3. Which of the following actions should be taken to harden applications and thereby make it more difficult for an attacker to perform reconnaissance on a network?

   a. Remove application banners from application greetings

   b. Apply patches to all applications

   c. Turn off unnecessary services

   d. Apply access control lists to edge routers

   e. Turn off essential services

4. What is the purpose of RFC 2827?

   a. It defines a range of network addresses to be used for private networks.

   b. It describes a method of mitigating DoS attacks.

   c. It describes the behavior of the TCP protocol.

   d. It defines site security procedures.

   e. It defines the behavior of the IP protocol.

5. Which feature of Cisco routers is considered an "anti-DoS" feature?

   a. NetFlow

   b. Fast switching

   c. Stateful firewall

   d. TCP intercept

   e. None of the above

6. Which of the following methods can you utilize to mitigate the effects of DoS attacks?

   a. NetFlow

   b. Traffic-rate limiting

   c. Fast switching

   d. Quality of service

   e. Stateful firewall

7. Which of the following is classified as an unauthorized access attack?

  a. An attacker connects to a web server and downloads publicly available files

  b. An attacker connects to an anonymous FTP server and downloads publicly available files

  c. An attacker connects to the SMTP port of a mail server and forges e-mail

  d. An attacker queries DNS for information about hosts on the network

  e. An attacker connects to the Telnet port of a system and repeatedly tries various username/password combinations until he gains entry to the system

8. What makes application layer attacks possible?

  a. Vulnerabilities in applications

  b. Poor access control lists

  c. Lack of proper firewall configuration

  d. Poor password choices

  e. None of the above

9. How can network and system administration personnel reduce the risk of an application layer attack?

  a. They can't; application layer attacks are inevitable

  b. Follow system administration best common practices

  c. Turn off applications

  d. Block application ports at the firewall

  e. All of the above

10. If an attacker is able to gain access to an internal server through a DMZ web server, what is the possible cause?

  a. The DMZ web server was not configured properly.

  b. The DMZ web server was vulnerable to exploitation.

  c. The edge router access control list was not blocking port 80.

  d. The firewall access control lists allowed for the DMZ web server to connect to the internal server.

  e. The internal server root password was weak.

The answers to the "Do I Know This Already?" quiz are found in Appendix A, "Answers to the 'Do I Know This Already?' Quizzes and Q&A Sections." The suggested choices for your next step are as follows:

- **8 or less overall score**—Read the entire chapter. This includes the "Foundation Topics" and "Foundation Summary" sections, and the "Q&A" section.

- **9 or more overall score**—If you want more review on these topics, skip to the "Foundation Summary" section and then go to the "Q&A" section. Otherwise, move to the next chapter.

Foundation Topics

Mitigating Reconnaissance Attacks

Reconnaissance attack mitigation centers on protecting the network from scouting forays by attackers. It is not possible to completely protect address range information in ARIN, APNIC, and RIPE or domain name information in a network registrar from being evaluated by an attacker. You must assume that an attacker can ferret out that information with relative ease. With that in mind, you should understand that, realistically, defense begins at the network perimeter, and starting it there involves two basic techniques: reducing the network posture visibility and hardening the application.

Network Posture Visibility

Reducing the visibility of the network posture involves reducing the number of services in the public-facing segment of the network to a minimum. This means that if a web server, an SMTP server, an FTP server, and a DNS server are situated in the DMZ of the Corporate Internet module, the only inbound ports open at the edge router are for web, e-mail, FTP, and DNS to those servers. All other ports are blocked with an access control list (ACL). If other hosts exist in the DMZ but access from the outside is not required, no traffic should reach these hosts through the edge router. This concept is shown in Figure 8-1. There are four servers behind the router:

- WWW

- DNS

- SMTP

- SQL

Figure 8-1 *Network Posture Visibility*

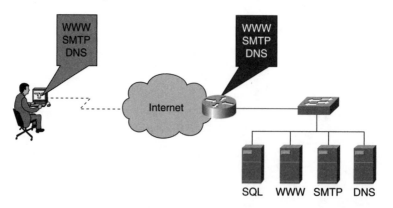

The attacker scans the network but only finds three servers—WWW, DNS, and SMTP servers. The fourth server is not visible to the attacker because the ACLs on the router deny access to the SQL server.

Application Hardening

Application hardening involves staying current on patches for all applications and reducing any information the applications may provide through service banners. It is possible to configure sendmail, a popular mail transport agent (MTA), so that it does not announce its version number when another MTA connects to it. Similarly, many Telnet and FTP daemons can be configured not to announce the operating system type or version number when a client connects. Removing banner information from the application makes reconnaissance much more difficult for an attacker.

Mitigating Denial of Service Attacks

Defeating DoS attacks or distributed DoS (DDoS) attacks (described in Chapter 6) begins by identifying the weak points in the network architecture where DoS attacks may have an advantage. Typically, weak points are located at the edge router. If an attacker launches a DDoS attack that is meant to consume the available network bandwidth, stopping the attack at the edge router does little good. Stopping a large DDoS attack requires coordination with the upstream ISP. DoS attack defense involves not just defending against a targeted DoS attack but also taking care to ensure that the network is not the source of a DoS attack Recall that DoS attacks attempt to inflict damage by flooding a network or a host with useless and undesired traffic. This traffic originates from a single host or multiple systems (in the case of DDoS) that an attacker has previously compromised. Preventing an attacker from compromising systems on the network in the first place prevents those systems from being the source of an attacker's DoS traffic. There are three primary methods of mitigating DoS attacks:

- Antispoof features

- Anti-DoS features

- Traffic-rate limiting

Antispoof Features

Antispoof features depend on RFC 2827 filtering. In short, although RFC 2827 is written mainly from an ISP perspective, it is equally applicable to networks of any size. RFC 2827 calls for filtering at the edge of the ISP network where customer networks connect. Traffic should be filtered at the edge by restricting outbound traffic to only those prefixes that are assigned to the customer. For example, in Figure 8-2, the ISP has assigned customer A the range 192.168.100.0/24 and customer B the range 192.168.101.0/24.

Figure 8-2   *RFC 2827 Filtering*

By applying filters at the ISP edge routers, the ISP can restrict traffic that is coming into the ISP network through those routers only to traffic that is assigned to those clients. The clients can implement egress filters according to the RFC 2827 guidelines as an additional filter to prevent their networks from becoming a source of DoS attacks.

Anti-DoS Features

The implementation of TCP intercept on Cisco routers also helps to mitigate DoS attacks, specifically attacks such as TCP SYN floods. Firewalls can also provide some measure of defense against TCP SYN floods by limiting the number of half-open connections permitted per host. TCP intercept works by requiring the router to intercept or "catch" the incoming TCP SYN requests from a client. The router responds to the SYN request by sending a SYN-ACK packet back and waiting for the client's final TCP ACK packet in order to complete the TCP three-way handshake. Once the three-way handshake is complete, the router replays the handshake to the server and then allows all further traffic between the server and client to continue. This feature protects a system whose incoming TCP SYN queue may be limited and thus liable to attack. This behavior is shown in Figure 8-3.

Figure 8-3   *TCP Intercept Operation*

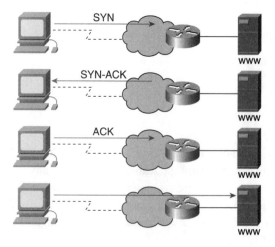

Traffic-Rate Limiting

An organization can implement, in cooperation with its ISP, traffic-rate limiting, whereby all nonessential traffic is given only a small fraction of the total bandwidth in the link. Additionally, an organization can implement quality of service (QoS) to identify permitted traffic and ensure that it is handled quickly while other, potentially unauthorized traffic is relegated to slower handling. Utilizing rate limits along with QoS shaping of traffic can greatly help to mitigate the impact of DoS and DDoS attacks.

Protecting Against Unauthorized Access

Mitigating unauthorized access is one of the easier mitigation techniques. Because an attacker must be able to access a port to gain unauthorized access to the system, the simple solution is to deny access to that port. For example, for an attacker to gain access to a system, she may need to Telnet to that system. By blocking Telnet access to systems at the router for DMZ systems and the firewall, you can prevent the attacker from reaching the Telnet port on the protected systems. Mitigation of unauthorized access comes down to implementing tight ACLs both on routers and on firewalls.

Mitigating Application Layer Attacks

Unfortunately, application layer attacks can never be completely eliminated. New vulnerabilities are being discovered across every platform and operating system. Additionally, as software becomes increasingly complex, the likelihood of a catastrophic vulnerability increases dramatically. Following system administration BCPs for host or server operating systems is the first step toward reducing the risk of an application layer attack. Additionally, the following is recommended:

- Keep current on all software patches, whether at the operating system level or the application level, for all systems active on the network

- Subscribe to mailing lists that provide information about emerging and existing vulnerabilities such as *bugtraq* and the *Computer Emergency Response Team* (CERT) mailing lists.

- Read the operating system and network logs and use available log-analysis tools to identify potential trends that may indicate an exploitive attempt against an application.

In addition to staying on top of current information as outlined in the preceding list, you should implement both host and network intrusion detection systems (IDSs) across the network. A network IDS (NIDS) monitors packets that are crossing the subnet. When a NIDS detects a potential attack, it can flag or terminate the session. A host-based IDS (HIDS) operates by inserting agents on hosts.

The agents then protect the host by detecting unauthorized activity or file modifications and responding to that activity. Because NIDSs typically work by using signatures of known attacks and then comparing network traffic to those signatures, it is susceptible to a potentially high rate of false alarms. It is critical that NIDSs be tuned properly to be most effective in detecting a true attack.

Guarding Against Trust Exploitation

Trust exploitation attacks can be mitigated through tight network access control and tight constraints on trust levels within a network. Systems in the DMZ should never be fully trusted by internal systems and the trust should be based on something other than the IP address of the trusted host.

Foundation Summary

The "Foundation Summary" section of each chapter lists the most important facts from the chapter. Although this section does not list every fact from the chapter that will be on your CSI exam, a well-prepared CSI candidate should at a minimum know all the details in each "Foundation Summary" section before taking the exam.

Network attacks include reconnaissance, unauthorized access, DoS, application layer, and trust exploitation attacks. For each type of attack, different methods can be used to mitigate the attack, but they are all based on BCPs and various concepts within the SAFE framework.

The effects of a reconnaissance attack can be reduced through a combination of a reduction in the network posture visibility and application hardening. Reducing network posture visibility includes reducing to a minimum the number of services in the public-facing segment of the network. Application hardening involves staying current on patches for the various applications on the network and reducing the amount of information provided by applications in the service banners.

DoS and DDoS attacks can be mitigated through the use of antispoofing, anti-DoS features in network equipment, and traffic-rate limiting. Antispoofing includes implementing RFC 2827 filtering both by the ISP at the edge router and at the client network.

Anti-DoS features that are available in Cisco equipment include the TCP intercept feature of routers, whereby the router "catches" the TCP SYN packet from the external client or server and responds for the target system. If the external client or server does not complete the TCP three-way handshake, the router or PIX Firewall drops the packets and the connection. This helps to protect systems from TCP SYN flood attacks.

Traffic-rate limiting is a method in which all nonessential traffic is given only a small fraction of the total bandwidth in the link. This can be used to identify important traffic to and from the network and to help to limit the damage caused by, say, an ICMP flood.

Mitigation of unauthorized access comes down to implementing tight ACLs both on routers and on firewalls and using network IDSs (NIDSs) and host-based IDSs (HIDSs).

Mitigation of application layer attacks can be accomplished by doing the following:

■   Keeping current on all software patches

- Subscribing to mailing lists such as *bugtraq* and the CERT mailing lists

- Reading the operating system and network logs and using available log-analysis tools

Additionally, NIDSs and HIDSs can be used to identify attacks that are crossing a subnet or reaching a host and trying to exploit a vulnerability.

Trust exploitation attacks can be mitigated through tight network access control and tight constraints on trust level within a network.

Q&A

As mentioned in the introduction, "All About the Cisco Certified Security Professional Certification," you have two choices for review questions. The questions that follow next give you a bigger challenge than the exam itself by using an open-ended question format. By reviewing now with this more difficult question format, you can exercise your memory better and prove your conceptual and factual knowledge of this chapter. The answers to these questions are found in Appendix A.

For more practice with exam-like question formats, including questions using a router simulator and multiple choice questions, use the exam engine on the CD-ROM.

1. What are the two basic methods of mitigating reconnaissance attacks?

2. What is network posture visibility reduction?

3. What steps should be taken to harden an application against attack?

4. DoS and DDoS attacks focus on what part of the network architecture?

5. What are the three primary methods of mitigating DoS and DDoS attacks?

6. What is RFC 2827 filtering and who does it?

7. In addition to traffic-rate limiting, what can be done to mitigate DoS attacks?

8. Why is it easy to mitigate unauthorized access attacks?

9. Why are application layer attacks always a security risk?

10. How can application layer attacks best be mitigated?

11. How do NIDSs help to mitigate application layer attacks?

12. How can HIDSs help to mitigate application layer attacks?

13. How can trust exploitation attacks be mitigated?

This chapter covers the following topics:

- Mitigating IP Spoofing Attacks

- Guarding Against Packet Sniffers

- Mitigating Password Attacks

- Mitigating Man-In-The-Middle Attacks

- Mitigating Port Redirection Attacks

- Guarding Against Virus and Trojan-Horse Applications

CHAPTER 9

Mitigating Sophisticated Network Attacks

This chapter covers mitigation techniques to counter the attacks described in Chapter 7, "Classifying Sophisticated Network Attacks." These techniques are based on the principles described in the SAFE blueprint and build on the techniques discussed in Chapter 8, "Mitigating Rudimentary Network Attacks." The attacks covered in this chapter include IP spoofing, packet sniffers, password attacks, man-in-the-middle attacks, port redirection, and virus and Trojan-horse applications.

Although this chapter, combined with Chapter 8, covers a fair amount of detail on mitigating attacks, the discussion is by no means exhaustive. Each attack is unique and has its own set of requirements for an effective defense. Nevertheless, this chapter provides a basis for network administrators to understand how to implement the principles in SAFE to better protect their networks against sophisticated network attacks.

"Do I Know This Already?" Quiz

The purpose of the "Do I Know This Already?" quiz is to help you decide if you really need to read the entire chapter. If you already intend to read the entire chapter, you do not necessarily need to answer these questions now.

The 11-question quiz, derived from the major sections in the "Foundation Topics" portion of the chapter, helps you determine how to spend your limited study time.

Table 9-1 outlines the major topics discussed in this chapter and the "Do I Know This Already?" quiz questions that correspond to those topics.

Table 9-1   *"Do I Know This Already?" Foundation Topics Section-to-Question Mapping*

Foundations Topics Section	Questions Covered in This Section
Mitigating IP Spoofing Attacks	1–3
Guarding Against Packet Sniffers	4–6
Mitigating Password Attacks	7–8

continues

Table 9-1 *"Do I Know This Already?" Foundation Topics Section-to-Question Mapping (Continued)*

Foundations Topics Section	Questions Covered in This Section
Mitigating Man-In-The-Middle Attacks	9
Mitigating Port Redirection Attacks	10
Guarding Against Virus and Trojan-Horse Applications	11

CAUTION The goal of self-assessment is to gauge your mastery of the topics in this chapter. If you do not know the answer to a question or are only partially sure of the answer, you should mark this question wrong for purposes of the self-assessment. Giving yourself credit for an answer you correctly guess skews your self-assessment results and might provide you with a false sense of security.

1. What RFC discusses suggested service provider filtering that restricts the traffic originating from an edge network to the IP address range assigned to that network?

   a. 1918

   b. 1745

   c. 973

   d. 2827

   e. 2828

2. What two methods are most effective in mitigating IP spoofing attacks?

   a. Access control

   b. Use of RFC 1918 addresses

   c. RFC 2827 filtering

   d. Strong authentication

   e. Cryptography

3. What type of trust model facilitates IP spoofing attacks?

   a. Strong

   b. Open

   c. User-based

   d. Closed

   e. IP address–based

4. Which of the following is a two-factor based authentication method?

   a. Passwords

   b. Cryptography

   c. One-time passwords

   d. IPSec

   e. Bank ATM

5. Antisniffer software works by what two methods?

   a. It detects changes in the response time of hosts to determine if the hosts are processing more traffic than their own.

   b. It identifies sniffing software running on a host.

   c. It can identify when a network interface goes into promiscuous mode.

   d. It can remotely see promiscuous packets that are captured by a host that is sniffing.

   e. There is no such thing as "antisniffer" software.

6. Why is cryptography an effective mitigation tool against sniffing?

   a. Cryptography is not an effective mitigation tool against sniffing.

   b. The attacker only sees data that appears to be a random string of bits.

   c. The key exchange masks the data being transmitted across the wire.

   d. An attacker cannot decode encrypted data without knowing the session key.

   e. Sniffing software cannot sniff encrypted packets.

7. Good passwords are characterized by which of the following?

   a. They have a minimum length of five characters.

   b. They have a combination of alphanumeric and nonalphanumeric characters.

   c. They are easy to remember.

   d. They are random.

   e. They have a minimum length of eight characters.

8. Which of the following are good password-testing tools?

   a. Ethereal

   b. John the Ripper

   c. LC4

   d. dsniff

   e. NetBIOS Audit Tool

9. Man-in-the-middle attacks can be effectively mitigated through which of the following techniques?

   a. Access control lists

   b. Strong authentication

   c. Patches

   d. Use of cryptography

   e. Firewalls

10. How are port redirection attacks successful?

    a. They rely on strong trust models between systems to allow a port on one host to connect to a port on another host.

    b. They rely on weak trust models between systems to allow a port on one host to connect to a port on another host.

    c. Port redirection attacks are not possible.

    d. They rely on poor authentication across hosts.

11. What is a key method of preventing virus and Trojan-horse applications from entering a network?

    a. Firewalls

    b. Router access lists

    c. Patches

    d. Intrusion detection

    e. Antivirus software

The answers to the "Do I Know This Already?" quiz are found in Appendix A, "Answers to the 'Do I Know This Already?' Quizzes and Q&A Sections." The suggested choices for your next step are as follows:

- **9 or less overall score**—Read the entire chapter. This includes the "Foundation Topics" and "Foundation Summary" sections, and the "Q&A" section.

- **10 or more overall score**—If you want more review on these topics, skip to the "Foundation Summary" section and then go to the "Q&A" section. Otherwise, move to the next chapter.

Foundation Topics

Mitigating IP Spoofing Attacks

Measures for mitigating IP spoofing attacks should be built into the defenses of both the enterprise network and the service provider. Although IP spoofing attacks cannot be completely eliminated, the threat they present can be reduced through access control and RFC 2827 filtering.

IP spoofing can function correctly only when devices use an IP address–based trust model for authentication, which permits or denies access to a host based on the IP address of the client. Additional authentication methods, such as cryptographic authentication or a strong two-factor authentication method using one-time passwords (OTPs), handily defeat IP spoofing attacks.

Access Control

The most effective means of mitigating IP spoofing is to properly configure access control. Denying access to any traffic that originates from an external network that claims to have a source address from the internal network reduces the effectiveness of IP spoofing. However, this method is truly effective only if the internal addresses are the only trusted addresses. This method is ineffective if external addresses, even a small set of them, are considered trusted.

RFC 2827 Filtering

As discussed in Chapter 8, RFC 2827 calls for filtering at the edge of the ISP network where customer networks connect. Traffic should be filtered at the edge by restricting traffic to only those prefixes that are assigned to the customer. Service provider customers can implement egress filters according to the RFC 2827 guidelines as an additional filter to prevent their networks from becoming a source of DoS attacks. For example, in Figure 9-1, the ISP has assigned customer A the range 192.168.100.0/24 and customer B the range 192.168.101.0/24.

Figure 9-1 *RFC 2827 Filtering*

Customer B
192.168.101.0/24

ISP

Customer A
192.168.100.0/24

By applying filters at the ISP edge routers, the ISP can restrict traffic that is coming into the ISP network through those routers to only traffic that is assigned to those clients. Note that the effectiveness of RFC 2827 filtering is significantly reduced if it is not implemented by all ISPs.

Guarding Against Packet Sniffers

Packet sniffers represent a significant threat to network security. Packet sniffers can capture traffic at a host, which jeopardizes your ability to maintain confidentiality and data integrity across the network.

Authentication

One of the most effective ways to defeat password attacks is to require strong passwords for administrator accounts and to provide users with proper training in selecting strong passwords for their own accounts. Many operating systems currently provide built-in password-testing tools to guide users in selecting strong passwords.

Another effective way to defeat password attacks is to use strong authentication, such as OTPs. Using OTPs is a two-factor authentication system that requires a person to have two items of information to complete the authentication. Typically, these items are something that the person has and something that the person knows. For example, many OTP systems use a token card to generate the password to be used. Token cards are hardware or software devices that generate a unique, random password either at timed intervals or on a per-use basis. The token card requires a personal identification number (PIN) to generate the proper OTP. In some cases, the randomly generated passwords are combined with the PIN to create a completely unique password for that one time. This method is very similar to the bank ATM. An account holder must have both their ATM card and knowledge of their PIN to access their account.

Switched Infrastructure

Switched infrastructures present a significant hurdle to packet sniffers by reducing the amount of traffic that is seen by the host that is doing the sniffing. The attacker has access only to the traffic that is destined for the specific port that the compromised host connects to. Although this does not completely eliminate the threat posed by packet sniffers, it greatly reduces their effectiveness.

Antisniffing Tools

Another method to mitigate packet sniffers is to use software or hardware that is designed to detect the use of packet sniffers. Third-party "antisniffer" tools are available that can detect changes in the response time of hosts to determine whether the hosts are processing more traffic than their own. Other software can run on the host and detect whether the network interface has entered promiscuous mode, which is necessary to facilitate sniffing activities.

Cryptography

Using cryptography is one of the most effective ways to mitigate packet sniffing. Essentially, encrypted communication renders packet sniffers irrelevant. A packet sniffer that is monitoring a cryptographic channel sees only data that appears to be a random string of bits. The original message is secure. Cryptography may involve the use of IPSec VPN tunnels, the use of the Secure Shell Protocol (SSH) to connect to another system, or the use of Secure Socket Layer (SSL).

Mitigating Password Attacks

Password attacks can be easily mitigated through the implementation of cryptographic authentication or the use of OTPs. However, not all devices, applications, or hosts support those authentication methods. Therefore, you may need to mitigate password attacks by disabling accounts after a set number of failed attempts at authentication. This helps to reduce the attacker's number of chances to crack an account through a brute-force method. Brute-force attacks involve the attacker simply trying various passwords until they finally gain access to an account on the system. These methods can be manual or automated.

Password Testing

Password testing involves the periodic attempt by administrators to crack account passwords. This is done by taking the password file and running it through a password-testing program such as LC4 (formerly known as L0phtCrack 4), Crack, or John the Ripper. These programs can apply case changes (change capitals letters to lowercase) and add nonalphanumeric characters to a list of known passwords. Although these tools may be seen as falling within the realm of the "black hat" community, they serve an essential purpose in identifying and correcting weak account passwords across systems.

User Education

Users should be educated on the content of "strong" passwords. They should be counseled regarding their choice of passwords by reminding them that passwords should not be the name of something they own, a family member's name, or the name of a pet. Effective security policies contain a password policy that guides users in how to generate strong passwords. The following guidelines can be used to define strong passwords. Passwords should

- Be at *least* eight characters in length

- Contain both upper- and lowercase characters

- Contain both alphanumeric and nonalphanumeric characters such as #, @, %, and $

Ideally, passwords are randomly generated. Unfortunately, those types of passwords are also the most difficult to remember, which leads users to write them down on paper, thereby creating additional risks.

Mitigating Man-In-The-Middle Attacks

Man-in-the-middle attacks can be mitigated effectively only through cryptography. If communication is encrypted, the attacker can capture only the cipher text. If, however, the attacker can determine or capture the session key, man-in-the-middle attacks become possible. A man-in-the-middle attack against an encrypted session can succeed only if attackers can insert themselves into the key-exchange process. Before an encrypted session can be set up, both parties must agree on a session key that will be used to encrypt traffic in both directions. To do so, both parties must either perform a Diffie-Hellman key exchange, whereby the session key is derived from a combination of private and public encryption keys, or communicate in some other fashion (preferably out-of-band) to agree on the session key. An attacker can insert themselves between the two parties in a man-in-the-middle attack in such a way that the attacker negotiates a separate session key with both parties and relays the communication sufficiently fast enough to keep up with the other two computers, as shown in Figure 9-2.

Figure 9-2 *Man-In-The-Middle Attack During Session Setup*

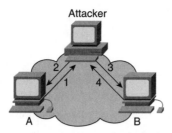

In Figure 9-2 system A initiates a key exchange in step 1. The attacker's system intercepts the key-exchange request and responds with a key that is forged to appear to come from system B (step 2). System B sends a key-exchange request (step 3) to system A and, before system A can respond, the attacker responds with his own key in step 4. In this way, the attacker sets up encrypted sessions with both system A and system B, and in each case masquerades as the other system. When system A sends traffic to system B, it is actually sent to the attacker's system, which can then copy the traffic for later analysis, forward it unmodified to system B, or forward it after some modification has been made to the message. If the attacker is able to keep up with the speed at which the two systems are communicating and he does nothing to give away his location in the data path, remaining completely unseen, as shown in Figure 9-2.

Mitigating Port Redirection Attacks

Mitigating port redirection requires the use of good trust models. Trust models can be implemented by proper access restrictions between hosts. As long as there is an implicit trust between hosts that is based on IP addresses, the problem of port redirection will not be solved. A HIDS can be used to detect and possibly prevent an attacker who is trying to install port redirection software, such as HTTPtunnel or NetCat, for use in a port redirection attack.

In Figure 9-3, the firewall permits any machine on the Internet to connect to the web server on the DMZ. Additionally, the firewall permits all traffic from the DMZ into the internal LAN and permits all traffic from the DMZ to the Internet. Finally, the firewall permits all traffic from the internal LAN going out.

An attacker can exploit a vulnerability in the web server to gain access to that host. Once access to the web server in the DMZ is obtained, the attacker can set up port redirection software to redirect traffic so that the traffic connects to the system on the internal LAN. In Figure 9-3, the web server TCP port 80 is redirected to connect to the Telnet port on the internal host. The attacker then connects to the web server on TCP port 80 and is automatically redirected to the Telnet port on the internal host. This allows the attacker to tunnel into the internal LAN through the firewall without violating the firewall policy.

Figure 9-3 *Port Redirection Attack*

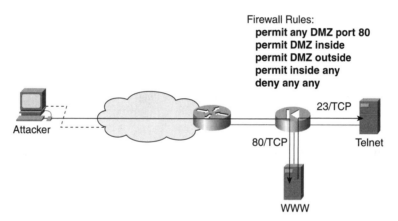

Guarding Against Virus and Trojan-Horse Applications

The most effective way to mitigate virus and Trojan-horse applications is to use antivirus software or a HIDS. These mitigation techniques can be deployed at the host and at the network level to prevent the entry of this attack vector into the network. The key point to remember is that these software applications rely on a database for the virus and Trojan-horse application signatures and the database must be kept up-to-date.

Foundation Summary

The "Foundation Summary" section of each chapter lists the most important facts from the chapter. Although this section does not list every fact from the chapter that will be on your CSI exam, a well-prepared CSI candidate should at a minimum know all the details in each "Foundation Summary" section before taking the exam.

Table 9-2 summarizes the various attacks discussed in this chapter and the primary methods that can be used to mitigate the attacks.

Table 9-2 *Mitigation Methods for Various Attacks*

Attack Type	Mitigation Methods
IP spoofing	Access control restrictions, and RFC 2827 filtering
Packet sniffers	Strong authentication (two-factor), switched infrastructure, antisniffing tools, and cryptography
Password attacks	Cryptographic authentication, OTPs, user education on strong passwords, and periodic password testing
Man-in-the-middle attacks	Cryptography
Port redirection	Strong trust models and access controls
Virus and Trojan-horse applications	Network antivirus software and a HIDS

Q&A

As mentioned in the introduction, "All About the Cisco Certified Security Professional Certification," you have two choices for review questions. The questions that follow next give you a bigger challenge than the exam itself by using an open-ended question format. By reviewing now with this more difficult question format, you can exercise your memory better and prove your conceptual and factual knowledge of this chapter. The answers to these questions are found in Appendix A.

For more practice with exam-like question formats, including questions using a router simulator and multiple choice questions, use the exam engine on the CD-ROM.

1. Describe the characteristics of a strong password.

2. What is two-factor authentication?

3. How can cryptography mitigate packet sniffers?

4. How can an attacker insert himself between two systems using cryptography in a man-in-the-middle attack?

5. How can Trojan-horse applications be mitigated?

6. RFC 2827 describes filtering by service providers at their edge devices. How can an enterprise network that is connecting through a service provider also benefit from RFC 2827 filtering?

7. Port redirection is effective when there is a poor or weak trust model between systems. How can an attacker use such an attack to gain access to the internal host through the DMZ web server shown earlier in Figure 9-3?

8. How do switched infrastructures affect packet sniffers?

9. What are two methods that antisniffer tools use to detect the possible presence of a sniffer?

10. How do password-testing tools work?

This chapter covers the following topics:

- Network Management Overview

- Network Management Protocols

CHAPTER 10

Network Management

Today's networks can consist of numerous different networked devices, each requiring a varying degree of management. The ability to remotely and securely manage each of these devices is crucial to any network administrator. For this reason, several network management protocols are available that help the network administrator access, monitor, log, report, and transfer information between the management console and the managed device. This management information flows bidirectionally; logging and reporting information flows from the managed device to the management console, while configuration, content, and firmware update data flows to the managed device from the management console.

This chapter presents a review of network management and the protocols that are used for that purpose.

"Do I Know This Already?" Quiz

The purpose of the "Do I Know This Already?" quiz is to help you decide if you really need to read the entire chapter. If you already intend to read the entire chapter, you do not necessarily need to answer these questions now.

The 12-question quiz, derived from the major sections in the "Foundation Topics" portion of the chapter, helps you determine how to spend your limited study time.

Table 10-1 outlines the major topics discussed in this chapter and the "Do I Know This Already?" quiz questions that correspond to those topics.

Table 10-1 *"Do I Know This Already?" Foundation Topics Section-to-Question Mapping*

Foundation Topics Section	Questions Covered in This Section
Network Management Overview	1–5
Network Management Protocols	6–12

> **CAUTION** The goal of self-assessment is to gauge your mastery of the topics in this chapter. If you do not know the answer to a question or are only partially sure of the answer, you should mark this question wrong for purposes of the self-assessment. Giving yourself credit for an answer you correctly guess skews your self-assessment results and might provide you with a false sense of security.

1. Name the two types of network management traffic flows that occur?

    a. Unidirectional

    b. In-band

    c. Bidirectional

    d. Channeled

    e. Out-of-band

2. Which network traffic management flow is considered the most secure?

    a. Unidirectional

    b. In-band

    c. Bidirectional

    d. Channeled

    e. Out-of-band

3. Which network traffic management flow is generally considered more cost-effective to implement?

    a. Unidirectional

    b. In-band

    c. Bidirectional

    d. Channeled

    e. Out-of-band

4. When using in-band network management, emphasis should be placed on which of the following?

    a. Performance

    b. Securing data

    c. Ease of management

    d. Traffic flow

5. If management protocols do not offer secure communications, then which of the following should be used to secure the in-band communications path?

   a. Telnet

   b. RFC 2827 filtering

   c. Access control lists

   d. IPSec

   e. Encrypted tunneling protocols

6. What port does SSH use for connections?

   a. UDP 443

   b. TCP 22

   c. TCP 25

   d. UDP 443

   e. TCP 23

7. Which of the following remote-access protocols is considered the least secure?

   a. SSH

   b. SSL

   c. Telnet

   d. HTTPS

8. Which of the following protocols transfer data in clear text?

   a. SSL

   b. HTTPS

   c. IPSec

   d. SSH

   e. TFTP

9. Which version of SNMP provides authentication and encryption?

   a. Version 1

   b. Version 2

   c. Version 3

   d. Version 2c

10. Which version of NTP supports authentication?

    a. Version 1

    b. Version 2

    c. Version 2c

    d. Version 3

    e. Version 3c

11. What two main components does SNMP use in its design?

    a. Agents

    b. Monitor

    c. Reporter

    d. Manager

12. When not using SNMPv3, it is recommended to do which of the following?

    a. Use read-write access

    b. Use read-only community strings

    c. Use authentication

    d. Use access control lists

The answers to the "Do I Know This Already?" quiz are found in Appendix A, "Answers to the 'Do I Know This Already?' Quizzes and Q&A Sections." The suggested choices for your next step are as follows:

■ **10 or less overall score**—Read the entire chapter. This includes the "Foundation Topics" and "Foundation Summary" sections, and the "Q&A" section.

■ **11 or more overall score**—If you want more review on these topics, skip to the "Foundation Summary" section and then go to the "Q&A" section. Otherwise, move to the next chapter.

Foundation Topics

Network Management Overview

Simply put, network management is a generic term that describes the execution of the set of functions that help to maintain, monitor, and troubleshoot the resources of a network. The traffic flow generated from these management actions can occur in what are generally referred to as either *in-band* or *out-of-band* flows hence giving the term in-band or out-of-band network management.

In-Band Network Management

The term *in-band network management* refers to the flow of management traffic that follows the same path as normal network data. In-band managed devices support various methods and protocols that facilitate remote management of the device while using the normal data flow. The section "Network Management Protocols," later in the chapter, provides more details on the protocols that provide this functionality.

Because management information is flowing over the same path as data traffic, in-band network management is usually seen to be less secure than out-of-band network management. This is primarily because administrative access to all managed devices is via the normal data flow and hence potentially liable to being administratively compromised by a network intruder.

Consequently, you should always keep in mind the potential security flaws associated with in-band network management and, wherever possible, implement techniques to minimize the chance of interception and modification of management data. Limiting network management to read-only access, using tunneling protocols, or using more secure variants of insecure management protocols are just some of the methods that you can use.

Out-of-Band Network Management

Out-of band network management refers to the flow of management traffic that does not follow the same path as normal network data. Normally, a parallel network or communications path is used for management purposes in this case. This path either directly interfaces to a dedicated network port on the device needing to be managed or terminates on a device, such as a terminal server, which then provides direct connection to the networked device's console port.

Generally, out-of-band management is considered more secure than in-band management because the network management segment is private and, hence, isolated from the normal data network.

Consequently, the out-of-band network management segment is less likely to be compromised by a network intruder. However, out-of-band network management is usually the least cost-effective means of network management because each managed device requires a dedicated connection to the private management network.

Mitigating Management Traffic Attacks

To mitigate management traffic attacks, consider the following points:

■   You should always use out-of-band management in preference to in-band management because it provides the highest level of security.

■   Where management traffic flows in-band, you need to place more emphasis on securing the transport of the management protocols. Consequently, you need to make this transport as secure as possible either by using a secure tunneling protocol, such as IPSec, to secure all management traffic or, if that is not possible, by using a secure management protocol.

■   If a device that requires management resides outside the network, then you should use an IPSec tunnel to manage that device. This tunnel should originate from the management network and terminate directly on the device.

■   Where management data cannot be secured due to device limitations, you should always be aware of the potential for data interception and falsification.

Network Management Protocols

Network management encompasses several different protocols that provide a wide variety of services that are used to manage a network. These services range from configuration management protocols, to monitoring and logging protocols, to time synchronization protocols.

Of primary concern when selecting which protocol type to use to achieve a particular management objective is the level of security that the proposed protocol provides. Inherently, some management protocols are much more secure than other types that might provide a similar function. Also, a different version of the same protocol might provide an enhanced level of security compared to older versions.

Table 10-2 shows a list of network management protocols that are commonly used to manage a typical network and the particular functionality that each provides.

Table 10-2 *Network Protocol Usage*

Protocol	Security Features	Network Management Protocol Usage
Secure Socket (SSH)	SSH encrypted payload, password authentication	Remote-access facilities
Secure Sockets Layer (SSL)	SSL encrypted payload, password authentication	Remote-access facilities
Telnet	Telnet clear text, password authentication	Remote-access facilities
System Log (syslog)	Clear text, no authentication	Reporting and logging facilities
Simple Network Management Protocol (SNMP)	Community string protected (password), clear text until version 3.0	Network monitoring and control facilities
Trivial File Transfer Protocol (TFTP)	No password protection, clear text	File management facilities
Network Time Protocol (NTP)	Cryptographic authentication from version 3 and later	Time synchronization facilities

The sections that follow address the functionality of each of the protocols listed in Table 10-2. For discussion purposes, protocols are grouped by network management usage type.

NOTE The protocols discussed in the next sections are not the only protocols available for use in the management of a network. These are just the most common ones that are used.

Remote-Access Protocols

The following remote-access protocols exist to assist a network administrator in the management of a network:

■ Telnet

■ SSH

■ SSL

These protocols provide varying degrees of security, ranging from data being sent in clear text to the use of strong encryption and authentication.

Telnet

Telnet is a terminal-emulation protocol that is commonly used on TCP/IP-based networks. Telnet allows remote access to managed devices in clear text and, hence, provides the least-secure remote-access method described here. The initiation of a Telnet session requires the user to log in to the device by entering valid authentication credentials, which normally consist of a username and password. This authentication either can take place locally on the remote device or can be passed to an authentication server such as a RADIUS or TACACS+ server.

Telnet uses TCP port 23 to establish connections.

SSH

SSH is a secure shell program that you can use to log in to another remote networked device and execute commands. It was developed by SSH Communications Security, Inc., and provides strong authentication and secure communications over insecure data links.

SSH provides protections from Domain Name System (DNS), IP spoofing, and IP source routing attacks. Should an intruder be successful in compromising a network, then they are only able to force an SSH session to be disconnected. An intruder is unable to play back or hijack the connection when encryption is enabled. Additionally, if an SSH session with encryption is used instead of a normal Telnet session, the login password and normal data are sent in cipher text, making it almost impossible for an intruder to collect passwords.

SSH uses TCP port 22 to establish connections, and its authentication methods include RSA, SecureID, and passwords.

SSL

SSL is a protocol that provides security and privacy over a connection. The protocol, developed by Netscape Communications Corporation, maintains the security and integrity of a communications link by using authentication and encryption.

SSL supports server and client authentication. When an SSL session is initiated, the server sends its public key to the client. The client then uses this public key to generate a random secret key that is sent back to the server, thus creating a secret key exchange for the session.

SSL uses TCP port 443. During the initial exchange or handshake process, the RSA public-key cryptosystem is used. After this key exchange is successful, several ciphers are available for use, including Rivest's Cipher 2 (RC2), RC4, International Data Encryption Algorithm (IDEA), Data Encryption Standard (DES), and Triple-DES (3DES).

> **NOTE** Recently, SSL has been merged with other protocols and authentication methods by the IETF into a new protocol known as Transport Layer Security (TLS).

Reporting and Logging Protocol: Syslog

Syslog is a transport mechanism that is used to send event messages across a network. These events can be the result of the starting and stopping of a process, a threshold being reached, or the reporting of the current status of some condition or process.

All syslog data is sent in clear text between the managed device and the logging server or management console. The protocol has no mechanism for authentication, and no message integrity checking is performed to ensure that data has not been manipulated while in transit. Consequently, an intruder could alter the data contained in syslog messages in an attempt to confuse the network administrator or even to disguise their actions.

Syslog uses UDP port 514. To mitigate against syslog attacks, encrypt syslog traffic within an IPSec tunnel wherever possible.

Monitoring and Control Protocol: Simple Network Management Protocol

SNMP is a widely used network control and monitoring protocol. Developed in the late 1980s, SNMP has become the de facto standard for internetwork management. SNMPv3 is the most recent version of SNMP and defines a secure version of this previously fairly insecure protocol. It supports message integrity, authentication, and encryption.

> **NOTE** The current version of Cisco IOS Release 12.2 supports SNMP versions 1, 2c, and 3.
>
> SNMPv1 is the original version of SNMP and is defined in RFC 1157. Security is based on community strings.
>
> SNMPv2c is an experimental IP defined in RFC 1901, RFC 1905, and RFC 1906. It uses the community string security model as defined in SNMPv1. The *c* in SNMPv2c stands for "community."
>
> SNMPv3 is the most recent version of SNMP and combines authentication with encryption of management data over the network. SNMPv3 is defined in RFCs 2273 through 2275. It supports username, MD5, or SHA authentication while supporting DES-56 encryption.

The SNMP system contains two primary elements:

- **A manager**—The manager is the interface that the network administrator uses to perform the network management functions. This interface is commonly referred to as the management console or management engine.

- **Agents**—Agents consist of hardware and software reporting activities in each network device being managed, which communicate with the manager. The data that is returned from these agents is structured in a hierarchal format called a Management Information Base (MIB). Each MIB defines what is obtainable from the managed device and what can be controlled in it. Agents can respond to specific requests from the SNMP manager or can be configured to report events as they occur by using a special message called an asynchronous trap.

Data that can only be received from a device but not written to the device via SNMP is referred to as *read-only access,* whereas information that can be read or written to a device is referred to as *read-write access.* This read-write access is controlled by *community strings*, which provide the very simple form of security found in the earlier versions of SNMP. However, these earlier versions of SNMP transmit community strings in clear text, so they are liable to being captured by a packet sniffer. Once these community strings are compromised, an intruder could reconfigure a remote device, via SNMP, if read-write access is allowed.

An additional level of security can be incorporated into SNMP by the use of access control lists (ACLs). These lists can be configured to restrict SNMP access to only nominated devices.

SNMP uses UDP ports 161 and 162. Agents listen on UDP port 161 while asynchronous traps are received on UDP port 162 at the management console.

To mitigate against SNMP attacks, unless you are using SNMPv3, it is recommended that you use SNMP read-only community strings. Also, restrict device access to only the management consoles by using SNMP access control. Finally, for added security, you can use a tunneling protocol such as IPSec to secure the transport.

File Management Protocols: Trivial File Transfer Protocol

TFTP is a TCP/IP file transfer protocol and is commonly used by many network devices to transfer configuration or system files across a network. Unlike FTP, TFTP does not have any directory or password capabilities. Data is sent in clear text, which leaves the TFTP transfer susceptible to a packet-sniffing attack; this can lead to sensitive data or configuration information being obtained.

TFTP uses UDP port 69 for control and uses the higher UDP ports, greater than 1023, for the data stream between the remote device and the TFTP server.

To mitigate against TFTP attacks, encrypt TFTP traffic within an IPSec tunnel wherever possible.

Time Synchronization Protocols: Network Time Protocol

NTP is a TCP/IP protocol that provides the facility to synchronize the time of network devices to a common time source. Simple Network Time Protocol (SNTP) is a more simplified client-only version of NTP and, hence, can only receive time from an NTP server; it cannot be used to provide time services to other systems.

The accurate synchronization of network device clocks is critical for the use of digital certificates and the timestamping of events. Consequently, a network administrator must trust the time source they intend to use for synchronization. It is normal to get NTP to synchronize its time from an authoritative time source such as an atomic or radio clock or from an Internet public time-server and then distribute this time across the network.

NTP version 3, defined in RFC 1305, supports a cryptographic authentication mechanism between peers. Without this authentication, it is possible for an attacker to perform a DoS attack on the system by sending bogus NTP data. This could then lead to digital certificates being expired and loss of service. It is also possible for an attacker to make their actions very difficult to trace should the system time get altered.

NTP uses UDP port 123 for time synchronization.

To mitigate against NTP attacks, it is recommended that you use version 3 cryptographic authentication and implement ACL restrictions to NTP synchronization peers.

Foundation Summary

The "Foundation Summary" section of each chapter lists the most important facts from the chapter. Although this section does not list every fact from the chapter that will be on your CSI exam, a well-prepared CSI candidate should at a minimum know all the details in each "Foundation Summary" section before taking the exam.

Table 10-3 shows a summary of the common network management protocols used, their function, and communication ports used in network management.

Table 10-3 *Network Protocol Summary*

Protocol	Security Features	Function	Ports
Secure Socket (SSH)	SSH encrypted payload, password authentication	Remote access	TCP port 22
Secure Sockets Layer (SSL)	SSL encrypted payload, password authentication	Remote access	TCP port 443
Telnet	Telnet clear text, password authentication	Remote access	TCP port 23
System Log (syslog)	Clear text, no authentication	Reporting and logging	UDP port 514
Simple Network Management Protocol (SNMP)	Community string protected (password), clear text until version 3.0.	Network monitoring and control	UDP port 161 UDP port 162
Trivial File Transfer Protocol (TFTP)	No password protection, clear text	File management	UDP port 69
Network Time Protocol (NTP)	Cryptographic authentication from version 3 and later	Time synchronization	UDP 123

Good design follows these guidelines:

- You should always use out-of-band management in preference to in-band management because it provides the highest level of security. However, for a cost-effective security deployment, you might have to use in-band management.

- Where management traffic flows in-band, you need to place more emphasis on securing the transport of the management protocols. Consequently, you need to make this transport as secure as possible by using a secure tunneling protocol, such as IPSec, when using insecure management protocols such as Telnet and TFTP.

- Encrypt TFTP traffic within an IPSec tunnel wherever possible to reduce the chance of it being intercepted.

- Unless you are using SNMPv3, it is recommended that you use SNMP read-only community strings. Also, restrict device access to only the management consoles by use of SNMP access control.

- To mitigate against NTP attacks, it is recommended that you use version 3 cryptographic authentication and implement ACL restrictions to NTP synchronization peers.

- If a device that requires management resides outside the network, you should use an IPSec tunnel to manage that device. This tunnel should originate from the management network and terminate directly on the device.

- You should use ACLs at all times to restrict access to management information. Any attempt from a nonmanagement address should be denied and logged.

- Enable RFC 2827 filtering, where appropriate, to prevent an attacker from spoofing management addresses.

- Where you cannot secure management data due to device limitations, always be aware of the potential for data interception and falsification.

Q&A

As mentioned in the introduction, "All About the Cisco Certified Security Professional Certification," you have two choices for review questions. The questions that follow next give you a bigger challenge than the exam itself by using an open-ended question format. By reviewing now with this more difficult question format, you can better exercise your memory and prove your conceptual and factual knowledge of this chapter. The answers to these questions are found in Appendix A.

For more practice with exam-like question formats, including questions using a router simulator and multiple choice questions, use the exam engine on the CD-ROM.

1. The flow of network management traffic that follows the same path as normal data is referred to as a(n) ____-band traffic flow.

2. Of the three remote-access protocols discussed in this chapter, which is the least secure and why?

3. What is the primary goal of SAFE in reference to network management?

4. Give the reason for using tunneling protocols with management protocols.

5. Out-of-band management normally uses a(n) _____ network for management traffic.

6. Name two usage categories that network management protocols provide?

7. A network administrator should always be aware of the level of _____ a management protocol provides.

8. What ports does SNMP use and what is the function of each port?

9. SSH is a secure shell program and provides protection from _____, _____, and _____ attacks.

10. What public-key cryptosystem does SSL use during the initial exchange or handshake process?

11. What version of SNMP should you use if you want to ensure that SNMP traffic is encrypted?

12. _____ management protocols should always be used in preference to _____ protocols.

13. NTP version 3 supports cryptographic authentication between peers. Why is this useful?

14. SSH can use what ciphers?

15. If you cannot secure management data for whatever reason, you should always be aware of the potential for what?

Part III covers the following Cisco CSI exam topics:

- Cisco security portfolio overview

- Perimeter security firewalls—Cisco PIX and Cisco IOS Firewall

- Intrusion protection—IDS and Cisco secure scanner

- Secure connectivity—Virtual Private Network solutions

- Secure connectivity—the 3000 Concentrator series

- Secure connectivity—Cisco VPN-optimized routers

- Identity—Access control solutions

- Security management—VMS and CSPM

- Cisco AVVID

Part III: Cisco Security Portfolio

This chapter covers the following topics:

- Perimeter Security

- Cisco Secure Intrusion Detection System

- Cisco Secure Scanner

- Selecting the Right Product

CHAPTER 11

Cisco Perimeter Security Products

The Cisco security strategy is to embed security throughout the network and integrate security services in all its products, making network security a transparent, scalable, and manageable aspect of any business infrastructure. The Cisco Secure product range combines a management framework, hardware devices, identity services, software functionalities, and applications into a single, secure infrastructure.

This is the first of two chapters that provide an overview of the Cisco Secure product range. This chapter concentrates on the perimeter security and intrusion detection offerings of this portfolio. Topics covered include the following:

- Routers

- Firewalls

- Intrusion detection

- Network vulnerability scanning

This chapter provides a brief overview to the functionality and positioning of each of the preceding products while giving design considerations to follow when securing a network.

"Do I Know This Already?" Quiz

The purpose of the "Do I Know This Already?" quiz is to help you decide if you really need to read the entire chapter. If you already intend to read the entire chapter, you do not necessarily need to answer these questions now.

The 12-question quiz, derived from the major sections in the "Foundation Topics" portion of the chapter, helps you determine how to spend your limited study time.

Table 11-1 outlines the major topics discussed in this chapter and the "Do I Know This Already?" quiz questions that correspond to those topics.

Table 11-1 *"Do I Know This Already?" Foundation Topics Section-to-Question Mapping*

Foundation Topics Section	Questions Covered in This Section
Perimeter Security	1–7
Cisco Secure Intrusion Detection System	8–10
Cisco Secure Scanner	11
Selecting the Right Product	12

CAUTION   The goal of self-assessment is to gauge your mastery of the topics in this chapter. If you do not know the answer to a question or are only partially sure of the answer, you should mark this question wrong for purposes of the self-assessment. Giving yourself credit for an answer you correctly guess skews your self-assessment results and might provide you with a false sense of security.

1.   Which of the following devices can provide perimeter security?

   a.   Switches

   b.   Routers

   c.   Servers

   d.   Firewalls

   e.   Hubs

2.   Which of the following are examples where perimeter security would be applied?

   a.   Intranet connection

   b.   Internet connection

   c.   An untrusted connection

   d.   A trusted connection

3.   The role of the perimeter router is to provide which of the following?

   a.   Authentication

   b.   Host denial of service

   c.   IP address spoofing mitigation

   d.   Reporting

   e.   Basic filtering

4. Which Cisco PIX Firewall is recommended for use in the small office/home office (SOHO) environment?

   a. PIX535

   b. PIX525

   c. PIX515

   d. PIX506

   e. PIX501

5. Which of the following products can provide a stateful packet-filter firewall?

   a. IDS sensor

   b. HIDS

   c. Cisco router

   d. NIDS

6. The FWSM is available for which product range?

   a. Cisco 3600 Series router

   b. PIX Firewall

   c. Cisco 7600 Series router

   d. Channeled

   e. Catalyst 6500 switch

7. VPN functionality is available in which of the following products?

   a. Catalyst switch

   b. Cisco IOS router

   c. IDS sensor

   d. Content engine

8. Which of the following are IDS sensors?

   a. Cisco Secure Scanner

   b. Cisco 4200 Series appliances

   c. Cisco IDSM

   d. Cisco FWSM

9. Which of the following can be used to manage IDS systems?

    a. CSPM

    b. VMS

    c. CiscoWorks

    d. CIDS

    e. NIDS

10. What are the main components of Cisco Secure IDS?

    a. IDS Reporter

    b. IDS Sensor

    c. IDS Scanner

    d. IDS Management Console

    e. IDS Logger

11. How many steps does the Cisco Secure Scanner use to identify network vulnerabilities?

    a. 1

    b. 2

    c. 3

    d. 4

    e. 5

12. Which Cisco router is recommended for use in the ROBO environment?

    a. Cisco 1600

    b. Cisco 1700

    c. Cisco 2600

    d. Cisco 3600

    e. Cisco 7200

The answers to the "Do I Know This Already?" quiz are found in Appendix A, "Answers to the 'Do I Know This Already?' Quizzes and Q&A Sections." The suggested choices for your next step are as follows:

- **10 or less overall score**—Read the entire chapter. This includes the "Foundation Topics" and "Foundation Summary" sections, and the "Q&A" section.

- **11 or more overall score**—If you want more review on these topics, skip to the "Foundation Summary" section and then go to the "Q&A" section. Otherwise, move to the next chapter.

Foundation Topics

Perimeter Security

In networking terms, a perimeter usually exists where a private network meets a public network. It can also be found internally in a private network where sensitive data may need to be protected from unauthorized access. However, more commonly, a perimeter is thought of as the entry point into a network for connections that are not to be trusted.

An Internet access point for a company is a typical example where you would apply perimeter security and hence control access to critical applications, services, and data so that only legitimate users and information can pass through the network.

Traditionally, perimeter security has been provided by a firewall that performs stateful inspections on packets and sessions to determine whether packets should be transmitted or dropped. Generally, firewalls protect from some of the vulnerabilities of the perimeter network.

Typical perimeter attacks or vulnerabilities are

- **Passive eavesdropping**—An intruder performs, for example, network packet sniffing or network snooping. The information gathered by eavesdropping can then be used to pose other attacks to the network.

- **Denial of service (DoS)**—An intruder attempts to deny network or networked computer services to legitimate users.

- **IP address spoofing**—An intruder manipulates the source IP address of his traffic to prevent detection.

- **Unauthorized access**—An intruder gains unauthorized access to networked computers or networking devices through any of a variety of means, such as social engineering or various exploitations.

- **Port scan**—An intruder uses an application that scans for active ports on a network device.

- **Data manipulation**—A network intruder captures, manipulates, and replays data sent over a communication channel.

- **Session replay or hijacking**—An intruder captures, manipulates, and replays a sequence of packets or application commands to cause an unauthorized action.

- **Rerouting attack**—An intruder manipulates routing updates to cause traffic to flow to unauthorized destinations.

- **Malicious destruction**—An intruder causes destruction to data on purpose.

Nowadays, perimeter security can use not only the traditional firewall but also other networking components, such as routers, and more specialized components, such as intrusion detection devices. The next few sections discuss routers and firewalls.

Routers

As shown in Figure 11-1, the perimeter router is the first line of defense for the Internet connection. Its basic role is to provide the following:

- Basic filtering

- IP address spoofing mitigation

- Protection of the firewall from direct attack

Figure 11-1 *Perimeter Router*

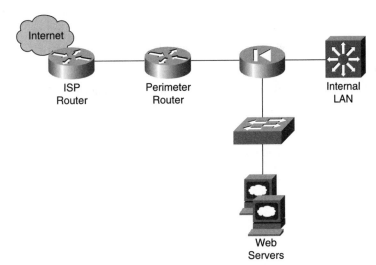

Many routers today have more advanced and powerful perimeter security features available for use in securing the perimeter connection. Cisco routers with Cisco IOS feature-rich software can provide some of the following advanced perimeter security features:

- Control of TCP/IP services

- Extensive access control list (ACL) functionality

- Network Address Translation

- Stateful packet-filter firewall

- IPSec support

- User authentication

This functionality is available across the breadth of the Cisco IOS router product portfolio from the SOHO/800 Series routers up to the enterprise and service provider class series of routers.

Further detailed information on the features available on Cisco routers can be found at Cisco.com by searching for "routers."

Firewalls

By definition, a *firewall* is a system or group of systems designed to prevent unauthorized access to or from a private network. Firewalls are generally implemented as a hardware device, but software versions are also available.

The method by which firewalls operate can be based on one of three technologies:

- **Packet filtering**—Limits the information that is permitted into a network based on the destination and source address.

- **Proxy server**—Requests connections between a client on the inside of the firewall and a client the outside of the firewall.

- **Stateful packet filtering**—Limits the information that is permitted into a network based not only on the destination and source address but also on the packet data content.

Cisco offers two lines of firewalls: Cisco IOS Firewalls and Cisco PIX Firewalls. The next two sections describe each type.

Cisco IOS Firewalls

The Cisco IOS Firewall is a Cisco IOS software option that is available with a wide range of routers. The Cisco IOS Firewall provides a stateful packet-filter firewall, which includes intrusion detection and authentication capabilities. These added security features enhance the existing security capabilities that are already present in the standard Cisco IOS router and offer sophisticated security and policy enforcement for connections within the perimeter.

The enhancements to the existing Cisco IOS security features (such as packet filters, authentication, and encryption) include the following:

- **Context-based access control (stateful, application-based filtering)**—Provides secure access control across the network perimeter by scrutinizing both source and destination addresses of traffic flows and by tracking each application's connection status.

- **Intrusion detection**—Currently, compares traffic flows to 59 default intrusion detection signatures and can direct the information from these comparisons to the Cisco Secure Policy Manager (CSPM) or a similar device.

- **Per-user authentication and authorization**—Integrates with either RADIUS or TACACS+ services.

- **Real-time alerts**—Provides real-time reporting of IDS alerts and other events.

- **VPN support**—Uses the IETF IPSec standard and other technologies such as L2TP tunneling. This support also includes the availability of optional IPSec hardware acceleration modules across most router platforms.

Currently, the Cisco IOS Firewall is available across a wide range of routers, from the SOHO/800 Series through the 7200 Series platforms.

You can find more detailed information about the Cisco IOS Firewall at Cisco.com by searching for "Cisco IOS Firewall."

Cisco PIX Firewalls

The Cisco PIX Firewall is a dedicated hardware firewall that is built around a secure, real-time, embedded operating system that provides excellent performance without comprising security. The PIX Firewall family spans the entire user application spectrum, from compact desktop firewalls for SOHO environments to carrier-class gigabit firewalls for the enterprise and service provider environments.

Recently a Firewall Service module (FWSM) has also become available for the Cisco Catalyst 6500 switch and Cisco 7600 Series routers, providing up to 5 Gbps of throughput.

The PIX Firewall is a stateful firewall appliance that provides a wide range of security and networking functionality and services. Some of these include the following:

- **Adaptive Security Algorithm (ASA)**—Maintains the secure perimeters between the networks that are controlled by the firewall. ASA is the heart of the PIX Firewall.

- **Authentication and authorization**—Integrates with either RADIUS or TACACS+ services.

- **Content filtering**—Integrates with URL packages and includes internal support for Java and ActiveX filtering.

- **Cut-through proxy**—After a user is authenticated, the firewall shifts the session flow directly between the source and destination, resulting in a marked increase in performance.

- **DHCP**—Provides DHCP services.

- **Network Address Translation (NAT) and Port Address Translation (PAT)**—Provides rich dynamic and static NAT and PAT capabilities.

- **Multimedia services**—Supports common multimedia applications.

- **Stateful firewall**—Monitors the traffic flow to verify that the destination of an inbound packet matches that of the source of a previous outbound packet.

- **URL filtering**—Supports URL filtering services.

- **VPN functionality**—Uses the IETF IPSec standard. This support also includes the availability of optional IPSec hardware VPN acceleration cards (VAC) starting at the mid-range models upwards.

You can find more detailed information about the Cisco Secure PIX Firewall at Cisco.com by searching for "PIX Firewall."

Cisco Secure Intrusion Detection System

The Cisco Secure IDS is a real-time intrusion detection system that is designed for enterprise and service provider deployments. It monitors all inbound and outbound network activity on selected segments within a network.

The system uses a signature database and looks for predetermined patterns of traffic flow that may indicate a network or system attack from someone attempting to break into or compromise a system. Using this information, the system detects, reports, and can terminate unauthorized activity throughout the network.

There are two major components to the Cisco Secure IDS:

- IDS sensor

- IDS Management Console

> **NOTE**   Cisco Secure IDS also uses a communication infrastructure based on the proprietary Post Office Protocol.

The following sections describe both major components of the Cisco Secure IDS.

Cisco Secure IDS Sensors

An IDS sensor can exist in one of two forms: a dedicated hardware device, or a software agent that resides on a specific host. The hardware version of the sensor is directly connected to a segment of the network that requires monitoring, whereas the software version resides on each specific host that requires monitoring.

These two types of IDS sensor give rise to what is commonly called network IDS (NIDS) and host IDS (HIDS), respectively. A NIDS is designed to support multiple hosts and uses hardware sensors, whereas a HIDS is set up to detect illegal actions within a single host and uses the software-based sensor. Figure 11-2 shows the deployment of the two types of IDS sensors.

Figure 11-2   *Typical NIDS and HIDS Deployment*

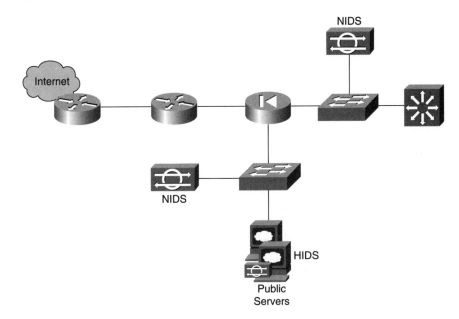

Cisco Secure NIDS and HIDS sensors are discussed in the following two sections.

Cisco Secure NIDS sensors

The Cisco Secure NIDS sensors are the muscle in the Cisco Secure IDS solution and consist of hardware appliances that are tuned for optimum performance and ease of maintenance.

> **NOTE**   Limited IDS capability is now available in many Cisco router platforms and in the Cisco Secure PIX Firewall Series.

Sensors constantly monitor network traffic in real time while looking for distinctive attack patterns in the traffic flow. Each sensor checks network traffic for a pattern match against one of the attack signatures in its signature database. This monitoring occurs through a specific monitoring interface on the sensor, whereas alarms are transmitted through the command and control interface to the management console.

When a traffic pattern triggers a signature response, the sensor logs the event and sends an alarm to the management console. The sensor also has several response options available that it can initiate when it detects an attack. These options are outlined in Table 11-2.

Table 11-2 *Sensor Response Options*

Response Action	Response Description
Alarm	Sensor reports the event to the Director (this occurs by default).
TCP reset	Sensor terminates the individual TCP connection if it senses that it has been involved in an attempted or actual attack.
IP blocking (shunning)	Sensor can automatically reconfigure an ACL on a router to block the attacker at the perimeter.
IP logging	Sensor records a log of the attacker's activities. This is a passive event and allows the attacker to continue.

Table 11-3 describes the Cisco IDS NIDS sensors that are currently available.

Table 11-3 *Cisco IDS NIDS Sensors*

Model	Performance (Mbps)	Response	Signature Coverage
4210	45	Reset, shun, and log	Full
4235	100	Reset, shun, and log	Full
4250	100	Reset, shun, and log	Full
IDSM	260	Shun	Full

Cisco Secure HIDS Sensors

The Cisco Secure HIDS sensor is a software agent that resides on the specific host that it is intended to monitor and protect. It safeguards the entire server by preventing known and unknown attacks. It uses a combination of behavioral rules and signatures to prevent attacks, rather than merely detecting and reporting them after they occur.

Currently, two versions of the Cisco Secure HIDS sensor are available: a Standard Edition Agent and a Server Edition Agent. Their functionality is shown in Table 11-4.

Table 11-4   *Cisco Secure HIDS Sensor Editions*

Agent Edition	Placement	Functionality
Standard	Hosts	Protects by evaluating requests to the operating system before they are processed
Server	Web servers	Includes the Standard Edition functionality but also protects the web server application and the web server API

The Standard Edition Agent is leveled for general host use. The Server Edition Agent, however, is aimed at public-facing devices, such as web servers, which require additional levels of security because of increased vulnerabilities.

IDS Management Console

The IDS management console (MC) is the platform that provides a single GUI management interface for the administrator. All IDS sensors report to this platform, and it is used to configure, log, and display alarms that are generated by the sensors.

IDS management consoles are available through the following platforms:

- Cisco Secure Policy Manager (CSPM)

- Cisco Secure IDS Director (CSID)

- CiscoWorks VPN/Security Management Solution (VMS)

You can find more detailed information about the Cisco Secure Intrusion Detection System at Cisco.com by searching for "IDS."

Cisco Secure Scanner

The Cisco Secure Scanner is a software application that offers a complete suite of network scanning tools and is designed to run on either the Windows or Solaris operating systems. The product was formerly called Cisco NetSonar.

This software suite provides the ability to configure a specific host on the network to become what is referred to as a *network scanner*. This scanning host is then capable of scanning all or a specific part of the network for known security threats. This makes the scanner an important asset in managing your network security.

The Cisco Secure Scanner identifies any possible network vulnerabilities by using the following four steps:

1. Gathers network device information.

2. Identifies potential vulnerabilities.

3. Confirms selected vulnerabilities.

4. Generates reports and graphs.

The network vulnerability information that is used in the analysis of the scan is collated from a managed database called the *network security database.* This database contains details of all currently known security vulnerabilities, grouped by operating system, and is managed by the Cisco Countermeasures Research Team (C-CRT), which frequently updates this database.

Selecting the Right Product

The products that are used and the complexity of the design that is implemented to secure any network perimeter will likely differ from one network to another, because each design can be influenced to varying degrees by numerous different factors. Just a few of the factors that can influence a design are

■   Budget

■   Security required

■   Services offered

■   Remote access

■   User numbers

■   Cost-effectiveness

■   Management

■   Connectivity required

Regardless of which products are used within a particular perimeter security design, they should always provide the required functionality specified by the customer.

Remember that if performance is an issue, you should use a dedicated security device to provide the required functionality rather than a more generic device that offers the service. For example, if a firewall is required, use a firewall instead of a router that provides firewall capability.

Table 11-5 outlines the recommendations of scalability for Cisco IOS Firewall and PIX Firewall deployments.

Table 11-5 *Cisco IOS Firewall and PIX Firewall Deployments*

Model	SOHO	ROBO	Regional Office	Enterprise/Service Provider
IOS Firewall	800 Series	1700 Series	2600/3600 Series	7200 Series
PIX Firewall	501	506E	515E-UR	525E-UR/535E-UR

The deployment of IDS within a network can be in a variety of locations and can be of either the NIDS or HIDS sensor type. Commonly deployed IDS locations and the sensor type that is used in each location are listed in Table 11-6.

Table 11-6 *Some Common IDS Deployment Areas*

Deployment Area	Sensor Type	Mitigation
Extranets	NIDS	Monitors traffic from partners
Intranets/internal	NIDS, HIDS	Protects internal critical systems and data
Internet access	NIDS, HIDS	Protects against threats from untrusted public networks; includes public services segment for web servers, and so on
Remote access	NIDS	Hardens perimeter

Additional design criteria can be found in Chapters 14, "Implementing Small SAFE Networks," and 16, "Implementing Medium-Sized SAFE Networks."

Foundation Summary

The "Foundation Summary" section of each chapter lists the most important facts from the chapter. Although this section does not list every fact from the chapter that will be on your CSI exam, a well-prepared CSI candidate should at a minimum know all the details in each "Foundation Summary" section before taking the exam.

Table 11-7 explains the different firewall technology types.

Table 11-7 *Firewall Technology Types*

Firewall Technology	Description
Packet filtering	Limits the information that is permitted into a network based on the destination and source address.
Proxy server	Requests connections between a client on the inside of the firewall and a client on the outside of the firewall.
Stateful packet filtering	Limits the information that is permitted into a network based not only on the destination and source address but also on the packet data content.

Table 11-8 highlights the three major components of the Cisco Secure IDS.

Table 11-8 *Cisco Secure IDS Components and Functionality*

Component	Product	Functionality
Sensor	NIDS—IDS 4200 Series, IDSM	Network sensing
	HIDS—Agent Software	Attack response
Management Console	CSPM	Sensor configuration
	CSID	Sensor monitoring
	VMS	Sensor management
		Sensor data collection
		Sensor data analysis
		Network security database

Table 11-9 describes the IDS sensor response options.

Table 11-9 *IDS Sensor Response Options*

Response Action	Response Description
Alarm	Sensor reports the event to the Director (this occurs by default).
TCP reset	Sensor terminates the individual TCP connection if it senses that it has been involved in an attempted or actual attack.
IP blocking (shunning)	Sensor can automatically reconfigure an ACL on a router to block the attacker at the perimeter.
IP logging	Sensor records a log of the attacker's activities. This is a passive event and allows the attacker to continue.

Table 11-10 explains the two editions of the Cisco Secure HIDS sensor.

Table 11-10 *Cisco Secure HIDS Sensor Editions*

Agent Edition	Placement	Functionality
Standard	Hosts	Protects by evaluating requests to the operating system before they are processed
Server	Web servers	Same as Standard Edition but also protects the web server application and the web server API

Table 11-11 outlines the recommendations of scalability for Cisco IOS Firewall and PIX Firewall deployments.

Table 11-11 *Cisco IOS Firewall and PIX Firewall Deployments*

Model	SOHO	ROBO	Regional Office	Enterprise/Service Provider
IOS Firewall	800 Series	1700 Series	2600/3600 Series	7200 Series
PIX Firewall	501	506E	515E-UR	525E-UR/535E-UR

Table 11-12 describes some common IDS deployment areas.

Table 11-12 *Common IDS Deployment Areas*

Deployment Area	Sensor Type	Mitigation
Extranets	NIDS	Monitors traffic from partners
Intranets/internal	NIDS, HIDS	Protects internal critical systems and data
Internet access	NIDS, HIDS	Protects against threats from untrusted public networks; includes public services segment for web servers, etc.
Remote access	NIDS	Hardens perimeter

Q&A

As mentioned in the introduction, "All About the Cisco Certified Security Professional Certification" you have two choices for review questions. The questions that follow next give you a bigger challenge than the exam itself by using an open-ended question format. By reviewing now with this more difficult question format, you can exercise your memory better and prove your conceptual and factual knowledge of this chapter. The answers to these questions are found in Appendix A.

For more practice with exam-like question formats, including questions using a router simulator and multiple choice questions, use the exam engine on the CD-ROM.

1. Define IDS.

2. What protocol do Cisco Secure IDS devices use to communicate with each other?

3. Traditionally, what devices provided perimeter security?

4. What are the three types of responses that a sensor can perform in reply to an attack?

5. What are the perimeter security features provided by a Cisco router?

6. Define a perimeter.

7. Network sensing, attack response, and device management are functions of what device?

8. What is the Cisco Secure Scanner?

9. Define stateful packet filtering.

10. Describe the two versions of Cisco Secure HIDS that are available.

This chapter covers the following topics:

- Secure Connectivity

- Identity Management—Cisco Secure Access Control Server

- Security Management

- Cisco AVVID

- Design Considerations

CHAPTER 12

Cisco Network Core Security Products

In the previous chapter, "Cisco Perimeter Security Products," you learned about the specific products available from the Cisco Secure security portfolio that are used to secure the perimeter of a network and those products that provide intrusion detection facilities for the network.

In this second chapter on the Cisco Secure product portfolio, we look at securing network connectivity, securing identity, security management, and Cisco Architecture for Voice, Video, and Integrated Data (AVVID).

"Do I Know This Already?" Quiz

The purpose of the "Do I Know This Already?" quiz is to help you decide if you really need to read the entire chapter. If you already intend to read the entire chapter, you do not necessarily need to answer these questions now.

The 14-question quiz, derived from the major sections in "Foundation Topics" portion of the chapter, helps you determine how to spend your limited study time.

Table 12-1 outlines the major topics discussed in this chapter and the "Do I Know This Already?" quiz questions that correspond to those topics.

Table 12-1   *"Do I Know This Already?" Foundation Topics Section-to-Question Mapping*

Foundation Topics Section	Questions Covered in This Section
Secure Connectivity	1–4
Identity Management	5–7
Security Management	8–11
Cisco AVVID	12–13
Design Considerations	14

> **CAUTION** The goal of self-assessment is to gauge your mastery of the topics in this chapter. If you do not know the answer to a question or are only partially sure of the answer, you should mark this question wrong for purposes of the self-assessment. Giving yourself credit for an answer you correctly guess skews your self-assessment results and might provide you with a false sense of security.

1. What technology is primarily used by Cisco to secure connectivity?

    a. Remote access

    b. Switching

    c. IPSec VPN

    d. Routing

    e. Intrusion detection

2. Which of the following can be used to provide Cisco Secure connectivity?

    a. Routers

    b. Switches

    c. Firewalls

    d. VPN 3000 Series

    e. IDS sensor

3. How many types of Cisco VPN clients are there?

    a. 1

    b. 2

    c. 3

    d. 4

    e. 5

4. Currently, how many models of the Cisco VPN 3000 Series Concentrator are available?

    a. 2

    b. 3

    c. 4

    d. 5

    e. 6

5. Cisco Secure Access Control Server supports which of the following authentication protocols?

   a. RADIUS

   b. X.25

   c. SMTP

   d. TACACS+

   e. POP3

6. What independent security functions are represented by AAA?

   a. Advertisement

   b. Accounting

   c. Authentication

   d. Allocation

   e. Authorization

7. Cisco Secure ACS is used to perform what primary function?

   a. Diagnostics

   b. Access control

   c. Filtering

   d. Sampling

   e. Reporting

8. Which of the following provide Cisco Security Management facilities?

   a. CSPM

   b. IPT

   c. IDSM

   d. FWSM

   e. VMS

9. Cisco VMS is made up of a set of web-based applications that provide which of the following facilities?

   a. Configuring

   b. Designing

   c. Monitoring

   d. Troubleshooting

   e. Marketing

10. What does the initialism CSPM represent?

   a. Cisco Server Policy Manager

   b. Cisco Security Policy Monitor

   c. Cisco Secure Policy Monitor

   d. Cisco Secure Policy Manager

   e. Cisco Security Policy Manager

11. CSPM is used to manage which of the following?

   a. Cisco PIX Firewall

   b. Cisco IP Telephony

   c. Cisco IOS routers

   d. Cisco IPSec VPN routers

   e. Cisco IDS sensors

12. Cisco AVVID Network Infrastructure components are?

   a. Reporters

   b. Clients

   c. Servers

   d. Network platforms

   e. Intelligent network services

13. Cisco AVVID consists of which building blocks?

    a. Network management

    b. Network infrastructure

    c. Service control

    d. Reporting facilities

    e. Communications services

14. What are common factors that can determine the choice of products in a design?

    a. Appearance

    b. Cost

    c. Customer requirements

    d. Manageability

    e. Functionality

The answers to the "Do I Know This Already?" quiz are found in Appendix A, "Answers to the 'Do I Know This Already?' Quizzes and Q&A Sections." The suggested choices for your next step are as follows:

- **12 or less overall score**—Read the entire chapter. This includes the "Foundation Topics" and "Foundation Summary" sections, and the "Q&A" section.

- **13 or more overall score**—If you want more review on these topics, skip to the "Foundation Summary" section and then go to the "Q&A" section. Otherwise, move to the next chapter.

Foundation Topics

Secure Connectivity

The Internet has evolved into an inexpensive, efficient form of doing business. The number of businesses that rely on the Internet to communicate with clients has increased and is still growing. The current techniques used for routing IP packets on the Internet, however, leave it vulnerable to security attacks such as spoofing, sniffing, and session hijacking, to name a few. As companies move from expensive, dedicated, secure connections to cost-effective use of the Internet, they require secure communications over what is generally described as an insecure network. Virtual private networks (VPNs) can reduce security risks and provide a more efficient use of Internet connections by reducing the number of dedicated leased lines.

With this knowledge, Cisco has embraced VPN technologies throughout its product range and now offers the most extensive VPN product portfolios available in the industry.

Cisco VPN-Enabled Routers

The Cisco IOS Software running in Cisco routers provides feature-rich IPSec VPN services with industry-leading routing and delivers a comprehensive VPN routing solution. The Cisco IOS Software combines IPSec VPN enhancements, such as strong 3DES encryption authentication using either digital certificates or preshared keys, with robust firewall, intrusion detection, and secure administrative capabilities.

The actual capability of the router to establish an IPSec VPN connection is determined by the software version running on the router rather than the actual hardware platform. Cisco provides, however, a suite of VPN-optimized routers, which currently range from the low-end Cisco SOHO/ 800 Series routers to headend connectivity with the Cisco 7200 Series routers.

Cisco IOS routers support both site-to-site VPNs between IPSec-compliant devices and client-to-site VPNs that terminate VPN sessions from various IPSec operating system–based clients such as the Cisco VPN Client.

You can find detailed information about the Cisco VPN-enabled routers at Cisco.com by searching for "routers."

Cisco Secure PIX Firewall

VPN functionality is provided within the Cisco Secure PIX Firewall product range and uses the industry-standard IPSec protocol suite to enable advanced VPN features. The PIX Firewall's

IPSec implementation is based on the same Cisco IOS IPSec found on Cisco routers. It provides high-performance VPN connectivity using 3DES encryption under most normal load conditions.

Cisco Secure PIX Firewalls support both site-to-site VPNs between IPSec-compliant devices and client-to-site VPNs that terminate VPN sessions from various IPSec operating system–based clients such as the Cisco VPN Client.

You can find detailed information about the Cisco VPN 3000 Series Concentrators at Cisco.com by searching for "PIX."

Cisco VPN 3000 Series Concentrator

The Cisco VPN 3000 Series Concentrator is a range of purpose-built, remote-access VPN devices that provide high performance, high availability, and scalability. The Cisco VPN 3000 Series Concentrator uses the most advanced state-of-the-art encryption and authentication techniques that are currently available within the industry.

The Cisco VPN 3000 Series Concentrator includes models that support a range of enterprise customers, from small businesses requiring 100 or fewer concurrent VPN connections to large organizations with up to 10,000 simultaneous connections.

Currently, the Cisco VPN 3000 Series Concentrator is available in five models:

- 3005

- 3015

- 3030

- 3060

- 3080

Table 12-2 presents a feature comparison for all models in the VPN 3000 Series Concentrator product range.

Table 12-2 *Cisco VPN 3000 Concentrator Product Comparison*

Feature	3005	3015	3030	3060	3080
Height (U)	1	2	2	2	2
Performance (Mbps)	4	4	50	100	100
Simultaneous users	100	100	1500	5000	10000

continues

Table 12-2   *Cisco VPN 3000 Concentrator Product Comparison (Continued)*

Feature	3005	3015	3030	3060	3080
Site-to-site tunnels	100	100	500	1000	1000
Encryption	SW	SW	HW	HW	HW
Memory (MB)	32	64	128	256	256
Power supplies	1	Up to 2	Up to 2	2	2
SEP modules	0	0	1	2	4
Upgradeable	N	Y	Y	Y	N

The Cisco VPN 3000 Series Concentrator is available in both nonredundant and redundant configurations. In addition, advanced routing capabilities are available, such as Open Shortest Path First (OSPF), Routing Information Protocol (RIP), and NAT.

You can find further information on the Cisco VPN 3000 Series Concentrators at Cisco.com by searching for "VPN 3000."

VPN Client

Two versions of Cisco VPN clients—a software-based client and a hardware-based client—represent integral parts of the Cisco VPN 3000 Series Concentrator product range.

Software Client

The Cisco VPN Software Client enables customers to establish secure, end-to-end encrypted (IPSec) tunnels to any Cisco VPN gateways or concentrators from a wide range of operating systems, including Microsoft Windows, Linux, and Solaris.

When a connection is established, VPN access policies and configurations are downloaded from the central gateway and pushed to the client, allowing simple deployment and management.

Currently, the Cisco VPN Software Client is compatible with the following Cisco products (Cisco Easy VPN servers):

■   Cisco VPN 3000 Series Concentrator version 3.0 and later

■   Cisco IOS Software–based platforms version 12.2(8)T and later

■   Cisco PIX Firewall version 6.0 and later

Key features and benefits of the VPN Software Client include the following:

■   Support for Windows, Linux, Solaris, and Mac operating systems

■ Intelligent peer availability detection

■ Simple Certificate Enrolment Protocol (SCEP)

■ Data compression (LZS)

■ Command-line options for connecting, disconnecting, and connection status

■ Configuration file with option locking

■ Support for Microsoft network login (all platforms)

■ Domain Name System (DNS) including DDNS/DHCP computer name population, Split DNS, Windows Internet Name Service (WINS), and IP address assignment

■ Load balancing and backup server support

■ Centrally controlled policies (including backup server list)

■ Integrated personal firewall (stateful firewall)

■ Client connection autoinitiation for wireless LAN environments

Hardware Client

The Cisco VPN 3002 Hardware Client is part of the Cisco VPN 3000 Series Concentrator family of products and combines the ease of use and high-scalability features of the software client while providing the reliability and stability of a hardware platform. It is available in two models, with or without an integral eight-port switch.

The Cisco VPN 3002 Hardware Client is a full-featured VPN client that supports 56-bit DES or 168-bit 3DES IPSec encryption. It has two modes of operation, a client mode and a network extension mode. The client mode emulates the operation of the software client in hardware, whereas the network extension mode provides the facility to establish a secure site-to-site connection with routable LAN addressing. Both modes use a "push" policy configuration technique and scale to very large numbers.

Key features and benefits of the VPN 3002 Hardware Client include the following:

■ Provides fast and easy deployment and scalability to thousands of sites

■ Includes Dynamic Host Control Protocol (DHCP) client and server compatibility for hundreds of stations behind the Cisco VPN 3002

■ Supports Port Address Translation (PAT) for hiding stations behind the Cisco VPN 3002 from external view and attack

■ Includes optional eight-port 10/100-Mbps autosensing switch

■ Supports client and network extension modes for application flexibility

- Works with any operating system, such as Windows, Mac, Linux, and Solaris.

- Eliminates the need to add or support VPN applications on a PC or workstation

- Operates seamlessly with existing applications

- Includes H.323 support in Client mode that allows users to host and access NetMeeting sessions or other H.323 applications

- Provides configurable Interface MTU, and Fragmentation Control Policy, including support for Path MTU Discovery (PMTUD)

Identity Management—Cisco Secure Access Control Server

As networks and network security have evolved, so too have the methods of controlling access to these networks and their associated resources. Traditionally, a static username and password were considered adequate to secure access to the corporate network. However, with time and the enterprise's need for stronger security, the introduction of stronger security techniques, such as one-time passwords, have been introduced.

One of the most significant problems in securing distributed systems is authentication; that is, ensuring that the parties to a conversation—possibly separated by a WAN and traversing untrusted systems and communications paths—are who they claim to be.

From a security point of view, this leads to two distinct areas of concern:

- Remote access to network resources from either dial-up or other remote services

- Access to the corporate internetworking devices

The Cisco solution to these concerns is the Cisco Secure Access Control Server (ACS). Cisco Secure ACS is a complete access control server that supports the industry-standard RADIUS protocol in addition to the Cisco proprietary TACACS+ protocol.

Cisco Secure ACS is a high-performance, highly scalable, centralized user access control framework. Cisco Secure ACS offers centralized command and control of user access from a web-based GUI and distributes those controls to hundreds or thousands of access gateways in your network.

With ACS, you can manage and administer user access for the following Cisco components:

- IOS routers

- VPNs

- Firewalls

- Dial and broadband digital subscriber line (DSL)

- Cable access solutions

- Voice over IP (VoIP)

- Cisco wireless solutions

- Cisco Catalyst switches via IEEE 802.1x access control

In addition, you can leverage the same ACS access framework to control administrator access and configuration for all network devices in your network that are enabled with TACACS+.

Advanced features include the following:

- Automatic service monitoring

- Database synchronization and importation of tools for large-scale deployments

- Lightweight Directory Access Protocol (LDAP) user authentication support

- User and administrative access reporting

- Dynamic quota generation

- Restrictions such as time of day and day of week

- User and device group profiles

Finally, Cisco Secure ACS provides authentication, authorization, and accounting (AAA) services to network devices that function as AAA clients, such as a network access servers, PIX Firewalls, or Cisco IOS routers.

AAA is an architectural framework for configuring a set of three independent security functions in a consistent manner. Table 12-3 shows the Cisco AAA Protocol Definition, which provides a modular way of performing AAA services.

Table 12-3 *Cisco AAA Protocol Definition*

Protocol	Description
Authentication	Provides the method of identifying users, including login and password dialog, challenge and response, messaging support, and encryption
Authorization	Provides the method for remote-access control, including one-time authorization or authorization for each service, per-user account list, and profile and user group support
Accounting	Provides the method for collecting and sending security server information used for billing, auditing, and reporting, such as user identities, start and stop times, executed commands, number of packets, and number of bytes

Security Management

Today's security deployments require more scalability than merely supporting a large number of devices. Many customers have limited staffing, yet are asked to perform numerous security-related tasks: manage myriad security devices; manage the security and network infrastructure; frequently update many remote devices; implement change control and auditing; enhance security without adding more headcount; or roll out remote-access VPN to all employees and monitor the VPN service. In response to these changing business needs, Cisco provides several centralized security management solutions, including

- CiscoWorks VPN/Security Management Solution

- Cisco Secure Policy Manager

CiscoWorks VPN/Security Management Solution

CiscoWorks VPN/Security Management Solution (VMS) is an integrated security management solution that forms an integral part of the SAFE blueprint for network security. VMS enables customers to deploy security infrastructures from small networks to large, complex, and widely distributed environments.

VMS features include the following:

- Scalability

- Centralized management

- Security monitoring

- Change management

VMS's strength is that it combines many administrative tasks that would normally be handled separately through a single integrated interface. This interface combines web-based tools for secure configuring, monitoring, and troubleshooting firewalls, VPNs, and both host- and network-based intrusion detection systems (HIDS and NIDS, respectively).

The VMS integrated package consists of the following applications:

- **CiscoWorks Resource Manager Essentials**—A powerful web-based management tool for inventory, configuration, and software control of Cisco routers and switches.

- **CiscoWorks VPN Monitor**—Collects, stores, and views VPN connectivity information for remote access and site-to-site VPN terminations.

- **CiscoWorks Cisco View**—Provides the common database, web, and desktop services that are used to integrate with other Cisco and third-party tools.

- **CiscoWorks CD One**—The CiscoWorks server desktop that provides the common interface for launching and navigating efficiently between the various tools and reports.

- **Cisco IDS Host Sensor**—Provides HIDS functionality.

- **CiscoWorks Auto Update Server Software**—Provides software management features using a pull model for initial configuration, configuration updates, operating system updates, and periodic configuration verification.

- **CiscoWorks Management Center for IDS Sensors**—Provides centralized management for the configuration of NIDS and switch IDS sensors.

- **CiscoWorks Management Center for VPN Routers**—Provides centralized management for the configuration and deployment of VPN connectivity.

- **CiscoWorks Management Center for PIX Firewalls**—Provides centralized management for the configuration of PIX Firewalls.

- **CiscoWorks Monitoring Center for Security**—Provides a unified server to capture, view, correlate, and report on events from NIDS, switch IDS, HIDS, PIX, and Cisco IOS devices.

Cisco Secure Policy Manager

Cisco Secure Policy Manager (CSPM), formerly Cisco Security Manager, is a centralized, scalable, comprehensive security policy management application for the Cisco Secure security portfolio. CSPM provides the administrator of a network the tools to centrally manage Cisco Secure PIX Firewalls, routers running Cisco IOS Firewall, Cisco IPSec VPN-enabled routers, and Cisco IDS sensors.

The CSPM's topology-based GUI allows administrators to visually define high-level security policies for multiple Cisco security devices. These policies can then be distributed from a central location, eliminating the costly, time-consuming practice of implementing security commands on a device-by-device basis. CSPM also provides the facility to import existing security policies as well as system-auditing functions, which include monitoring, event notification, and web-based reporting.

CSPM's main features are as follows:

- **Security policy management**—Via CSPM's GUI, network-wide security policies can be created to manage Cisco security devices without requiring extensive device knowledge and dependency on the command-line interface (CLI).

- **Cisco firewall management**—CSPM provides the administrator the facility to easily define perimeter security policies for Cisco Secure PIX Firewalls and Cisco IOS routers running the firewall feature set.

- **Cisco VPN router management** —The CSPM GUI allows for the easy configuration of intranet/extranet IPSec VPNs based on Cisco PIX Firewalls and the Cisco suite of VPN routers running the Cisco IOS IPSec software.

- **Notification and reporting system**—CSPM provides basic auditing tools to monitor, alert, and report Cisco security device and policy activity, thereby keeping the network administrator readily informed of network-wide events. CSPM also complements and interoperates with third-party monitoring, billing, and reporting systems.

- **Network operations**—CSPM incorporates many network operational features, including topology import from CiscoWorks, CLI policy mapping, command diff, admin password aging, and policy query

- **Windows 2000–based system**—CSPM provides an easy-to-use Windows-based user interface.

Cisco AVVID

This section looks at the design concept of the Cisco AVVID. Cisco AVVID is the only enterprise-wide, standards-based network architecture that provides the foundation for today's converged networks. Cisco AVVID provides the roadmap for combining your business and technology strategies into one cohesive model and encompasses the following:

- Converged client devices

- Hardware and software

- Directory services

- Call processing

- Telephony and data applications

- Network management

- Service and support

Cisco AVVID provides the baseline infrastructure that enables enterprises to design networks that scale to meet Internet business demands while delivering the e-business infrastructure and intelligent network services that are essential for rapid deployment of emerging technologies and new Internet business.

Cisco AVVID consists of several building blocks, including

- Network infrastructure

- Service control

- Communication services

Network Infrastructure

Cisco AVVID Network Infrastructure provides an enterprise foundation that combines IP connectivity with security, high availability, and QoS. Table 12-4 shows the network infrastructure components defined within Cisco AVVID.

Table 12-4   *Cisco AVVID Network Infrastructure Components*

Component	Description
Clients	Network clients include Cisco IP Phones, wireless devices, PCs, and laptops. These standards-based devices can be interconnected and functionality can be added through intelligent network services.
Network platforms	The network platforms comprise routers, gateways and switches, servers, firewalls, and other devices. This layer of the architecture provides the basis for a complete networking solution.
Intelligent network services	The intelligent network services are platforms, network services, appliances, and management that allow business rules and policies to be reflected in network performance.

Service Control

The Service Control interface joins the Internet technologies to the Internet business solutions. This software element performs network fine-tuning and optimization, and its functionality is provided through the following:

- VPN/security control

- Perimeter control

- Call control

- QoS/policy control

- Video media control

- Content distribution control

- Wireless access control

- Directory control

Communication Services

The convergence of media types is enabling richer interactions and greater personalization of applications and services, including

- Unified communications

- Intelligent contact management

- Collaboration

- Multimedia viewing

Detailed information on Cisco AVVID can be found at Cisco.com by searching for "AVVID."

Design Considerations

The Cisco Security Products Portfolio offers a wide diversity of products with an equally wide range of features and functionality. Consequently, the network architect gains an unusually high level of flexibility in the products that are available to satisfy any particular security requirements that are needed in a design.

Common factors affecting the choice of products in any design are as follows:

- Cost

- Size of network

- Functionality

- Manageability

- Scalability

- Customer requirements

Network architects consider these factors when choosing products to meet a specific customer requirement. For example, if a customer requires an Internet connection with firewall capability, the network architect can use either a Cisco IOS Firewall router solution or an independent Internet router with a standalone PIX firewall. The choice is dictated by budget, customer specifications, and various other design criteria.

Foundation Summary

The "Foundation Summary" section of each chapter lists the most important facts from the chapter. Although this section does not list every fact from the chapter that will be on your CSI exam, a well-prepared CSI candidate should at a minimum know all the details in each "Foundation Summary" section before taking the exam.

Table 12-5 shows a feature comparison for all models in the VPN 3000 Series Concentrator product range.

Table 12-5 *Cisco VPN 3000 Concentrator Product Comparison*

Feature	3005	3015	3030	3060	3080
Height (U)	1	2	2	2	2
Performance (Mbps)	4	4	50	100	100
Simultaneous users	100	100	1500	5000	10000
Site-to-site tunnels	100	100	500	1000	1000
Encryption	SW	SW	HW	HW	HW
Memory (MB)	32	64	128	256	256
Power supplies	1	Up to 2	Up to 2	2	2
SEP modules	0	0	1	2	4
Upgradeable	N	Y	Y	Y	N

AAA is an architectural framework for configuring a set of three independent security functions in a consistent manner. Table 12-6 shows the Cisco AAA Protocol Definition, which provides a modular way of performing these services.

Table 12-6 *Cisco AAA Protocol Definition*

Protocol	Description
Authentication	Provides the method of identifying users, including login and password dialog, challenge and response, messaging support, and encryption.
Authorization	Provides the method for remote-access control, including one-time authorization or authorization for each service, per-user account list, and profile and user group support.
Accounting	Provides the method for collecting and sending security server information used for billing, auditing, and reporting, such as user identities, start and stop times, executed commands, number of packets, and number of bytes.

Table 12-7 shows the network infrastructure components defined within Cisco AVVID.

Table 12-7 *Cisco AVVID Network Infrastructure Components*

Component	Description
Clients	Network clients include Cisco IP Phones, wireless devices, PCs, and laptops. These standards-based devices can be interconnected and functionality can be added through intelligent network services.
Network platforms	The network platforms comprise routers, gateways, switches, servers, firewalls, and other devices. This layer of the architecture provides the basis for a complete networking solution.
Intelligent network services	The intelligent network services are platforms, network services, appliances, and management that allow business rules and policies to be reflected in network performance.

Q&A

As mentioned in the introduction, "All About the Cisco Certified Security Professional Certification," you have two choices for review questions. The questions that follow next give you a bigger challenge than the exam itself by using an open-ended question format. By reviewing now with this more difficult question format, you can exercise your memory better and prove your conceptual and factual knowledge of this chapter. The answers to these questions are found in Appendix A.

For more practice with exam-like question formats, including questions using a router simulator and multiple choice questions, use the exam engine on the CD-ROM.

1. What does AVVID stand for?

2. Which two authentication protocols does Cisco Secure ACS use?

3. Currently, what models are available for the Cisco 3000 Series Concentrator?

4. The Cisco _____ and the Cisco ___ Series routers are entry-level VPN-enabled routers.

5. What two operating modes are available to the Cisco VPN 3000 Hardware Client?

6. What does AAA stand for?

7. Cisco ___ and _____ are two security management solutions available from Cisco.

8. Name the principle building blocks of the AVVID design.

9. Identity management can be achieved by using what Cisco product?

10. What two types of VPNs are supported by the PIX Firewall?

11. The capability of a Cisco router to support VPN connectivity is determined by what?

12. What is the Cisco VPN 3000 Series Concentrator?

Part IV covers the following Cisco CSI exam topics:

- Small network design overview

- Small network Corporate Internet module

- Small network Campus module

- Small network implementation—ISP router

- Small network implementation—IOS Firewall features and configuration

- Small network implementation—PIX Firewall

- Medium network Corporate Internet module

- Medium network Corporate Internet module design guidelines

- Medium network Campus module

- Medium network Campus module design guidelines

- Medium network WAN module

- Medium network implementation—ISP router

- Medium network implementation—edge router

- Medium network implementation—IOS Firewall

- Medium network implementation—PIX Firewall

- Medium network implementation—NIDS

- Medium network implementation—HIDS

Part IV: Designing and Implementing SAFE Networks

- Medium network implementation—VPN Concentrator

- Medium network implementation—Layer 3 switch

- Remote-User network design overview

- Remote-User network key devices

- Remote-User network threat mitigation

- Remote-User network software access option

- Remote-User network remote site firewall option

- Remote-User network remote site router option

- Remote-User network hardware VPN client option

This chapter covers the following topics:

- Components of SAFE Small Network Design

- Corporate Internet Module

- Campus Module

- Branch Versus Headend/Standalone Considerations for Small Networks

CHAPTER 13

Designing Small
SAFE Networks

The principle goal of Cisco SAFE blueprints is to provide to interested parties best-practice information on how to design and implement secure networks. SAFE serves as a guide to network architects who are examining the security requirements of their networks. SAFE blueprints combat security threats by using a modular method that allows for the creation of a scalable, corporate-wide security solution.

This is the first of three chapters that cover the specific design requirements of the "SAFE: Extending the Security Blueprint to Small, Midsize, and Remote-User Networks" (SAFE SMR) design model. The focus of this chapter is the specific security design requirements of the small network.

"Do I Know This Already?" Quiz

The purpose of the "Do I Know This Already?" quiz is to help you decide if you really need to read the entire chapter. If you already intend to read the entire chapter, you do not necessarily need to answer these questions now.

The nine-question quiz, derived from the major sections in the "Foundation Topics" portion of the chapter, helps you determine how to spend your limited study time.

Table 13-1 outlines the major topics discussed in this chapter and the "Do I Know This Already?" quiz questions that correspond to those topics.

Table 13-1 *"Do I Know This Already?" Foundation Topics Section-to-Question Mapping*

Foundation Topics Section	Questions Covered in This Section
Components of SAFE Small Network Design	1
Corporate Internet Module in Small Networks	2–6
Campus Module in Small Networks	7–9

> **CAUTION** The goal of self-assessment is to gauge your mastery of the topics in this chapter. If you do not know the answer to a question or are only partially sure of the answer, you should mark this question wrong for purposes of the self-assessment. Giving yourself credit for an answer you correctly guess skews your self-assessment results and might provide you with a false sense of security.

1. The SAFE small network design consists of which of the following modules?

    a. ISP module

    b. Campus module

    c. Remote User module

    d. Corporate Internet module

    e. E-Commerce module

2. Which of the following are components of the Corporate Internet module?

    a. Firewall

    b. Management server

    c. Corporate users

    d. Layer 3 switch

    e. DNS server

3. VPN connectivity is terminated in the Corporate Internet module.

    a. True

    b. False

4. What is the most likely point of attack in the Corporate Internet module?

    a. Firewall

    b. Switch

    c. Router

    d. Public services

    e. ISP router

5. It is common to avoid using private VLANs on the public services segment of the Corporate Internet module.

   a. True

   b. False

6. What provides network-level protection, stateful filtering of traffic, and VPN termination within the Corporate Internet module?

   a. VPN concentrator

   b. Cisco IOS Firewall

   c. Layer 2 switch

   d. PIX Firewall

   e. Public server

7. The Campus module of the small network design contains which of the following?

   a. Filtering

   b. Layer 2 functionality

   c. Corporate users

   d. Public servers

   e. Intranet servers

8. In the small network design, user authentication is implemented within the Campus module.

   a. True

   b. False

9. Because no Layer 3 services are used within the Campus module, the small network design places an emphasis on what?

   a. Routing

   b. Host security

   c. Filtering

   d. Connectivity

   e. Application security

The answers to the "Do I Know This Already?" quiz are found in Appendix A, "Answers to the 'Do I Know This Already?' Quizzes and Q&A Sections." The suggested choices for your next step are as follows:

- **7 or less overall score**—Read the entire chapter. This includes the "Foundation Topics" and "Foundation Summary" sections, and the "Q&A" section.

- **8 or more overall score**—If you want more review on these topics, skip to the "Foundation Summary" section and then go to the "Q&A" section. Otherwise, move to the next chapter.

Foundation Topics

The design philosophy behind the SAFE blueprint was first introduced in Chapter 2, "SAFE Design Fundamentals." This chapter builds on the objectives of that design philosophy by combining them with the desired network functionality required for a small network.

The small network is like most networks connected to the Internet. Internal users require access to external resources, whereas external users might need access to internal resources. Consequently, this can leave the network open to various types of threats both from internal users and from users on the publicly addressable hosts. When designing any security solution, you must always be aware of the potential for these types of threats.

The small network can be designed in two ways: as a headend or standalone configuration or as a branch configuration. The design recommendations for each of these two configuration types are similar, but some functionality found in the branch configuration might be superfluous because it is provided for in the headend configuration of the network.

For the discussion purposes of this chapter, in addition to presenting the headend or standalone configuration, any specific design changes in relation to a branch configuration are also given.

Components of SAFE Small Network Design

The following two modules and their associated devices, shown in Figure 13-1, make up the small network design:

■ Corporate Internet module

■ Campus module

> **NOTE**   Figure 13-1 also shows an ISP module, for clarity, but it is not considered a part of the small network design model.

The Corporate Internet module provides connectivity to the Internet and terminates any VPN connectivity. Traffic for public services such as mail, web, file transfer, and name lookups are also terminated at the Corporate Internet module.

The Campus module incorporates the internal Layer 2 switching, including corporate users, corporate intranet servers, and management servers.

Figure 13-1   *Small Network Model*

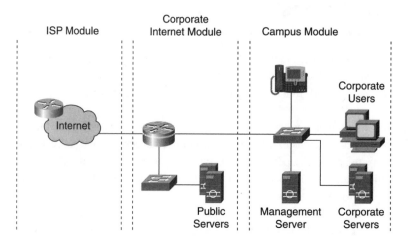

Corporate Internet Module in Small Networks

The Corporate Internet module provides internal users connectivity to Internet services and provides Internet users access to information on the corporate public servers. This module also provides remote access for remote locations and telecommuters through the use of VPN connectivity.

Several key devices make up the Corporate Internet module. These devices are described in Table 13-2.

Table 13-2   *Corporate Internet Module Devices*

Device	Description
Mail server	Acts as a relay between the Internet and the intranet mail servers and scans for mail-based attacks
DNS server	Serves as the authoritative external DNS server and relays internal requests to the Internet
Web/file server	Provides public information about the organization
Firewall or Cisco IOS Firewall router	Provides network-level protection of resources, stateful filtering of traffic, and VPN termination for remote sites and users
Layer 2 switch	Ensures that data from managed devices can only cross directly to the Cisco IOS Firewall and provides private VLAN support

As shown in Figure 13-2, either a Cisco IOS Firewall router or a PIX Firewall is used within the Corporate Internet module. The particular choice of hardware platform depends on the specific network requirements and any associated design criteria. Design considerations are discussed in subsequent sections of this chapter.

Figure 13-2 *Small Network Corporate Internet Module*

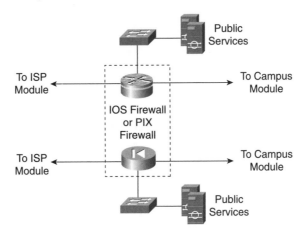

Mitigating Threats in the Corporate Internet Module

The most likely point of attack within the Corporate Internet module is on the public services segment. Positioned on this segment are the publicly addressed servers. Table 13-3 shows the anticipated threats and mitigation actions expected on this segment.

Table 13-3 *Corporate Internet Module Threats and Threat Mitigation*

Threat	Threat Mitigation
Application layer attacks	Mitigated through HIDSs on the public servers
DoS	Limited through the use of CAR* at ISP edge and TCP setup controls at firewall
IP spoofing	Mitigated through RFC 2827 and RFC 1918 filtering at ISP edge and local firewall
Network reconnaissance	Mitigated through HIDS detecting reconnaissance and by the use of protocol filtering to limit visibility
Packet sniffers	Mitigated through use of a switched infrastructure and HIDS to limit exposure
Password attacks	Mitigated by limiting the services available to brute force; operating system and IDS can detect the threat

continues

Table 13-3 *Corporate Internet Module Threats and Threat Mitigation (Continued)*

Threat	Threat Mitigation
Port redirection	Mitigated through restrictive filtering and HIDS to limit attack
Trust exploitation	Mitigated through restrictive trust model and private VLANs to limit trust-based attacks
Unauthorized access	Mitigated through filtering at the firewall
Virus and Trojan-horse attacks	Mitigated through virus scanning at the host level

*CAR = committed access rate

Figure 13-3 displays the threat-mitigation roles of each of the devices found within the Corporate Internet module.

Figure 13-3 *Small Network Corporate Internet Module Threat-Mitigation Roles*

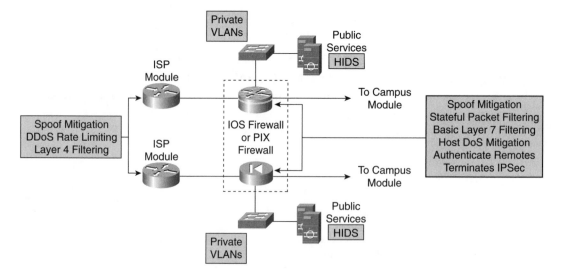

Design Guidelines for the Corporate Internet Module

The small network model represents a scaled-down security-centric network design with all the security and VPN functionality that is found within a single device. As described earlier and shown in Figure 13-2, two options are available within this design model:

- Cisco IOS router

- Firewall

The first option uses a Cisco IOS router with firewall and VPN functionality. This option provides the greatest flexibility within the small network design because the router is capable of supporting not only the firewall and VPN functionality but also the advanced features now offered to Cisco IOS routers, such as QoS and multiprotocol support.

The second option available in the small network design is to use a dedicated firewall, but because most firewalls are Ethernet-only devices, deployment issues might arise if a WAN termination is required for the ISP circuit. If WAN connectivity is required, a router must be used in the design. However, using a dedicated firewall does have the advantage of easier configuration of security services, and a dedicated firewall can provide improved performance when performing firewall functions.

Whichever option is finally chosen, stateful firewall inspection is used to examine traffic in all directions, to ensure that only legitimate traffic crosses the firewall.

Filtering and Access Control

Even before any traffic reaches the firewall, it is ideal to implement some form of security filtering on the perimeter traffic flow. Table 13-4 shows the filter parameters that can be applied to perimeter traffic flow.

Table 13-4   *Perimeter Traffic Flow Filtering*

Filter Location	Flow	Filter Description	Mitigation
ISP router	Egress	ISP rate limits nonessential traffic that exceeds a predefined threshold	DDoS
ISP router	Egress	RFC 1918 and RFC 2827 filtering	IP spoofing
Router or firewall	Ingress	RFC 1918 and RFC 2827 filtering	IP spoofing — verifies ISP filtering
Router or firewall	Ingress	VPN- and firewall-specific traffic	Unauthorized access

The stateful firewall also provides connection-state enforcement and detailed filtering for sessions initiated through the firewall. Additionally, the advance features within the software protect against TCP synchronization (TCP SYN) attacks on the publicly facing servers by controlling the limits on half-open sessions that are transiting the firewall.

With reference to the public services segment, the filtering of traffic should control not only the flow of traffic destined to specific addresses and ports on the public services segment but also the flow of traffic from the segment. This additional level of filtering prevents an attacker who may have compromised one of the public servers from using that server as a platform to launch further attacks on the network.

For example, if an intruder has managed to circumvent the firewall and HIDS security features on a public-facing DNS server, that server should be permitted only to reply to requests, not to originate requests. This prevents an intruder from using this compromised platform to launch additional attacks.

Finally, the use of private VLANs on the demilitarized zone (DMZ) switch prevents a compromised server from being used to attack other servers on the same segment. The implementation of private VLANs is especially important because this type of vulnerability is not detectable by the firewall.

Intrusion Detection

Every server on the public services segment should be configured with HIDS software, which allows for the monitoring of rogue activity at the operating system level. HIDS can also be configured to monitor certain common server applications. Additionally, all public service applications, such as the web, mail, and DNS services, should be hardened as much as possible so that unnecessary responses cannot be used to assist an intruder in network reconnaissance.

The advanced software features found in Cisco PIX Firewalls and Cisco IOS Firewall routers provide some limited NIDS functionality. They can normally drop many types of attacks without the use of an IDS management station, but obviously dropped events are not reported. However, because these devices are not specifically designed for intrusion detection, it is possible that a degradation in performance of the device might occur. If performance degradation does occur, the drop in performance is normally acceptable when compared to the benefits gained from an increase in attack visibility.

VPN Connectivity

The firewall or Cisco IOS Firewall router provides VPN connectivity for the small network design. Authentication of remote sites and remote users can be accomplished by using preshared keys or the use of an access control server located in the Campus module.

Design Alternatives for the Corporate Internet Module

Usual deviations from these design guidelines normally include the breaking out of the functional components in the network from a single device to individual, specific devices or an increase in network capacity. When these functions are broken out, the design begins to take on the look of the medium-sized network design, which is discussed in Chapter 16, "Implementing Medium-Sized SAFE Networks." Before you decide that you have to adopt the complete design for a medium-sized network, however, it may be worth considering the placement of a Cisco VPN 3000 Series Concentrator or router on the DMZ to offload processing of VPN traffic. The addition of this device also increases the manageability of VPN connectivity.

Campus Module in Small Networks

The Campus module of the small network design, which is shown in Figure 13-4, provides end-user workstations, corporate intranet servers, management servers, and the associated Layer 2 functionality via a single switch.

Figure 13-4 *Small Network Campus Module*

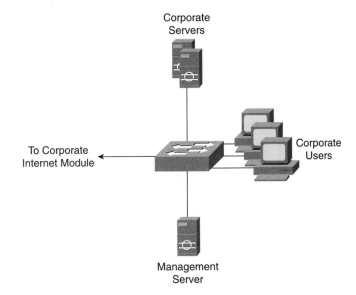

Four key devices make up the Campus module, which are highlighted in Table 13-5.

Table 13-5 *Campus Module Devices*

Device	Description
Corporate server	Provides services to internal users such as e-mail, file, and printing services
Layer 2 switch	Provides Layer 2 connectivity and also supports private VLANs
Management host	Provides management services, such as authentication, through RADIUS and TACACS+, HIDS, syslog, and other general management services
User workstation	Provides data services to authorized users on the network

Mitigating Threats in the Campus Module

Within the small network Campus module, each device plays a threat-mitigation role, as shown in Figure 13-5. Table 13-6 lists the expected threats and mitigation actions found within this module.

Figure 13-5 *Small Network Campus Module Threat-Mitigation Roles*

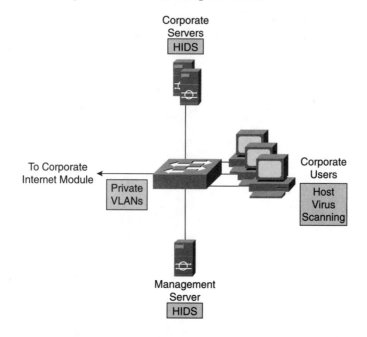

Table 13-6 *Campus Module Threats and Threat Mitigation*

Threat	Threat Mitigation
Application layer attacks	Operating systems, devices, and applications are kept up to date with the latest security fixes and are protected by HIDSs.
Packet sniffers	A switched infrastructure limits the effectiveness of sniffing.
Port redirection	HIDSs prevent port redirection agents from being installed.
Trust exploitation	Private VLANs prevent hosts on the same subnet from communicating unless necessary.
Unauthorized access	HIDSs and application access control are used to mitigate unauthorized access.
Virus and Trojan-horse applications	Host-based virus scanning and host intrusion prevention prevents most viruses and many Trojan horses.

Design Guidelines for the Campus Module

The small network Campus module provides connectivity for the corporate and management servers and also corporate users. Private VLANs can be used within the switch to mitigate trust-exploitation attacks between the devices. For example, corporate users might not require inter-user communications and only need to communicate directly with corporate servers. This functionality can be provided by using private VLANs.

Because the Campus module has no Layer 3 services within its design, there is an increased emphasis on application and host security because of the open nature of the internal network. Consequently, HIDSs have been installed on key devices within the campus, including the corporate servers and management systems.

Design Alternatives for the Campus Module

The placement of a filtering device, such as a firewall or router, to control the flow of management traffic between the management server and the rest of the network provides an increased level of security. Also, if the level of trust within the organization is high, it is possible to consider removing the HIDS from the design but this is not recommended.

Branch Versus Headend/Standalone Considerations for Small Networks

When considering the small network design requirements in a branch role rather than a headend or standalone role, the following should be noted:

- VPN connectivity for remote users is normally not required because it is provided for by the corporate headquarters.

- Management servers and hosts are normally located at the corporate headquarters, requiring management traffic to traverse the site-to-site VPN connection.

Foundation Summary

The "Foundation Summary" section of each chapter lists the most important facts from the chapter. Although this section does not list every fact from the chapter that will be on your CSI exam, a well-prepared CSI candidate should at a minimum know all the details in each "Foundation Summary" section before taking the exam.

The key devices that make up the Corporate Internet module are highlighted in Table 13-7.

Table 13-7 *Corporate Internet Module Devices*

Device	Description
Mail server	Acts as a relay between the Internet and the intranet mail servers and also scans for mail-based attacks
DNS server	Serves as the authoritative external DNS server and relays internal requests to the Internet
Web/file server	Provides public information about the organization
Firewall or Cisco IOS Firewall router	Provides network-level protection of resources, stateful filtering of traffic, and VPN termination for remote sites and users
Layer 2 switch	Ensures that data from managed devices can only cross directly to the Cisco IOS Firewall and provides private VLAN support

Table 13-8 summarizes the Corporate Internet module threats and mitigation techniques.

Table 13-8 *Corporate Internet Module Threats and Threat Mitigation*

Threat	Threat Mitigation
Application layer attacks	Mitigated through HIDSs on the public servers
DoS	Limited through use of CAR at ISP edge and TCP setup controls at firewall
IP spoofing	Mitigated through RFC 2827 and RFC 1918 filtering at ISP edge and local firewall
Network reconnaissance	Mitigated through HIDS detecting reconnaissance and by the use of protocol filtering to limit visibility
Packet sniffers	Mitigated through switched infrastructure and HIDS to limit exposure

Table 13-8 *Corporate Internet Module Threats and Threat Mitigation (Continued)*

Threat	Threat Mitigation
Password attacks	Mitigated by limiting the services available to brute force; operating system and IDS can detect the threat
Port redirection	Mitigated through restrictive filtering and HIDSs to limit attack
Trust exploitation	Mitigated through restrictive trust model and private VLANs to limit trust-based attacks
Unauthorized access	Mitigated through filtering at the firewall
Virus and Trojan-horse attacks	Mitigated through virus scanning at the host level

Table 13-9 shows the filter parameters that can be applied to perimeter traffic flow.

Table 13-9 *Perimeter Traffic Flow Filtering*

Filter Location	Flow	Filter Description	Mitigation
ISP router	Egress	ISP rate limits nonessential traffic that exceeds a predefined threshold	DDoS
ISP router	Egress	RFC 1918 and RFC 2827 filtering	IP spoofing
Router or firewall	Ingress	RFC 1918 and RFC 2827 filtering	IP spoofing—verifies ISP filtering
Router or firewall	Ingress	VPN- and firewall-specific traffic	Unauthorized access

The four key devices that make up the Campus module are highlighted in Table 13-10.

Table 13-10 *Campus Module Devices*

Device	Description
Corporate servers	Provides services to internal users such as e-mail, file, and printing services
Layer 2 switch	Provides Layer 2 connectivity and also supports private VLANs
Management host	Provides management services, such as authentication, through RADIUS and TACACS+, HIDS, syslog, and other general management services
User workstation	Provides data services to authorized users on the network

Table 13-11 lists the expected threats and mitigation actions found within the Campus module.

Table 13-11 *Campus Module Threats and Threat Mitigation*

Threat	Threat Mitigation
Application layer attacks	Operating systems, devices, and applications are kept up to date with the latest security fixes and are protected by HIDSs.
Packet sniffers	A switched infrastructure limits the effectiveness of sniffing.
Port redirection	HIDSs prevent port redirection agents from being installed.
Trust exploitation	Private VLANs prevent hosts on the same subnet from communicating unless necessary.
Unauthorized access	HIDSs and application access control are used to mitigate unauthorized access.
Virus and Trojan-horse applications	Host-based virus scanning and host intrusion prevention prevents most viruses and many Trojan horses.

Q&A

As mentioned in the Introduction, "All About the Cisco Certified Security Professional Certification," you have two choices for review questions. The questions that follow next give you a more rigorous challenge than the exam itself by using an open-ended question format. By reviewing now with this more difficult question format, you can exercise your memory better and prove your conceptual and factual knowledge of this chapter. The answers to these questions are found in Appendix A.

For more practice with exam-like question formats, including questions using a router simulator and multiple choice questions, use the exam engine on the CD-ROM.

1. What modules are found within the small network design?

2. Where are private VLANs used in the small network design?

3. What two security devices can be used in the Corporate Internet module to connect to the ISP module?

4. Where would you use intrusion detection in the small network design?

5. VPN functionality is provided by what devices in the small network design?

6. The Corporate Internet module connects to which modules?

7. What are the two configuration types available in the small network design?

8. The Campus module provides functionality to what components?

9. Because no Layer 3 services are available in the Campus module, an increased emphasis is placed on _____ and _____ security.

10. What is a common design deviation in the Corporate Internet module?

11. The Corporate Internet module provides what services?

Reference

Convery, Sean, and Roland Saville. "SAFE: Extending the Security Blueprint to Small, Midsize, and Remote-User Networks." Cisco Systems, Inc., 2001.

This chapter covers the following topics:

- General Implementation Recommendations

- Using the ISP Router in Small Networks

- Using the Cisco IOS Firewall Router in Small Networks

- Using the PIX Firewall in Small Networks

- Alternative Implementations

CHAPTER 14

Implementing Small SAFE Networks

In Chapter 13, "Designing Small SAFE Networks," you looked in detail at the small network design requirements and guidelines that are recommended to secure a small network. In this chapter, you use those design recommendations as a basis for examining the specific configuration requirements that are necessary to achieve the desired functionality for each component of a small network.

> **NOTE** The configuration shown in this chapter highlights only the code that is required to achieve the specific security requirement of the design that is under discussion. Complete configurations are not shown nor are all the available options for a specific feature under discussion.
>
> Also, this chapter assumes that the reader is familiar with the devices that are used in the small network design and, in particular, has an understanding of the command sets that are used for each of the device types shown.

"Do I Know This Already?" Quiz

The purpose of the "Do I Know This Already?" quiz is to help you decide if you really need to read the entire chapter. If you already intend to read the entire chapter, you do not necessarily need to answer these questions now.

The 10-question quiz, derived from the major sections in the "Foundation Topics" portion of the chapter, helps you determine how to spend your limited study time.

Table 14-1 outlines the major topics discussed in this chapter and the "Do I Know This Already?" quiz questions that correspond to those topics.

Table 14-1 *"Do I Know This Already?" Foundation Topics Section-to-Question Mapping*

Foundation Topics Section	Questions Covered in This Section
General Implementation Recommendations	1
Using the ISP Router in Small Networks	2–3
Using the Cisco IOS Firewall Router in Small Networks	4–7
Using the PIX Firewall in Small Networks	8–9
Alternative Implementations	10

CAUTION The goal of self-assessment is to gauge your mastery of the topics in this chapter. If you do not know the answer to a question or are only partially sure of the answer, you should mark this question wrong for purposes of the self-assessment. Giving yourself credit for an answer you correctly guess skews your self-assessment results and might provide you with a false sense of security.

1. The functionality of the ISP module can be incorporated into which component of the small network design?

   a. PIX Firewall

   b. IDS sensor

   c. Cisco IOS Firewall router

   d. Layer 3 switch

   e. Public server

2. The primary role of the ISP router is to provide which of the following?

   a. VPN connectivity

   b. WAN connectivity

   c. Firewall filtering

   d. IP spoofing mitigation

   e. DDoS mitigation

3. Rate-limit filtering for DDoS mitigation affects all traffic.

   a. True

   b. False

4. Which of the following is provided by the Cisco IOS Firewall router?

   a. IDS services

   b. WAN connectivity

   c. Switching

   d. Filtering

   e. RAS services

   f. Firewall

5. Cisco IOS Firewall inspection can occur only on traffic that is transiting the public (Internet) interface.

   a. True

   b. False

6. IDS inspection services are enabled on the Cisco IOS Firewall router using which command?

   a. ip inspect

   b. ip audit

   c. ip access-group

   d. ip ids

   e. ip service

7. Which of the following services are commonly available on the public services segment?

   a. NTP

   b. FTP

   c. SMTP

   d. SSL

   e. WWW

   f. TFTP

   g. DNS

8. The PIX Firewall provides IDS services.

   a. True

   b. False

9. Filtering is applied to an interface in a PIX Firewall using which command?

   a. access-class

   b. access-list

   c. access-group

   d. access-rule

   e. ip access-group

10. When the small network model is used as a branch, which of the following is true?

   a. It is normal not to have a public services segment

   b. It is normal to terminate remote VPN users

   c. Branch LANs are normally routable across the WAN

   d. It is normal not to have a firewall

   e. None of the above

The answers to the "Do I Know This Already?" quiz are found in Appendix A, "Answers to the 'Do I Know This Already?' Quizzes and Q&A Sections." The suggested choices for your next step are as follows:

- **8 or less overall score**—Read the entire chapter. This includes the "Foundation Topics" and "Foundation Summary" sections, and the "Q&A" section.

- **9 or more overall score**—If you want more review on these topics, skip to the "Foundation Summary" section and then go to the "Q&A" section. Otherwise, move to the next chapter.

Foundation Topics

General Implementation Recommendations

In the SAFE small network implementation, we will look at the specific configuration requirements for the following components:

- Internet service provider (ISP) router

- Cisco IOS Firewall router

- PIX Firewall

These three components are the major networked devices that can be used within the small network. Technically, the ISP router is not part of the small network design, but because it plays a major role in the overall design aspects, it is included here for completeness. Also, the functionality of the ISP router can be integrated in some circumstances within the Cisco IOS Firewall router, thus eliminating it from the design.

> **NOTE** Discussion on the implementation of the Campus module in the small network is not undertaken in this chapter because this module involves only a basic configuration on the Layer 2 switch or involves application-specific configuration, which is outside the scope of this chapter.

As a review of the options explained in Chapter 13, Figure 14-1 illustrates the small network modules and their respective devices.

Figure 14-1 *Small Network Devices*

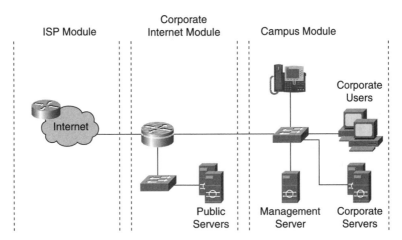

General configuration guidelines on effective tightening of security on Cisco routers and switches are listed in Appendix B, "General Configuration Guidelines for Cisco Router and Switch Security." Readers should familiarize themselves with the content of this appendix because these commands are not shown in the following sections but play an important role in the overall implementation.

Using the ISP Router in Small Networks

The primary purpose of the ISP router is to provide connectivity from the small network to a provider's network. The ISP router also provides mitigation against DDoS attacks and IP address spoofing attacks.

Distributed Denial of Service Attacks

DDoS mitigation can be provided at the egress of the ISP router through the use of rate limiting of nonessential traffic that exceeds prespecified thresholds. Obviously, the criteria used to identify nonessential traffic are critical because the flow of production traffic could be affected. To implement rate limiting, committed access rate (CAR) filtering can be used by following these steps:

Step 1   Define an ACL to select nonessential traffic:

```
access-list 100 permit non-essential-traffic-criteria1 any
access-list 100 permit non-essential-traffic-criteria2 any
```

Step 2   Apply the **rate-limit** command to the interface:

```
rate-limit input access-group rate-limit 100 8000 1500 20000 conform-action
    drop exceed-action drop
```

To prevent TCP SYN-flooding attacks, another form of a DoS attack, a feature called TCP intercept can be implemented by following these steps:

Step 1   Define an ACL to select the host(s) or network to be protected. In this example, only the destination is being specified.

```
access-list 105 permit tcp any host-or-network-to-protect
```

Step 2   Apply the **tcp intercept** command:

```
ip tcp intercept list 105
```

IP Spoofing Attacks

IP spoofing mitigation can be provided at the egress of the ISP router through the use of RFC 1918 and RFC 2827 filtering. The implementation of these filters is described in the sections that follow.

RFC 1918 Filtering

RFC 1918 filtering prevents source address spoofing of the private address ranges, as shown in the following sample configuration:

```
access-list 101 deny ip 10.0.0.0 0.255.255.255 any
access-list 101 deny ip 172.16.0.0 0.15.255.255 any
access-list 101 deny ip 192.168.0.0 0.0.255.255 any
access-list 101 permit ip any any
```

This ACL is then applied to the ingress interface of the ISP router by using the command **ip access-group 101 in**.

RFC 2827 Filtering

With RFC 2827 filtering at the ingress point of the ISP network, any traffic with a source address that is not part of the organization's public address space is filtered out by using

```
access-list 102 permit ip valid-public-source-address(es) any
```

This ACL is then applied to the ingress interface of the ISP router by using the command **ip access-group 102 in**.

The next section looks at the implementation requirements that need to be applied when a Cisco IOS Firewall router is used in the small network.

Using the Cisco IOS Firewall Router in Small Networks

This section details the implementation and configuration of the Cisco IOS Firewall router in the small network standalone model. The Cisco IOS Firewall router provides all of the required functionality in a single device, including a stateful firewall, IDS services, filtering, and WAN connectivity.

This section highlights the security aspects of the Cisco IOS Firewall configuration and does not include general router configuration nor WAN connectivity details. Details on the configuration changes of this router in a branch scenario are discussed in subsequent sections of the chapter. The primary features and configuration examples that are presented in this section cover the following:

■ Cisco IOS Firewall configuration

■ IDS configuration

■ VPN configuration

■ Internal traffic filtering

- Public services traffic filtering

- Public traffic filtering

Cisco IOS Firewall Implementation

The implementation of the Cisco IOS stateful firewall is implemented as follows:

Step 1   Because the router is configured with a public services segment or demilitarized zone (DMZ), two separate sets of firewall inspection rules need to be configured. The first set is configured for traffic from the inside of the firewall that is destined for the Internet or the DMZ. The second set is set up for traffic from the Internet that is destined for the DMZ only.

The following commands configure the router's firewall inspection rules for transmissions from inside the firewall to the Internet or DMZ:

```
ip inspect name IN_FW tcp
ip inspect name IN_FW udp
ip inspect name IN_FW ftp
ip inspect name IN_FW smtp
ip inspect name IN_FW sqlnet
ip inspect name IN_FW realaudio
ip inspect name IN_FW h323
```

The following commands configure the router's firewall inspection rules for Internet-to-DMZ transmissions:

```
ip inspect name OUT_FW tcp
ip inspect name OUT_FW udp
ip inspect name OUT_FW ftp
ip inspect name OUT_FW h323
```

NOTE   Not all of the available firewall inspection rules are shown in the previous examples. Inspection rules can be amended as required.

Step 2   These two rule sets are then applied to their respective interfaces where they inspect the traffic that is transiting those interfaces.

The IN_FW inspection rule set is applied to the inside interface of the router by using the command **ip inspect IN_FW in**. The OUT _FW inspection rule set is applied to the outside interface of the router by using the command **ip inspect OUT_FW in**.

IDS Implementation

The implementation of basic Cisco IOS IDS services and reporting to the syslog server is achieved in the Cisco IOS Firewall router by following these steps:

Step 1   Define the IDS rules:

```
ip audit notify log
ip audit po max-events 100
ip audit name IDS info action alarm
ip audit name IDS attack action alarm drop reset
```

Step 2   Apply the IDS rules to each interface that requires monitoring by using the command **ip audit IDS in**.

VPN Implementation

The implementation of VPN connectivity in the small network to remote branches is achieved by following these steps:

Step 1   Define the cryptographic policy and preshared key that are required for the connection:

```
crypto isakmp policy 10
encr 3des
authentication pre-share
group 5
crypto isakmp key crypto-key address peer-address
```

Step 2   Define the cryptographic transform set that is to be used for the VPN connection:

```
crypto ipsec transform-set transform-set-name esp-3des esp-sha-hmac
```

Step 3   Define the crypto map:

```
crypto map crypto-map-name 10 ipsec-isakmp
set peer peer-IP-address
set transform-set transform-set-name
match address 110
```

Step 4   Define the traffic that is to be encrypted by using an ACL. This can be for both user and management traffic:

```
access-list 110 permit traffic-to-be-encrypted
```

Step 5   Assign the crypto map to the outside interface:

```
crypto map crypto-map-name
```

Internal Traffic Filtering

By using an inbound ACL, you can filter traffic that is entering from the inside interface. This filtering is applied to the inside interface by using the command **ip access-group 120 in**. You should consider using the following common access list definitions.

Allow ssh management access to the public services network devices:

```
access-list 120 permit tcp host management-host-IP host PS-device-IP eq 22
```

Allow internal user access to the public services, such as web and FTP services:

```
access-list 120 permit tcp internal-network host public-server-IP eq http
access-list 120 permit tcp internal-network host public-server-IP eq ftp
```

Allow the internal mail server to communicate with the public mail server:

```
access-list 120 permit tcp host internal-mail-server-IP host public-mail-server-IP eq smtp
```

Allow the internal Domain Name System (DNS) server to communicate with the public DNS server:

```
access-list 120 permit udp host internal-DNS-IP host public-DNS-IP eq domain
```

Allow outbound Internet Control Message Protocol (ICMP) traffic:

```
access-list 120 permit icmp any any
```

Deny all other access to the public services segment:

```
access-list 120 deny ip any public-services-network
```

Allow the router to synchronize time:

```
access-list 120 permit udp host time-server-IP host router-inside-IP eq ntp
```

Allow management access to the router:

```
access-list 120 permit tcp management-server-IP host router-inside-IP eq 22
```

Block access to the outside interface of the router:

```
access-list 120 deny ip internal-network host outside-router-IP
```

Permit all other traffic to the outside:

```
access-list 120 permit ip any any
```

Block and log any other traffic:

```
access-list 120 deny ip any any log
```

Public Services Traffic Filtering

By using an inbound ACL, you can filter traffic that is entering from the public services interface. This filtering is applied to the public services interface by using the command **ip access-group 130 in**. You should consider using the following common ACL definitions.

Allow mail services between the public and internal mail servers:

```
access-list 130 permit tcp host public-mail-server-IP host internal-mail-server-IP eq smtp
```

Allow HIDS traffic from the public server to the management server:

```
access-list 130 permit tcp host public-server-IP host management-server-IP eq 5000
```

Allow any network device that is on the public services segment to synchronize time with the router:

```
access-list 130 permit udp host PS-network-device-IP host internal-time-server-IP eq ntp
```

Allow management traffic to flow from public services segment network devices:

```
access-list 130 permit ip host PS-network-device-IP host management-server-IP
```

Deny all other connections to the internal network from the public services segment:

```
access-list 130 deny ip any internal-network
```

Allow all mail and DNS traffic that originates from the public services server:

```
access-list 130 permit tcp host public-server-IP any eq smtp
access-list 130 permit udp host public-server-IP any eq domain
```

Block all other traffic and log it:

```
access-list 130 deny ip any any log
```

Public Traffic Filtering

You can use an inbound ACL to filter traffic that is entering from the public (Internet) interface. This filtering is applied to the public interfaceby using the command **ip access-group 140 in**. You should consider the following common ACL definitions.

If required, allow traffic from remotes sites:

```
access-list 140 permit ip remote-site-A-network internal-network
access-list 140 permit ip remote-site-B-network internal-network
```

Apply RFC 1918 filtering. If RFC 1918 addresses are used remotely, these rules require modification accordingly.

```
access-list 140 deny ip 10.0.0.0 0.255.255.255 any
access-list 140 deny ip 172.16.0.0 0.15.255.255 any
access-list 140 deny ip 192.168.0.0 0.0.255.255 any
```

If required, allow IPSec traffic from the remote sites to terminate on the router:

```
access-list 140 permit udp host remote-peer-IP host router-outside-IP eq isakmp
access-list 140 permit esp host remote-peer-IP host router-outside-IP
```

> **NOTE** In earlier implementations of IPSec and Cisco IOS Firewall, it may be necessary to add an additional entry to the preceding ACL to identify the actual traffic that needs to be encrypted through the VPN on top of those already defined.

If required, allow management traffic from the remote sites. This can be either a global statement, as shown in the subsequent command, or made more specific by electing to specify services.

```
access-list 140 permit ip host remote-router-IP host management-server-IP
```

Allow access to the services that are available on the public services segment via the public NAT address:

```
access-list 140 permit tcp any host public-NAT-IP eq ftp
access-list 140 permit tcp any host public-NAT-IP eq www
access-list 140 permit tcp any host public-NAT-IP eq smtp
access-list 140 permit tcp any host public-NAT-IP eq 443
access-list 140 permit udp any host public-NAT-IP eq domain
```

Deny all other traffic and log it:

```
access-list 140 deny ip any any log
```

In the next section, you look at the implementation requirements that need to be applied when a PIX Firewall is used in the small network.

Using the PIX Firewall in Small Networks

This section details the implementation and configuration of the PIX Firewall in the small network standalone model. WAN connectivity is provided by an ISP-supplied device. The configuration shows only the ACLs and cryptographic parameters that are required for the PIX Firewall to operate as a headend device.

This section covers the following primary features and configuration examples:

■ Outside interface filtering

■ Inside interface filtering

■ DMZ interface filtering

■ IDS configuration

■ VPN configuration

Outside Interface Filtering

By using an ACL, you can filter traffic that is entering from the outside (Internet) interface. This filtering is applied to the outside interface by using the **access-group** command. You should consider the following common ACL definitions.

Allow access to the services that are available on the public services segment:

```
access-list outside_access_in permit tcp any host public-NAT-IP eq ftp
access-list outside_access_in permit tcp any host public-NAT-IP eq www
access-list outside_access_in permit tcp any host public-NAT-IP eq smtp
access-list outside_access_in permit tcp any host public-NAT-IP eq 443
access-list outside_access_in permit udp any host public-NAT-IP eq domain
```

If required, allow traffic from remotes sites:

```
access-list outside_access_in permit ip remote-site-A-network internal-network
access-list outside_access_in permit ip remote-site-B-network internal-network
```

Apply RFC 1918 filtering. If RFC 1918 addresses are used remotely, these rules require modification accordingly.

```
access-list outside_access_in deny ip 10.0.0.0 0.255.255.255 any
access-list outside_access_in deny ip 172.16.0.0 0.15.255.255 any
access-list outside_access_in deny ip 192.168.0.0 0.0.255.255 any
```

If required, allow management traffic from the remote sites. This can be either a global statement, as shown in the command that follows, or made more specific by electing to specify services.

```
access-list outside_access_in permit ip host remote-device-IP host management-server-IP
```

Allow echo reply to internally generated traffic:

```
access-list outside_access_in permit icmp any public-NAT-IP echo-reply
```

Internal Traffic Filtering

By using an ACL, you can filter traffic that is entering from the inside interface. This filtering is applied to the inside interface by using the **access-group** command. You should consider the following common ACL definitions.

Allow management access to the public services network devices:

```
access-list inside_access_in permit tcp host management-host-IP host PS-device-IP eq 22
```

Allow internal user access to the public services, such as web and FTP services:

```
access-list inside_access_in permit tcp internal-network host public-server-IP
eq service
```

Allow the internal mail server to communicate with the public mail server:

```
access-list inside_access_in permit tcp host internal-mail-server-IP
host public-mail-server-IP eq smtp
```

Allow the internal DNS server to communicate with the public DNS server:

```
access-list inside_access_in permit udp host internal-DNS-IP host public-DNS-IP
eq domain
```

Allow outbound ICMP traffic:

```
access-list inside_access_in permit icmp any any echo
```

Deny all other access to the public services segment:

```
access-list inside_access_in deny ip any public-services-network
```

Permit all other traffic to the outside:

```
access-list inside_access_in permit ip any any
```

Public Services Traffic Filtering

Using an ACL, traffic that is entering from the DMZ interface can be filtered. This filtering is applied to the DMZ interface by using the **access-group** command. You should consider the following common ACL definitions.

Allow mail services between the public and internal mail servers:

```
access-list dmz_access_in permit tcp host public-mail-server-IP
host internal-mail-server-IP eq smtp
```

Allow echo replies from the internal network:

```
access-list dmz_access_in permit icmp public-services-network internal-network
eq echo-reply
```

Allow HIDS traffic from the public server to the management server:

```
access-list dmz_access_in permit tcp host public-server-IP host management-server-IP
eq 5000
```

Allow management traffic to flow from public services segment network devices:

```
access-list dmz_access_in permit ip host PS-network-device-IP host management-server-IP
```

Deny all other connections to the internal network from the public services segment:

```
access-list ps_access_in deny ip any internal-network
```

Allow all mail and DNS traffic originating from the public services server:

```
access-list ps_access_in permit tcp host public-server-IP any eq smtp
access-list ps_access_in permit udp host public-server-IP any eq domain
```

IDS Configuration

The implementation of IDS services on a PIX Firewall can be achieved by using the following commands:

```
ip audit name IDS info action alarm
ip audit name IDS attack action alarm drop reset
ip audit interface outside IDS
ip audit interface inside IDS
ip audit interface dmz IDS
```

VPN Configuration

The implementation of VPN services on a PIX Firewall can be achieved by using the following commands.

To configure remote-site VPNs, use the following commands:

```
no sysopt route dnat
crypto ipsec transform-set REMOTESITES esp-3des esp-md5-hmac
crypto map REMOTE 10 ipsec-isakmp
crypto map REMOTE 10 match address remote-sites
crypto map REMOTE 10 set peer peer-IP-A
crypto map REMOTE 10 set transform-set REMOTESITES
crypto map REMOTE interface outside
isakmp enable outside
isakmp key key address IP-address netmask 255.255.255.255
isakmp identity address
```

```
isakmp policy 10 authentication pre-share
isakmp policy 10 encryption 3des
isakmp policy 10 hash md5
isakmp policy 10 group 2
isakmp policy 10 lifetime 28800
access-list remote-sites permit ip internal-network remote-site-network
```

To configure remote-access VPN users, use the following commands:

```
vpngroup RASVPN address-pool vpnpool
vpngroup RASVPN dns-server dns-address
vpngroup RASVPN default-domain domain-name
vpngroup RASVPN idle-time 1800
vpngroup RASVPN password password
ip local pool vpnpool start-IP-range-end-IP-range
```

Alternative Implementations

The implementation examples shown so far have been based on the small network design model in which the small network is being used in a standalone or headend configuration.

If the small network is considered a branch of a larger network, the implementation of the small network in this design model is slightly different than that previously discussed. These differences are as follows:

■ Corporate resources are normally centralized at the corporate headquarters; therefore, the use of a local public services segment is redundant. Under this circumstance, all related configuration is removed.

■ To provide site-to-site connectivity between offices, IPSec over Generic Routing Encapsulation (GRE) can be used. If you use GRE, you must amend cryptographic parameters to allow IPSec transport mode to be used and then modify the associated filtering to reflect this change.

■ Remote users normally terminate at the corporate headquarters rather than on the small network. Under this circumstance, all related configuration is removed.

Foundation Summary

The "Foundation Summary" section of each chapter lists the most important facts from the chapter. Although this section does not list every fact from the chapter that will be on your CSI exam, a well-prepared CSI candidate should at a minimum know all the details in each "Foundation Summary" section before taking the exam.

The following three components are the major networked devices that can be used within the small SAFE network:

■ ISP router

■ Cisco IOS Firewall router

■ PIX Firewall

Technically, the ISP router is not part of the small network design, but it plays a major role in the overall design. The functionality of the ISP router can be integrated in some circumstances within the Cisco IOS Firewall router, thus eliminating it from the design. The primary purpose of the ISP router is to provide the following:

■ Connectivity from the small network to a provider's network

■ Mitigation against DDoS attacks and IP address spoofing attacks.

The Cisco IOS Firewall router provides all the required functionality of the small network in a single device that includes the following:

■ A stateful firewall

■ IDS services

■ Filtering

■ WAN connectivity

The primary features and configuration examples presented in this chapter include

■ Cisco IOS Firewall configuration

■ IDS configuration

■ VPN configuration

■ Internal traffic filtering

■ Public services traffic filtering

■ Public traffic filtering

For a PIX Firewall in the small network standalone model, WAN connectivity is provided by an ISP-supplied device.

The primary features and configuration examples of the PIX Firewall covered in this chapter include

■ Outside interface filtering

■ Inside interface filtering

■ DMZ interface filtering

■ IDS configuration

■ VPN configuration

If the small network is considered a branch of a larger network, the implementation of the small network in this design scenario is then slightly different. These differences are as follows:

■ Corporate resources are normally centralized at the corporate headquarters; therefore, the use of a local public services segment is redundant. All related configuration is removed under this circumstance.

■ To provide site-to-site connectivity between offices, IPSec over GRE is used. This requires the amendment of cryptographic parameters to allow the use of IPSec transport mode and the modification of associated filtering.

■ Remote users normally terminate at the corporate headquarters rather than on the small network. All related configuration is removed under this circumstance.

Q&A

As mentioned in the introduction, "All About the Cisco Certified Security Professional Certification," you have two choices for review questions. The questions that follow next give you a bigger challenge than the exam itself by using an open-ended question format. By reviewing now with this more difficult question format, you can exercise your memory better and prove your conceptual and factual knowledge of this chapter. The answers to these questions are found in Appendix A.

For more practice with exam-like question formats, including questions using a router simulator and multiple choice questions, use the exam engine on the CD-ROM.

1. What is RFC 2827 filtering?

2. What public services should be available to Internet users?

3. What is the command to implement a Cisco IOS Firewall rule set to an interface?

4. What technique is used to perform rate limiting within the ISP router?

5. How do you implement RFC 1918 filtering?

6. How should traffic that is flowing from the internal network to the public services segment be restricted?

7. How are remote users affected in the small network when the small network is used in a branch configuration?

8. What commands are used to implement IDS services on the PIX Firewall in the small network design?

9. What is the importance of the **isakmp key** command?

This chapter covers the following topics:

- Components of SAFE Medium-Sized Network Design

- Corporate Internet Module in Medium-Sized Networks

- Campus Module in Medium-Sized Networks

- WAN Module in Medium-Sized Networks

- Branch Versus Headend/Standalone Considerations for Medium-Sized Networks

15

Designing Medium-Sized SAFE Networks

As mentioned in Chapter 13, "Designing Small SAFE Networks," the principle goal of Cisco SAFE blueprints is to provide to interested parties best-practice information on how to design and implement secure networks. SAFE serves as a guide to network architects who are examining the security requirements of their networks and uses a modular format to combat security threats. This enables the creation of scalable, corporate-wide security solutions.

In this second of three chapters covering the design requirements of the "SAFE: Extending the Security Blueprint to Small, Midsize, and Remote-User Networks" (SAFE SMR) design model, you examine the specific security design requirements of the SAFE medium-sized network.

Readers should be aware that information within this chapter builds on the topics already discussed in Chapter 4, "Understanding SAFE Network Modules," and Chapter 13, "Designing Small SAFE Networks." In Chapter 4, you were introduced to the modules and their various components that make up the SAFE SMR model. In Chapter 13, you applied the information from Chapter 4 to small networks, including the role of each module and the specific components that make up the small network design.

This chapter takes the process a step further to discuss the design aspects of the modules and their various components that make up the medium-sized network.

"Do I Know This Already?" Quiz

The purpose of the "Do I Know This Already?" quiz is to help you decide if you really need to read the entire chapter. If you already intend to read the entire chapter, you do not necessarily need to answer these questions now.

The 12-question quiz, derived from the major sections in the "Foundation Topics" portion of the chapter, helps you determine how to spend your limited study time.

Table 15-1 outlines the major topics discussed in this chapter and the "Do I Know This Already?" quiz questions that correspond to those topics.

Table 15-1 *"Do I Know This Already?" Foundation Topics Section-to-Question Mapping*

Foundation Topics Section	Questions Covered in This Section
Components of SAFE Medium-Sized Network Design	1–2
Corporate Internet Module in Medium-Sized Networks	3–6
Campus Module in Medium-Sized Networks	7–10
WAN Module in Medium-Sized Networks	11–12

CAUTION The goal of self-assessment is to gauge your mastery of the topics in this chapter. If you do not know the answer to a question or are only partially sure of the answer, you should mark this question wrong for purposes of the self-assessment. Giving yourself credit for an answer you correctly guess skews your self-assessment results and might provide you with a false sense of security.

1. The SAFE medium-sized network design consists of which of the following modules?

   a. ISP module

   b. Campus module

   c. PSTN module

   d. Corporate Internet module

   e. WAN module

2. How many configuration options are there within the design for a medium-sized network?

   a. 1

   b. 2

   c. 3

   d. 4

   e. 5

3. Which of the following are components of the medium-sized network Corporate Internet module?

   a. Firewall

   b. Management server

   c. NIDS appliance

   d. Layer 3 switch

   e. Edge router

4. Perimeter traffic filtering is performed by which of the following medium-sized network Corporate Internet module devices?

    a. VPN concentrator

    b. ISP router

    c. Edge router

    d. Firewall

    e. Access server

5. Remote access is provided by which of the following medium-sized network Corporate Internet module devices?

    a. Firewall

    b. VPN concentrator

    c. Layer 2 switch

    d. Edge router

    e. Access server

6. Only a HIDS is used in the medium-sized network Corporate Internet Module.

    a. True

    b. False

7. The medium-sized network Campus module provides Layer 3 services.

    a. True

    b. False

8. Which of the following are components of the medium-sized network Campus module?

    a. Inside router

    b. Corporate servers

    c. VPN concentrator

    d. WAN router

    e. Management servers

    f. ISP router

    g. Layer 2 switch

    h. NIDS sensor

9. Where is an IDS used in the medium-sized network Campus module?

   a. Management VLAN

   b. Corporate servers

   c. Core switch

   d. Management servers

   e. Access switches

10. The medium-sized network Campus module uses a flat Layer 2 topology.

    a. True

    b. False

11. What are the main components found in the medium-sized network WAN module?

    a. Switch

    b. IDS appliance

    c. Router

    d. Firewall

    e. Access server

12. Access control is used in the medium-sized network WAN module.

    a. True

    b. False

The answers to the "Do I Know This Already?" quiz are found in Appendix A, "Answers to the 'Do I Know This Already?' Quizzes and Q&A Sections." The suggested choices for your next step are as follows:

■ **10 or less overall score**—Read the entire chapter. This includes the "Foundation Topics" and "Foundation Summary" sections, and the "Q&A" section.

■ **11 or more overall score**—If you want more review on these topics, skip to the "Foundation Summary" section and then go to the "Q&A" section. Otherwise, move to the next chapter.

Foundation Topics

The implementation decisions that are recommended in the "SAFE SMR" white paper are based on numerous factors, including required network functionality and certain design objectives, which are discussed in Chapter 2, "SAFE Design Fundamentals."

Again, as in the SAFE small network design, two possible configurations are available in the SAFE medium-sized network design: a headend or standalone configuration and a branch configuration. The design recommendations for these two configuration types are very similar, but some of the functionality found in the branch configuration might be superfluous because it is provided in the headend configuration of the network.

For discussion purposes, the headend or standalone configuration is used but specific design changes are detailed for use of the branch configuration.

Components of SAFE Medium-Sized Network Design

Within the SAFE SMR model, the medium-sized network design consists of three modules:

■ Corporate Internet module

■ Campus module

■ WAN module

Figure 15-1 shows six modules; however, the Public Switched Telephone Network (PSTN), Internet Service Provider (ISP), and Frame Relay/ATM modules are shown for clarity but are not considered a part of the medium-sized network design model:

■ ISP module

■ PSTN module

■ Frame Relay/ATM module

■ Corporate Internet module

■ WAN module

■ Campus module

Figure 15-1 *Medium-Sized Network Model*

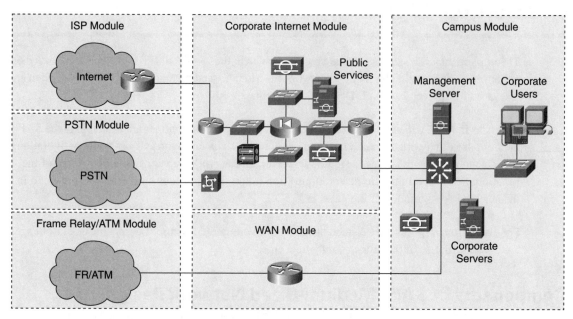

As with the small network design model, the medium-sized network Corporate Internet module provides connectivity to the Internet, terminates any VPN traffic, and provides access to public services such as e-mail, web, file transfer, and Domain Name System (DNS). In the design for a medium-sized network, this module also provides the termination of dial-in services. Within the Campus module of the SAFE medium-sized network, shown in Figure 15-1, you'll find all the internal Layer 2 and Layer 3 switching infrastructure, including all corporate users, corporate intranet servers, and management servers.

Finally, the WAN module, found within the SAFE medium-sized network and shown in Figure 15-1, provides for the termination of remote sites using private WAN connections such as ATM or Frame Relay.

Corporate Internet Module in Medium-Sized Networks

The Corporate Internet module provides internal users with connectivity to Internet services and provides Internet users access to information on the corporate public servers. This module also provides remote access for remote locations and telecommuters through the use of VPN connectivity as well as traffic from traditional dial-in users.

The various key devices that make up the Corporate Internet module are outlined in Table 15-2.

Table 15-2 *Corporate Internet Module Devices*

Device	Description
Dial-in server	Terminates analog connections and authenticates individual remote users
DNS server	Serves as the authoritative external DNS server and relays internal requests to the Internet
Edge router	Provides basic filtering and Layer 3 connectivity to the Internet
File/web server	Provides public information about the organization
Firewall	Provides network-level protection of resources, stateful filtering of traffic, granular security of remote users, and VPN connectivity for remote sites
Layer 2 switch	Provides Layer 2 connectivity for devices and can also provide private VLAN support
SMTP server	Acts as a relay between the Internet and the intranet mail servers and provides content security of mail
NIDS appliance	Provides Layer 4-to-Layer 7 monitoring of key network segments in the module
VPN concentrator	Authenticates individual remote users and terminates their IPSec tunnels

The devices that constitute the Corporate Internet module in the medium-sized network design are shown in Figure 15-2. As you can see, the medium-sized network builds on the complexity of the small network design, which was previously discussed in Chapter 13. This added complexity results from the addition of a specific VPN device for remote-access users' termination, the placement of NIDS sensors on key segments of the module, the provision of an edge router, and the facility to accommodate PSTN remote-user access in the design.

Figure 15-2 *Medium-Sized Network Corporate Internet Module*

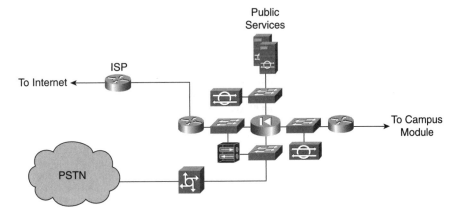

Mitigating Threats in the Corporate Internet Module

The most likely point of attack within the Corporate Internet module is on the public services segment. Positioned on this segment are the publicly addressed servers. The expected threats on the public services segment and the mitigation actions to counter them are described in Table 15-3.

Table 15-3 *Corporate Internet Module—Threats Against Public Services and Threat Mitigation*

Threat	Threat Mitigation
Application layer attacks	Mitigated by using HIDSs and NIDSs
DoS	Mitigated by using committed access rate (CAR) at the ISP edge and TCP setup controls at the firewall to limit exposure
IP spoofing	Mitigated by using RFC 2827 and RFC 1918 filtering at ISP edge and edge router of the medium-sized network
Network reconnaissance	Mitigated by using IDS; protocols are filtered to limit effectiveness
Packet sniffers	Mitigated by using a switched infrastructure and a HIDS to limit exposure
Password attacks	Mitigated by limiting the services that are available to brute force; the operating system and IDS can detect the threat
Port redirection	Mitigated by using restrictive filtering and a HIDS to limit attacks
Trust exploitation	Mitigated by using a restrictive trust model and private VLANs to limit trust-based attacks
Unauthorized access	Mitigated by using filtering at the ISP, edge router, and corporate firewalls
Virus and Trojan-horse attacks	Mitigated by using a HIDS, virus scanning at the host level, and content filtering on e-mail

The VPN services that are found within the Corporate Internet module of the medium-sized network design are also vulnerable to attack. The expected threats and mitigation actions for these services are described in Table 15-4.

Table 15-4 *Corporate Internet Module—Threats Against VPN Services and Threat Mitigation*

Threat	Threat Mitigation
Man-in-the-middle attacks	Mitigated by encrypting remote traffic
Network topology discovery	Mitigated by using ACLs on the ingress router to limit access to the VPN concentrator and firewall and, if terminating VPN traffic, to Internet Key Exchange (IKE) and Encapsulating Security Payload (ESP) from the Internet

Table 15-4 *Corporate Internet Module—Threats Against VPN Services and Threat Mitigation (Continued)*

Threat	Threat Mitigation
Packet sniffers	Mitigated by using a switched infrastructure to limit exposure
Password attacks	Mitigated by using one-time passwords (OTPs)
Unauthorized access	Mitigated by using firewall filtering and by preventing traffic on unauthorized ports

The threat-mitigation roles performed by the various devices that are found within the medium-sized corporate Internet module are shown in Figure 15-3.

Figure 15-3 *Medium-Sized Network Corporate Internet Module Threat-Mitigation Roles*

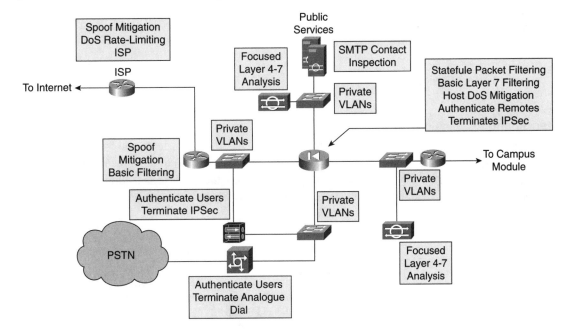

Design Guidelines

The Corporate Internet module in the medium-sized network design consists of the following key devices, which have different functional roles within the design:

- **ISP router**—Provides Internet connectivity

- **Edge router**—Provides a demarcation point between the ISP and the network

- **Firewall**—Provides stateful filtering and site-to-site VPN termination

- **Intrusion detection**—Detects attacks from permitted firewall traffic

- **Remote-access VPN**—Provides secure connectivity for remote users

- **Dial-in access users**—Provides secure connectivity for remote users

- **Layer 2 switch**—Provides Layer 2 connectivity

- **Inside router**—Provides Layer 3 separation and routing between the Corporate Internet and Campus modules

The various roles that the preceding devices play can be broken down into the following more general areas, which are described in depth next:

- Filtering and access control

- Intrusion detection

- Remote access

- Layer 2 services

- Layer 3 services

Filtering and Access Control

Within the medium-sized network design, the ISP router, the edge router, and the firewall provide filtering and access control of perimeter traffic. It is generally ideal to implement some form of security filtering on the perimeter traffic flow even before that traffic hits the firewall. Table 15-5 outlines the filter parameters that can be applied on the ISP and edge routers to restrict perimeter traffic flow, and the corresponding threat mitigation.

Table 15-5 *Perimeter Traffic Flow Filtering*

Filter Location	Flow	Filter Description	Mitigation
ISP router	Egress	The ISP rate-limits nonessential traffic that exceeds a predefined threshold	DDoS
ISP router	Egress	RFC 1918 and RFC 2827 filtering	IP spoofing
Edge router	Ingress	Coarse IP filtering for expected traffic	General attacks
Edge router	Ingress	RFC 1918 and RFC 2827 filtering	IP spoofing—verifies ISP filtering
Edge router	Ingress	VPN- and firewall-specific traffic filtering	Unauthorized access

The primary function of the stateful firewall within the medium-sized network design is to provide connection-state enforcement and detailed filtering for sessions that are initiated through the firewall.

The firewall consists of two segments—a public services segment and a remote-access segment. The firewall also acts as a termination point for site-to-site IPSec VPN tunnels for both production and management traffic from remote sites. Additionally, the advanced features within the software protect against TCP synchronization (TCP SYN) attacks on the publicly facing servers by controlling the limits on half-open sessions through the firewall.

With reference to the public services segment, the filtering of traffic should control not only the flow of traffic destined to specific addresses and ports on the public services segment but also the flow of traffic from the segment. This additional level of filtering prevents an attacker who may have compromised one of the public servers from using that server as a platform to launch further attacks on the network. For example, if an intruder has managed to circumvent the firewall and IDS security features on a public-facing DNS server, that server should be permitted only to reply to requests, not to originate a request. This prevents an intruder from using a compromised platform to launch additional attacks.

Finally, the use of private VLANs on the demilitarized zone (DMZ) switches prevents a compromised server from being used to attack other servers on the same segment. This type of vulnerability is not detectable by the firewall, so the implementation of private VLANs is especially important.

Intrusion Detection

Within the medium-sized network design, both HIDS and NIDS are used. The placement of a NIDS appliance on the public services segment provides the facility to detect attacks that have already been permitted by the firewall. Most commonly, these attacks are application layer attacks that are aimed at specific services. Because traffic at this point has been permitted through the firewall, the NIDS appliance should be configured to act in a restrictive mode for matched signatures.

Every server on the public services segment should be configured with a HIDS, which enables you to monitor any rogue activity at the operating system level. A HIDS can also be configured to monitor certain common server applications. Additionally, all public services applications, such as web, e-mail, and DNS services, should be hardened as much as possible so that any unnecessary responses cannot be used to assist an intruder in network reconnaissance.

The placement of a NIDS appliance on the segment between the inside interface of the firewall and the internal router provides for a final analysis of traffic that detects even the most determined of attacks. Traffic on this segment has already been filtered by the firewall and should consist only of these elements: responses to internally initiated requests, traffic from the remote-access segment, and traffic from selected ports of the public servers on the public services segment.

A typical example of an attack that might be encountered on this segment is one in which the attacker compromises one of the public servers on the public services segment. The attacker could then use the compromised server to launch further attacks against the internal network. Consequently, any response to an attack on this segment that is recognized should be more severe than on other segments in the network, because an attack here normally indicates that a server has been compromised. You should seriously consider implementing TCP resets or shunning in response to any detected attack.

Remote Access

Remote-access connectivity in the medium-sized network design is provided by the use of remote-access VPNs and traditional dial-in services. VPN connectivity is provided through the use of a VPN concentrator, whereas dial-in services are provided through the use of an access server.

By using a remote-access VPN concentrator, remote VPN users can be offered secure connectivity. When a remote user initiates a VPN session, the VPN concentrator authenticates the remote user's credentials by querying an access control server (ACS), located on the internal network, before allowing the remote user access to the network. This ACS can interact with a one-time password (OTP) server, if required, to validate the user's credentials.

After the user is authenticated, a specific IPSec policy can be sent from the VPN concentrator to the client to determine the characteristics of the remote connection. Characteristics such as the tunnel mode, encryption standards, and data-integrity standards to be used are passed in the IPSec policy. The following IPSec parameters are recommended in the SAFE medium-sized network design: no split tunneling (tunnel everything); use Triple Data Encryption Standard (3DES) for encryption; and use Secure Hash Algorithm/Hash-Based Message Authentication Code (SHA/HMAC) for data integrity. Finally, granular control over remote VPN users is achieved by placing the VPN concentrator in front of the firewall. By doing this, the VPN tunnels terminate in front of the firewall and thereby permit the filtering of these remote users as their traffic transits the firewall.

Traditional dial-in remote users are catered to within the medium-sized network design by the use of an ACS with built-in modems. User authentication is achieved by the use of the Challenge Handshake Authentication Protocol (CHAP) and, as in the remote-access VPN service, an ACS. Once authenticated, the users are allocated an IP address from an IP pool of addresses. As with the remote VPN users, you can achieve granular control of the dial-in users when the access server is placed on a separate segment, in front of the firewall, enabling you to apply appropriate filtering as dial-in user traffic transits the firewall.

Layer 2 Services

Layer 2 connectivity between devices in the Corporate Internet module is provided by the use of individual switches on each segment rather than a single switch using multiple VLANs. The placement of individual switches on each segment of the firewall allows for the physical separation of segments and helps to mitigate against a switch being compromised by misconfiguration. Each switch also provides private VLAN support, if required, for its corresponding segment.

Layer 3 Services

An inside router is placed in the medium-sized network design to provide Layer 3 separation and routing between the Corporate Internet and Campus modules. This router performs no filtering of any kind and provides a demarcation point between the routed intranet and the Corporate Internet module and, hence, the outside of the network. To mitigate against DoS attacks using routing updates, it is recommended that you use authenticated routing updates.

Design Alternatives

The Corporate Internet module discussed in the previous section can have a number of alternative designs, which are summarized in the following list and then explored in more detail:

- The basic filtering of the edge router can be replaced with the advanced functionality of a Cisco IOS Firewall router

- A NIDS appliance can be placed on the outside of the firewall

- The inside router located between the firewall and the Campus module can be removed

- A form of content inspection can be added, such as URL filtering

Replacing the basic filtering of the edge router with the advanced functionality of a Cisco IOS Firewall router provides not only general filtering but also a second stateful firewall within the design. Having two stateful firewalls provides more of a defense-in-depth approach to security within the module.

Placing a NIDS appliance on the outside of the firewall enables you to monitor the types of attacks the network is experiencing and the effectiveness of the ISP and edge filters. Because this configuration has the potential to generate a high number of alarms, you must carefully set up the IDS and filtering parameters. You should consider setting up a separate monitoring station to report these events so that you don't miss legitimate alarms from other segments.

By removing the inside router that is located between the firewall and the Campus module, the Layer 3 functionality provided by this router could be offered within the Campus module.

However, that would force the functions of the Corporate Internet module to rely on another area of the network.

The placement of some form of content inspection, such as URL filtering, could be added.

Campus Module in Medium-Sized Networks

The Campus module of the medium-sized network design provides end-user workstations, corporate intranet servers, management servers, and the associated Layer 2 and Layer 3 functionality that is required by the network.

The various key devices that make up the campus module are described in Table 15-6.

Table 15-6   *Campus Module Devices*

Device	Description
ACS	Provides authentication services to the network devices
Corporate servers	Provides services to internal users, such as e-mail, file, and printing services
Layer 2 switch	Provides Layer 2 connectivity and supports private VLANs
Layer 3 switch	Provides route and switch production and management traffic within the Campus module, provides distribution layer services to the building switches, and supports advanced services such as traffic filtering
NIDS appliance	Provides Layer 4-to-Layer 7 monitoring of key network segments in the module
NIDS host	Provides alarm aggregation for all NIDS devices in the network
OTP server	Authenticates one-time password information that is relayed from the ACS
SNMP management host	Provides SNMP management for devices
Syslog host(s)	Aggregates log information for firewall and NIDS hosts
System admin host	Provides configuration, software, and content changes on devices
User workstations	Provides data services to authorized users on the network

The devices that constitute the Campus module in the medium-sized network design are shown in Figure 15-4. As you can see, the medium-sized network builds on the small network design, previously discussed in Chapter 13. The new features that appear in the medium-sized network Campus module are a Layer 3 switch and a NIDS sensor.

Figure 15-4 *Medium-Sized Network Campus Module*

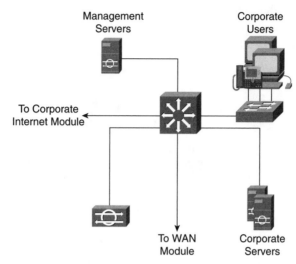

Management Servers

Corporate Users

To Corporate Internet Module

To WAN Module

Corporate Servers

Mitigating Threats in the Campus Module

Expected threats against the Campus module and the mitigation actions to counter them are described in Table 15-7.

Table 15-7 *Threats Against Campus Module and Threat Mitigation*

Threat	Threat Mitigation
Application layer attacks	Mitigated by keeping operating systems, devices, and applications up to date with the latest security fixes and protected by HIDSs
IP spoofing	Mitigated by using RFC 2827 filtering to prevent source-address spoofing
Packet sniffers	Mitigated by using a switched infrastructure to limit the effectiveness of sniffing
Password attacks	Mitigated by using an ACS to enforce strong two-factor authentication for key applications
Port redirection	Mitigated by using HIDSs to prevent port redirection agents from being installed
Trust exploitation	Mitigated by using private VLANs to prevent hosts on the same subnet from communicating unless necessary
Unauthorized access	Mitigated by using HIDS and application access control
Virus and Trojan-horse applications	Mitigated by using host-based virus scanning

The threat-mitigation roles that are performed by the various devices found within the medium-sized Campus module are shown in Figure 15-5.

Figure 15-5 *Medium-Sized Network Campus Module Threat-Mitigation Roles*

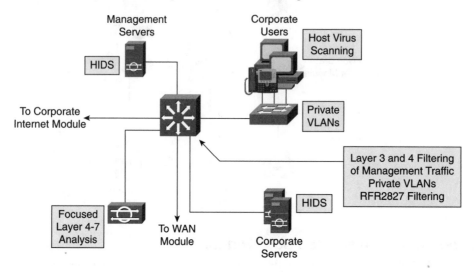

Design Guidelines

The medium-sized network Campus module consists of several key devices that provide the necessary Layer 2 and Layer 3 connectivity and other functional requirements of the corporate campus network. The functionality and connectivity are provided by the following devices:

■ Core switch

■ Access switches

■ IDSs

Core Switch

The main purpose of the campus core switch is to provide the following services:

■ Routing and switching for management and production data

■ Distribution layer services for the building access switches

■ Corporate and management server connectivity

■ Traffic filtering

The Campus module uses a Layer 3 core switch in preference to a Layer 2 core switch for four reasons:

■ The use of multiple VLANs has been implemented in the design, allowing the corporate servers, management servers, user connectivity functions, WAN module, and Corporate Internet module to all reside on individual VLANs.

■ By using separate VLANs with access control, inter-VLAN traffic filtering can be introduced, which can mitigate the chance of users on one VLAN accessing confidential information on another VLAN of the network. For example, a network that contains administration, engineering, finance, and sales departments might segment off the finance server to a specific VLAN and filter access to it, ensuring that only finance staff have access. For performance reasons, it is important that this access control be implemented on a hardware platform that can deliver filtered traffic at near-wire rates. This setup generally dictates the use of Layer 3 switching, as opposed to more traditional dedicated routing devices.

■ To mitigate against trust-exploitation attacks and address spoofing, private VLANs and RFC 2827 filtering should be used on the corporate user and corporate server VLANs.

■ Extensive filtering should be used on the management VLAN to control the flow of management traffic between both local devices and devices located at remote sites. Both Layer 3 and Layer 4 access control should be implemented to restrict traffic flow between managed hosts and the management servers. This filtering should only permit the specific management protocols and services that are required between the managed device and management server.

Access Switches

The role of the access or building switches within the Campus module is to provide Layer 2 connectivity to corporate users.

Because users generally do not require direct host-to-host communication, private VLANs are implemented on the access switches to mitigate against trust-exploitation attacks. To mitigate against virus attacks, host-based virus scanning is implemented on user workstations.

Intrusion Detection in the Campus Module

The medium-sized network Campus module supports both HIDS and NIDS. A HIDS is used on each of the corporate intranet and management servers, and a single NIDS appliance is connected to the core switch. The switch port that connects the NIDS appliance is configured as a monitoring port, which can be used to mirror all VLAN traffic that requires monitoring within the switch. Generally, though, few attacks should be detected by this NIDS appliance because it is looking for potential attacks originating from within the Campus module itself.

Design Alternatives

The Campus module discussed in the previous section can have the following alternative designs:

■ If the medium-sized network is small enough, the access or building switches can be removed. The removed Layer 2 functionality is then provided by connecting the devices directly to the core switch. Any private VLAN configuration that is lost with the removal of the access switches is offered by the core switch and still mitigates against trust-exploitation attacks.

■ The external NIDS appliance can be replaced by an integrated IDS module that fits into the core switch. This configuration option offers increased performance benefits because the IDS appliance sits directly on the backplane of the switch.

If performance is not an issue, it is possible to replace the Layer 3 switch with a Layer 2 switch and provide inter-VLAN routing by use of an external router.

WAN Module in Medium-Sized Networks

The inclusion of the WAN module in the medium-sized network design is feasible only if there is a requirement to connect to a remote site using a private circuit such as Frame Relay or ATM.

The design of a WAN module includes only one device, a Cisco IOS Firewall router, which provides routing, access-control, and QoS mechanisms to remote locations.

The WAN module and its associated components is shown in Figure 15-6.

Figure 15-6 *Medium-Sized Network WAN Module*

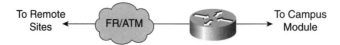

Mitigating Threats in the WAN Module

The expected threats on the WAN module and the mitigation actions to counter them are outlined in Table 15-8.

Table 15-8 *Threats Against WAN Modules and Threat Mitigation*

Threat	Threat Mitigation
IP spoofing	Mitigated by using Layer 3 filtering on the router
Unauthorized access	Mitigated by using simple access control on the router, which can limit the types of protocols to which branches have access

Figure 15-7 shows the threat-mitigation roles performed by the components of the medium-sized network WAN module.

Figure 15-7   *Medium-Sized Network WAN Module Threat-Mitigation Roles*

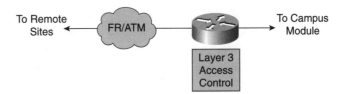

Design Guidelines

The level of security placed within the WAN module depends on the level of trust at the remote sites and the ISP that is supplying the WAN connectivity. ACLs on the interfaces of the router can be used to control the flow of traffic both inbound and outbound among the remote sites and the medium-sized network.

Design Alternatives

The following are possible design alternatives to the WAN module previously discussed:

■ To provide an additional level of security and information privacy, you can use IPSec VPNs across the WAN link.

■ You can use a Cisco IOS Firewall router as the WAN router so that you can use its firewall features to provide an additional level of security. This stateful firewall provides enhanced access control when compared to the basic access control discussed previously.

Branch Versus Headend/Standalone Considerations for Medium-Sized Networks

When considering the medium-sized network design requirements in a branch role rather than a headend or standalone role, it is possible to eliminate some components from the design, keeping the following points in mind:

■ If a private WAN link is used to connect to the corporate headquarters, it is possible to omit the entire Corporate Internet module unless local Internet connectivity is required.

■ If an IPSec VPN is used to connect to the corporate headquarters, it is possible to omit the WAN module from the design.

- If the corporate headquarters provides the services, a VPN concentrator or dial-access router might not be needed for remote-access services.

- Management servers and hosts are normally located at the corporate headquarters, which means that management traffic must traverse either the private WAN link or the IPSec VPN connection. Management traffic can easily flow across the private WAN link, but when an IPSec VPN is used, some devices are located outside of the VPN tunnel and therefore require some alternate form of management. This might require the use of a separate IPSec tunnel that terminates on the actual device, or the device might have to be managed by other means, such as Secure Socket Header or something similar.

Foundation Summary

The "Foundation Summary" section of each chapter lists the most important facts from the chapter. Although this section does not list every fact from the chapter that will be on your CSI exam, a well-prepared CSI candidate should at a minimum know all the details in each "Foundation Summary" section before taking the exam.

Within the SAFE SMR model, the medium-sized network design consists of three modules:

- Corporate Internet module

- Campus module

- WAN module

The Corporate Internet module consists of the key devices outlined in Table 15-9.

Table 15-9 *Corporate Internet Module Devices*

Device	Description
Dial-in server	Terminates analog connections and authenticates individual remote users
DNS server	Serves as the authoritative external DNS server and relays internal requests to the Internet
Edge router	Provides basic filtering and Layer 3 connectivity to the Internet
File/web server	Provides public information about the organization
Firewall	Provides network-level protection of resources, stateful filtering of traffic, granular security of remote users, and VPN connectivity for remote sites
Layer 2 switch	Provides Layer 2 connectivity for devices and can also provide private VLAN support
Mail server	Acts as a relay between the Internet and the intranet mail servers and provides content security of mail
NIDS appliance	Provides Layer 4-to-Layer 7 monitoring of key network segments in the module
VPN concentrator	Authenticates individual remote users and terminates their IPSec tunnels

The most likely point of attack within the Corporate Internet module is on the public services segment. Positioned on this segment are the publicly addressed servers. The anticipated threats against publicly addressed servers and the mitigation actions to counter them are described in Table 15-10.

Table 15-10 *Threats Against Corporate Internet Module Public Services and Threat Mitigation*

Threat	Threat Mitigation
Application layer attacks	Mitigated by using HIDSs and NIDSs
Denial of service	Mitigated by using CAR at the ISP edge and TCP setup controls at the firewall to limit exposure
IP spoofing	Mitigated by using RFC 2827 and RFC 1918 filtering at ISP edge and edge router of the medium-sized network
Network reconnaissance	Mitigated by using IDS protocols filtered to limit effectiveness
Packet sniffers	Mitigated by using a switched infrastructure and HIDS to limit exposure
Password attacks	Mitigated by limiting the services that are available to brute force; operating system and IDS can detect the threat
Port redirection	Mitigated by using restrictive filtering and HIDS to limit attack
Trust exploitation	Mitigated by using a restrictive trust model and private VLANs to limit trust-based attacks
Unauthorized access	Mitigated by using filtering at the ISP, edge router, and corporate firewall
Virus and Trojan-horse attacks	Mitigated by using HIDS, virus scanning at the host level, and content filtering on e-mail

The VPN services that are found within the Corporate Internet module of the medium-sized network design are also vulnerable to attack. The expected threats and the mitigation actions for these services are outlined in Table 15-11.

Table 15-11 *Threats Against VPN Services of a Corporate Internet Module and Threat Mitigation*

Threat	Threat Mitigation
Man-in-the-middle attacks	Mitigated by encrypting remote traffic
Network topology discovery	Mitigated by using ACLs on the ingress router to limit access to the VPN concentrator and firewall, if terminating VPN traffic, to IKE and ESP from the Internet
Packet sniffers	Mitigated by using a switched infrastructure to limit exposure
Password attacks	Mitigated by using OTPs
Unauthorized access	Mitigated by using firewall filtering and by preventing traffic on unauthorized ports

Table 15-12 describes the filter parameters that can be applied on the ISP and edge routers to restrict perimeter traffic flow and the corresponding threat mitigation.

Table 15-12 *Perimeter Traffic Flow Filtering*

Filter Location	Flow	Filter Description	Mitigation
ISP router	Egress	The ISP rate-limits nonessential traffic that exceeds a predefined threshold	DDoS
ISP router	Egress	RFC 1918 and RFC 2827 filtering	IP spoofing
Edge router	Ingress	Coarse IP filtering for expected traffic	General attacks
Edge router	Ingress	RFC 1918 and RFC 2827 filtering	IP spoofing—verifies ISP filtering
Edge router	Ingress	VPN- and firewall-specific traffic	Unauthorized access

The key devices that make up the Campus module are described in Table 15-13.

Table 15-13 *Campus Module Devices*

Device	Description
ACS	Provides authentication services to the network devices
Corporate servers	Provides services to internal users such as e-mail, file, and printing services
Layer 2 switch	Provides Layer 2 connectivity and supports private VLANs
Layer 3 switch	Provides route and switch production and management traffic within the Campus module, provides distribution layer services to the building switches, and supports advanced services such as traffic filtering
NIDS appliance	Provides Layer 4-to-Layer 7 monitoring of key network segments in the module
NIDS host	Provides alarm aggregation for all NIDS devices in the network
OTP server	Authenticates OTP information that is relayed from the ACS
SNMP Management Host	Provides SNMP management for devices
Syslog host(s)	Aggregates log information for firewall and NIDS hosts
System admin host	Provides configuration, software, and content changes on devices
User workstations	Provides data services to authorized users on the network

Within the medium-sized network Campus module, the expected threats and the mitigation actions to counter them are outlined in Table 15-14.

Table 15-14 *Threats Against a Campus Module and Threat Mitigation*

Threat	Threat Mitigation
Application layer attacks	Mitigated by keeping operating systems, devices, and applications up to date with the latest security fixes and protected by HIDS
IP spoofing	Mitigated by using RFC 2827 filtering to prevent source-address spoofing
Packet sniffers	Mitigated by using a switched infrastructure to limit the effectiveness of sniffing
Password attacks	Mitigated by using an ACS to enforce strong two-factor authentication for key applications
Port redirection	Mitigated by using HIDSs to prevent port redirection agents from being installed
Trust exploitation	Mitigated by using private VLANs to prevent hosts on the same subnet from communicating unless necessary
Unauthorized access	Mitigated by using HIDS and application access control
Virus and Trojan-horse applications	Mitigated by using host-based virus scanning

The Cisco IOS Firewall router in the WAN module provides routing, access-control, and QoS mechanisms to remote locations.

Within the WAN module, the expected threats and the mitigation actions to counter them are outlined in Table 15-15.

Table 15-15 *WAN Module Threats and Threat Mitigation*

Threat	Threat Mitigation
IP spoofing	Mitigated by using Layer 3 filtering on the router
Unauthorized access	Mitigated by using simple access control on the router, which can limit the types of protocols to which branches have access

Q&A

As mentioned in the introduction, "All About the Cisco Certified Security Professional Certification," you have two choices for review questions. The questions that follow next give you a bigger challenge than the exam itself by using an open-ended question format. By reviewing now with this more difficult question format, you can exercise your memory better and prove your conceptual and factual knowledge of this chapter. The answers to these questions are found in Appendix A.

For more practice with exam-like question formats, including questions using a router simulator and multiple choice questions, use the exam engine on the CD-ROM.

1. What modules are found within the medium-sized network design?

2. At what locations in the medium-sized network design are private VLANs used?

3. What devices in a medium-sized network design provide VPN connectivity?

4. Where would you use intrusion detection in the medium-sized network design?

5. Traditional dial-in users are terminated in which module of the medium-sized network design?

6. What type of filter is used to prevent IP spoofing attacks?

7. In the medium-sized network design, the ACS is located in which module?

8. What is facilitated by the use of a Layer 3 switch within the Campus module?

9. What services does the Campus module provide?

10. In the SAFE medium-sized network design, what are the recommended IPSec policy parameters?

11. What services does the Corporate Internet module provide?

Reference

Convery, Sean and Roland Saville. "SAFE: Extending the Security Blueprint to Small, Midsize, and Remote-User Networks." Cisco Systems, Inc., 2001.

This chapter covers the following topics:

- General Implementation Recommendations

- Using the ISP Router in Medium-Sized Networks

- Using the Edge Router in Medium-Sized Networks

- Using the Cisco IOS Firewall Router in Medium-Sized Networks

- Using the PIX Firewall in Medium-Sized Networks

- Network Intrusion Detection System Overview

- Host Intrusion Detection System Overview

- VPN 3000 Series Concentrator Overview

- Configuring the Layer 3 Switch

CHAPTER 16

Implementing Medium-Sized SAFE Networks

In Chapter 15, "Designing Medium-Sized SAFE Networks," you looked in detail at the design requirements and guidelines that are recommended to secure the medium-sized network. In this chapter, you use an understanding of those design recommendations to examine the specific configuration requirements to achieve the desired functionality for each component of the medium-sized network.

> **NOTE** The configuration that is shown in this chapter highlights only the code that is required to achieve the specific security requirements of the design that is under discussion. Complete configurations are not shown, nor are all the available options for a specific feature discussed.
>
> It is also assumed that you are familiar with the devices that are used in the medium-sized network implementation and, in particular, have an understanding of the commands and tasks that are required to configure the various devices that are detailed in this chapter.

"Do I Know This Already?" Quiz

The purpose of the "Do I Know This Already?" quiz is to help you decide if you really need to read the entire chapter. If you already intend to read the entire chapter, you do not necessarily need to answer these questions now.

The 15-question quiz, derived from the major sections in the "Foundation Topics" portion of the chapter, helps you determine how to spend your limited study time.

Table 16-1 outlines the major topics discussed in this chapter and the "Do I Know This Already?" quiz questions that correspond to those topics.

Table 16-1 *"Do I Know This Already?" Foundation Topics Section-to-Question Mapping*

Foundation Topics Section	Questions Covered in This Section
General Implementation Recommendations	1
Using the ISP Router in Medium-Sized Networks	2–3
Using the Edge Router in Medium-Sized Networks	4–5

continues

Table 16-1 *"Do I Know This Already?" Foundation Topics Section-to-Question Mapping (Continued)*

Foundation Topics Section	Questions Covered in This Section
Using the Cisco IOS Firewall Router in Medium-Sized Networks	6
Using the PIX Firewall in Medium-Sized Networks	7–9
Network Intrusion Detection System Overview	10–11
Host Intrusion Detection System Overview	12
VPN 3000 Series Concentrator Overview	13
Configuring the Layer 3 Switch	14–15

CAUTION The goal of self-assessment is to gauge your mastery of the topics in this chapter. If you do not know the answer to a question or are only partially sure of the answer, you should mark this question wrong for purposes of the self-assessment. Giving yourself credit for an answer you correctly guess skews your self-assessment results and might provide you with a false sense of security.

1. Which of the following components are found within the SAFE medium-sized network model?

    a. Cache engine

    b. PIX Firewall

    c. Edge router

    d. Layer 3 switch

    e. Voice gateway

2. The ISP router provides which of the following attack-mitigation services?

    a. IP address spoofing

    b. ARP spoofing

    c. DDoS

    d. Password attack

    e. Port redirection

3. The ISP router provides which of the following filtering types?

    a. RFC 1918

    b. RFC 1819

    c. RFC 2728

    d. RFC 1928

    e. RFC 2827

4. The edge router in the medium-sized network provides which of the following?

    a. VPN connectivity

    b. DDoS mitigation

    c. A demarcation point between the ISP and the network

    d. WAN connectivity

    e. Remote access

5. In the medium-sized network design, what filtering role(s) does the edge router undertake?

    a. Coarse IP filtering

    b. Desktop user filtering

    c. LAN filtering

    d. Reinforces ISP filtering

    e. Intrusion detection

6. Can the Cisco IOS Firewall functionality be incorporated into the edge router's role?

    a. Yes

    b. No

7. In the medium-sized network design, how many interfaces does the PIX Firewall use?

    a. 1

    b. 2

    c. 3

    d. 4

    e. 5

8. What devices are physically terminated on the remote-access VLAN?

   a. PIX Firewall

   b. Edge router

   c. Internal router

   d. VPN concentrator

   e. Remote-access server

9. In the medium-sized network design, site-to-site VPN connectivity terminates on the VPN concentrator?

   a. True

   b. False

10. In the medium-sized network, only a HIDS is used.

   a. True

   b. False

11. Where are NIDS appliances normally placed in the medium-sized network?

   a. Remote-access VLAN

   b. Public services VLAN

   c. ISP VLAN

   d. Inside VLAN/L3 Switch

   e. Management VLAN

12. What is the name given to the software element of the HIDS installed on the host being protected?

   a. Monitor

   b. Agent

   c. Client

   d. Sniffer

   e. Manager

13. Remote-access users connect to the medium-sized network by using which of the following devices?

    a. NIDS appliance

    b. Edge router

    c. PIX Firewall

    d. VPN concentrator

    e. Layer 3 switch

14. How many VLANs are used within the Campus module of the medium-sized network design?

    a. 2

    b. 3

    c. 4

    d. 5

    e. 6

15. Within the Campus module of the medium-sized network design, access filtering takes place on which of the following VLANs?

    a. Corporate Internet module link

    b. Corporate servers

    c. Corporate users

    d. WAN link

    e. Management

The answers to the "Do I Know This Already?" quiz are found in Appendix A, "Answers to the 'Do I Know This Already?' Quizzes and Q&A Sections." The suggested choices for your next step are as follows:

- **12 or less overall score**—Read the entire chapter. This includes the "Foundation Topics" and "Foundation Summary" sections, and the "Q&A" section.

- **13 or more overall score**—If you want more review on these topics, skip to the "Foundation Summary" section and then go to the "Q&A" section. Otherwise, move to the next chapter.

Foundation Topics

General Implementation Recommendations

In the SAFE medium-sized network implementation, we will look at the specific configuration requirements for the following components:

■ ISP router

■ Edge router

■ Cisco IOS Firewall router

■ PIX Firewall

■ Network intrusion detection system (NIDS)

■ Host intrusion detection system (HIDS)

■ VPN concentrator

■ Layer 3 switch

Figure 16-1 illustrates the medium-sized network modules and their respective devices.

Figure 16-1 *Medium-Sized Network Devices*

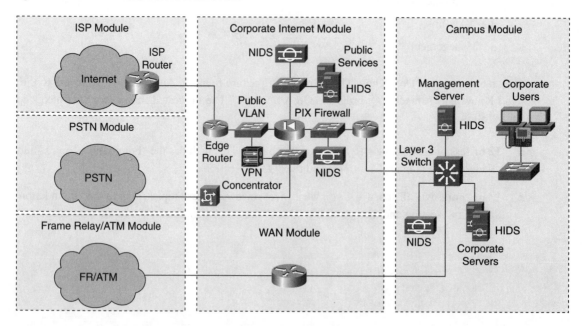

General configuration guidelines for effectively tightening security on Cisco routers and switches are provided in Appendix B, "General Configuration Guidelines for Cisco Router and Switch Security." You should familiarize yourself with the content of this appendix because the commands that it presents (which are not shown in this chapter) play an important role in the overall implementation.

Using the ISP Router in Medium-Sized Networks

The primary purpose of the ISP router is to provide connectivity from the medium-sized network to a ISP's network. It also provides mitigation against DDoS and IP address spoofing attacks.

Distributed Denial of Service Attacks

DDoS mitigation can be provided at the egress of the ISP router through the use of rate limiting nonessential traffic that exceeds prespecified thresholds. Obviously, the criteria used to identify nonessential traffic are critical because the flow of production traffic could be affected. To implement rate limiting, committed access rate (CAR) filtering can be used through the following steps:

Step 1   Define an ACL to select nonessential traffic:

```
access-list 100 permit non-essential-traffic-criteria1 any
access-list 100 permit non-essential-traffic-criteria2 any
```

Step 2   Apply the **rate-limit** command to the interface:

```
rate-limit input access-group rate-limit 100 8000 1500 20000 conform-action
    drop exceed-action drop
```

IP Spoofing Attacks

IP spoofing mitigation can be provided at the egress of the ISP router through the use of RFC 1918 and RFC 2827 filtering. To implement these filters, use the filtering that is described in the sections that follow.

RFC 1918 Filtering

RFC 1918 filtering prevents source address spoofing of the private address ranges. The following ACL is then applied to the ingress interface of the ISP router by using the command **ip access-group 101 in**:

```
access-list 101 deny ip 10.0.0.0 0.255.255.255 any
access-list 101 deny ip 172.16.0.0 0.15.255.255 any
access-list 101 deny ip 192.168.0.0 0.0.255.255 any
access-list 101 permit ip any any
```

RFC 2827 Filtering

With RFC 2827 filtering at the ingress point of the ISP network, any traffic with a source address that is not part of the organization's public address space is filtered out by using the following:

```
access-list 102 permit ip valid-public-source-address(es) any
```

The preceding ACL is then applied to the ingress interface of the ISP router by using the command **ip access-group 102 in**.

Using the Edge Router in Medium-Sized Networks

It may be helpful to refer to Figure 16-1 to see where the edge router is located within the medium-sized network model. The edge router is the demarcation point between the ISP and the network. Its role is to provide coarse IP filtering of expected traffic and to reinforce the filtering provided by the ISP.

ISP Traffic Filtering

By using an inbound ACL, you can filter traffic that is arriving from the ISP router. This filtering is applied to the public services interface by using the command **ip access-group 140 in**. You should consider using the following common ACL definitions.

Apply RFC 1918 filtering. If RFC 1918 addresses are used remotely, these rules require modification accordingly.

```
access-list 140 deny ip 10.0.0.0 0.255.255.255 any
access-list 140 deny ip 172.16.0.0 0.15.255.255 any
access-list 140 deny ip 192.168.0.0 0.0.255.255 any
```

Deny any outside device from spoofing a public VLAN network address:

```
access-list 140 deny ip public-VLAN-network any
```

If required, allow IPSec traffic from the remote users or remote sites to either the PIX Firewall or VPN concentrator:

```
access-list 140 permit udp host remote-peer-IP host PIX-public-IP eq isakmp
access-list 140 permit esp host remote-peer-IP host PIX-public-IP
access-list 140 permit udp any host VPN-concentrator-public-IP eq isakmp
access-list 140 permit esp any host VPN-concentrator-public-IP
```

Restrict all other access to the public VLAN devices:

```
access-list 140 deny ip any host public-VLAN-device-IP
```

Permit all other connections to the public VLAN:

```
access-list 140 permit ip any public-VLAN-network
```

Deny and log all other traffic:

```
access-list 140 deny ip any any log
```

Public VLAN Traffic Filtering

By using an inbound ACL, you can filter traffic that is entering from the public VLAN interface. This filtering is applied to the public VLAN interface by using the command **ip access-group 120 in**. You should consider using the following common ACL definitions.

Allow management access to the edge router:

```
access-list 120 permit tcp host management-host-NAT-IP host public-VLAN-IP
```

Allow other public VLAN devices to use the edge router as a time server:

```
access-list 120 permit udp public-VLAN-network host public-VLAN-IP eq ntp
```

Allow outbound Internet Control Message Protocol (ICMP) traffic from the public VLAN devices:

```
access-list 120 permit icmp public-VLAN-network any
```

Deny all other access to the edge router:

```
access-list 120 deny ip any host public-VLAN-IP log
```

Permit all other public VLAN sourced traffic to the outside:

```
access-list 120 permit ip public-VLAN-network any
```

Block and log any other traffic:

```
access-list 120 deny ip any any log
```

Using the Cisco IOS Firewall Router in Medium-Sized Networks

If required, you can adopt a defense-in-depth approach within the medium-sized network design. This alternative design incorporates the functionality of the Cisco IOS Firewall and the functionality of the edge router in a single device.

The implementation of this configuration requires that the edge router filtering, which was described in the previous section, be added to the Cisco IOS Firewall configuration, as explained next.

To implement the Cisco IOS Firewall, use the following steps:

Step 1   Configure the firewall inspection rules:

```
ip inspect name FIREWALL tcp
ip inspect name FIREWALL udp
ip inspect name FIREWALL ftp
ip inspect name FIREWALL smtp
```

> **NOTE**   Not all of the available firewall inspection rules are shown in the preceding examples. Inspection rules can be amended as required.

Step 2   Apply the defined inspection rules so that traffic that is transiting the interface is inspected.

The firewall inspection rule set is applied to the public VLAN interface of the edge router by using the command **ip inspect FIREWALL in**.

Referring to Figure 16-1, you can see that the next component within the medium-sized network is the PIX Firewall, which is discussed in the next section.

Using the PIX Firewall in Medium-Sized Networks

This section details the implementation and configuration of the PIX Firewall in the medium-sized network. The PIX Firewall in the medium-sized network model uses four interfaces: an inside interface, an outside interface, a remote-access segment interface, and a public services segment interface.

The configuration shows only the ACLs and cryptographic parameters that are required to achieve the required functionality.

The primary features and configuration examples that are described in this chapter cover the following:

■   Outside interface filtering

■   Inside interface filtering

■   Public services segment filtering

■   Remote-access segment filtering

■   VPN configuration

Outside Interface Filtering

By using an ACL, you can filter traffic that is entering from the outside (public VLAN) interface. This filtering is applied to the outside interface by using the **access-group** command. You should consider using the following common ACL definitions.

Allow access to the services that are available on the public services segment:

```
access-list outside_access_in permit tcp any host public-NAT-IP eq ftp
access-list outside_access_in permit tcp any host public-NAT-IP eq www
access-list outside_access_in permit tcp any host public-NAT-IP eq smtp
access-list outside_access_in permit tcp any host public-NAT-IP eq 443
access-list outside_access_in permit udp any host public-NAT-IP eq domain
```

If required, allow traffic from remote sites:

```
access-list outside_access_in permit ip remote-site-A-network internal-network
access-list outside_access_in permit ip remote-site-B-network internal-network
```

Apply RFC 1918 filtering. If RFC 1918 addresses are used remotely, these rules require modification accordingly.

```
access-list outside_access_in deny ip 10.0.0.0 0.255.255.255 any
access-list outside_access_in deny ip 172.16.0.0 0.15.255.255 any
access-list outside_access_in deny ip 192.168.0.0 0.0.255.255 any
```

If required, allow management traffic from the remote sites. You can either make this statement global, as the following shows, or make it more specific by specifying particular services:

```
access-list outside_access_in permit ip host remote-device-IP  host
   management-server-IP
```

Allow echo replies to internally generated traffic:

```
access-list outside_access_in permit icmp any public-NAT-IP echo-reply
```

Allow traffic from the public VLAN devices to the management servers for syslog, TACACS+, and TFTP:

```
access-list outside_access_in permit host public-VLAN-device-IP  host
   management-server-IP eq syslog
access-list outside_access_in permit host public-VLAN-device-IP  host
   management-server-IP eq tftp
access-list outside_access_in permit host public-VLAN-device-IP  host
   management-server-IP eq tacacs
```

Inside Interface Filtering

By using an ACL, you can filter traffic that is entering from the inside interface. This filtering is applied to the inside interface by using the **access-group** command. You should consider using the following common ACL definitions.

Allow management access to the public services network devices:

```
access-list inside_access_in permit tcp host management-host-IP host PS-device-IP
   eq 22
```

Allow internal user access to public services such as web and FTP services:

```
access-list inside_access_in permit tcp internal-network host public-server-IP
  eq service
```

Allow the internal mail server to communicate with the public mail server:

```
access-list inside_access_in permit tcp host internal-mail-server-IP
  host public-mail-server-IP eq smtp
```

Allow the internal DNS server to communicate with the public DNS server:

```
access-list inside_access_in permit udp host internal-DNS-IP host public-DNS-IP eq domain
```

Allow outbound ICMP traffic:

```
access-list inside_access_in permit icmp any any echo
```

Deny all other access to the public services segment:

```
access-list inside_access_in deny ip any public-services-network
```

Permit all other traffic to the outside:

```
access-list inside_access_in permit ip any any
```

Public Services Segment Filtering

By using an ACL, you can filter traffic that is entering from the public services interface. This filtering is applied to the public services interface by using the **access-group** command. You should consider using the following common ACL definitions.

Allow mail services between the public and internal mail servers:

```
access-list ps_access_in permit tcp host public-mail-server-IP
  host internal-mail-server-IP eq smtp
```

Allow echo replies from the internal network:

```
access-list ps_access_in permit icmp public-services-network internal-network
  eq echo-reply
```

Allow HIDS traffic from the public server to the management server:

```
access-list ps_access_in permit tcp host public-server-IP host management-server-IP
  eq 5000
```

Allow management traffic to flow from the public services segment network devices:

```
access-list ps_access_in permit ip host PS-network-device-IP host management-server-IP
```

Deny all other connections to the internal network from the public services segment:

```
access-list ps_access_in deny ip any internal-network
```

Allow all mail and DNS traffic that originates from the public services server:

```
access-list ps_access_in permit tcp host public-server-IP any eq smtp
access-list ps_access_in permit udp host public-server-IP any eq domain
```

Remote-Access Segment Filtering

By using an ACL, you can filter traffic that is entering from the remote-access interface. This filtering is applied to the RS interface by using the **access-group** command. You should consider using the following common ACL definitions.

Allow traffic from the remote-access segment devices to the management servers for syslog, TACACS+, and TFTP:

```
access-list remote_access_in permit host ra-segment-device-IP host
    management-server-IP eq syslog
access-list remote_access_in permit host ra-segment-device-IP host
    management-server-IP eq tftp
access-list remote_access_in permit host ra-segment-device-IP host
    management-server-IP eq tacacs
```

Allow remote-access users to access the services that are available on the public services segment:

```
access-list remote_access_in permit tcp ra-user-pool-network host public-server-IP
    eq ftp
access-list remote_access_in permit tcp ra-user-pool-network host public-server-IP
    eq www
access-list remote_access_in permit tcp ra-user-pool-network host public-server-IP
    eq smtp
access-list remote_access_in permit tcp ra-user-pool-network host public-server-IP
    eq 443
access-list remote_access_in permit udp ra-user-pool-network host public-server-IP
    eq domain
```

Permit remote-access users' traffic to the Internet and internal network:

```
access-list remote_access_in permit ip ra-user-pool-network any
```

Allow remote-access segment devices to synchronize time with the internal time server:

```
access-list remote_access_in permit udp ra-segment-device-IP host time-server-IP
    eq ntp
```

VPN Configuration

You can implement VPN services on a PIX Firewall by using the commands that are described next.

To configure remote-site VPNs, use the following commands:

```
no sysopt route dnat
crypto ipsec transform-set REMOTESITES esp-3des esp-md5-hmac
crypto map REMOTE 10 ipsec-isakmp
crypto map REMOTE 10 match address remote-sites
crypto map REMOTE 10 set peer peer-IP-A
crypto map REMOTE 10 set transform-set REMOTESITES
crypto map REMOTE interface outside
isakmp enable outside
isakmp key key address IP-address netmask 255.255.255.255
isakmp identity address
isakmp policy 10 authentication pre-share
isakmp policy 10 encryption 3des
isakmp policy 10 hash md5
isakmp policy 10 group 2
isakmp policy 10 lifetime 28800
access-list remote-sites permit ip internal-network remote-site-network
```

Network Intrusion Detection System Overview

An in-depth look at the implementation of a NIDS is beyond the scope of this book. Furthermore, the configuration that is required to implement any NIDS depends on the system to be used. Within the medium-sized network design, NIDS appliances are used within the following:

■ Public services segment

■ Inside PIX Firewall segment

■ Layer 3 core switch

Figure 16-1 shows the deployment of these NIDS sensors within the medium-sized network.

A NIDS works by using dedicated, hardened devices known as sensors, which analyze all network traffic that is received on the NIDS's interfaces. These sensors can monitor many hosts and, if configured properly, many different network segments. If you expand your network by adding new servers, you do not need to change the NIDS setup.

Adding more sensors gives the following benefits:

■ **Traffic levels**—With the introduction of Gigabit Ethernet, more than one IDS sensor easily provides the interface capacity of new networks.

■ **Performance**—As traffic increases, it may be necessary to introduce new sensors to cope with the increased capacity.

■ **Network implementation**—The security policy or network design may require sensors in more than one location to monitor for different types of traffic.

Sensors have three crucial elements that must be specified in accordance with the network design:

- **Connectivity**—Network interface cards must be able to connect into the network (Ethernet, Fast Ethernet, Gigabit Ethernet, Token Ring, and FDDI are all options).

- **Processor**—Sensors must have adequate processing power to deal with the amount of traffic.

- **Memory**—Intrusion detection analysis is memory intensive.

NOTE   As mentioned at the beginning of this section, an in-depth look at NIDS deployment is beyond the scope of this book. You may have had some exposure to NIDS deployment by preparing for other CCSP exams. If not, however, you should familiarize yourself with the implementation and configuration steps required to deploy a NIDS. You should draw from practical experience and rely on reference material such as the CCSP course and Cisco Press self-study guides.

The remainder of this section summarizes the important features and facts that you should be aware of, at a minimum, regarding NIDSs:

To set up a NIDS sensor, perform the following steps:

Step 1   Configure the sensor's network settings.

Step 2   Define the list of hosts that are authorized to manage the sensor.

Step 3   Configure remote-management services.

Step 4   Configure SSH settings.

Step 5   Configure the sensor's date and time.

Step 6   Change the password for the account that is used to access the IDS Device Manager (IDM).

By default, the sensor logs all events locally by severity and type.

The sensor can transfer archived copies of log files off line to an FTP server. This facility requires the following:

- Network access to the FTP server

- FTP username and password

- Directory with write permissions

The IP logging feature captures packets from an attacking host. The IP log file is in tcpdump format:

- Logs packets automatically when IP log is a signature response

- Logs packets if the source address is entered manually

- Requires that event logging is enabled

The sensor has parameters that affect the sensing function that are not necessarily specific to a particular signature or set of signatures. The following are the global sensing parameters:

- Internal network

- Sensing properties

- Level of traffic logging

The following provides an overview of signatures:

- The sensing engines and signatures are the core technologies of the Cisco IDSs.

- The sensing engines use the signature information to determine if the network traffic is considered malicious activity.

- The sensing engines are designed to perform pattern matching, stateful pattern matching, protocol decodes, and heuristic methods.

- The IDS Director enables the network security administrator to view the signatures, which are categorized by the following:

  — Signature groups

  — TCP connection signatures

  — UDP connection signatures

  — String signatures

  — ACL violation signatures

- Basic signature configuration includes the following:

  — Enabling or disabling the signature

  — Assigning the severity level

  — Assigning the signature action

Complete the following tasks to start using IDS Event Viewer (IEV):

Step 1   Add the IEV host as a remote event destination.

Step 2   Download the IEV software from the sensor.

Step 3   Install the IEV software on the host.

Step 4   Reboot the IEV host to start IDS services.

Step 5   Add IDS devices that the IEV will monitor.

Host Intrusion Detection System Overview

An in-depth look at the implementation of a HIDS is beyond the scope of this book. Furthermore, the configuration that is required to implement any HIDS depends on the software that is used.

Within the medium-sized network design, HIDSs are implemented on all servers, as shown in Figure 16-1.

A HIDS is a host-based, real-time, intrusion-prevention and security-enforcement system that is designed to protect system resources and applications.

The main installed elements of a HIDS are the following:

- Agents that are installed on each host you want to protect

- The console, a GUI application that lets you monitor agent and system activity and manage HIDSs

- A database of signatures and all other information relevant to the host sensor system

A HIDS provides the facility that audits log files on a server and also the file systems and other resources. It can monitor individual operating system processes and protect resources that exist only on a specific server.

A simple form of a HIDS is event logging. However, event logging requires resource-intensive operations to analyze these logs. Current HIDSs run an agent on the server, which monitors and protects the resources.

An added advantage of a HIDS is that it can analyze secured communications after the data has been decrypted (a normal NIDS cannot analyze HTTPS traffic).

A console server is used for all HIDS agent reporting. This server must also be protected by a HIDS.

VPN 3000 Series Concentrator Overview

An in-depth look at the implementation of the VPN 3000 Series Concentrator within the medium-sized network design is beyond the scope of this book.

Within the medium-sized network design, the VPN concentrator is implemented on a transit VLAN off the PIX Firewall, as demonstrated in Figure 16-1. This configuration allows for the granular control of remote-user traffic that is accessing the medium-sized network.

The Cisco VPN 3000 Series Concentrator is a purpose-built, remote-access VPN platform and client software that incorporates high availability, high performance, and scalability with the most advanced encryption and authentication techniques available today.

Remote users establish secure connections via the use of a software client. Cryptographic parameters are negotiated during connection to the concentrator. Other features include

- Dynamically pushed VPN-policy configuration on a per-group basis that eliminates the need for manual client configuration

- Support for internal IP addresses, primary and secondary Windows Internet Name Service (WINS), and Domain Name System (DNS)

- Split-tunnel or no-split-tunnel options on a per-group basis

- Support for policy-database support either locally on the router or via RADIUS

- Authentication of users via extended authentication

- The latest revisions of the mode configuration and extended authentication IKE extensions

> **NOTE**   As mentioned at the beginning of this section, an in-depth look at VPN 3000 Series Concentrator deployment is beyond the scope of this book. To obtain your CCSP certification, you should familiarize yourself with the implementation and configuration steps that are required to deploy the VPN 3000 Series Concentrator. You should draw from practical experience and rely on reference material, such as the CCSP course and Cisco Press self-study guides.

The following is a summary of the basic configuration requirements that you should be aware of, at a minimum, regarding the VPN 3000 Series Concentrator:

- IKE proposals

- Group configuration

- Identity

- General configuration

- IPSec

Configuring the Layer 3 Switch

The Layer 3 core switch that is found in the Campus module of the medium-sized network design provides the following functionality:

■   VLAN segregation

■   Access filtering

You can implement this functionality by using the configurations discussed in the following sections.

VLAN Segregation

VLAN segregation within the Campus module, as shown in Figure 16-1, uses the following five VLANs:

■   VLAN10—Corporate Internet module link

■   VLAN11—Corporate servers

■   VLAN12—Corporate users

■   VLAN13—WAN module link

■   VLAN20—Management

The configuration in Example 16-1 defines the preceding VLANS.

Example 16-1 *Defining VLANs*

```
interface Vlan10
 description ** Link to Corporate Internet Module ***
 ip address corporate-internet-VLAN-IP mask
!
interface Vlan11
 description ** Corporate Servers ***
 ip address corporate-server-VLAN-IP mask
!
interface Vlan12
 description ** Corporate Users ***
 ip address corporate-user-VLAN-IP mask
!
interface Vlan13
 description ** Link to WAN Module ***
 ip address WAN-module-VLAN-IP mask
!
interface Vlan20
 description ** Management ***
 ip address management-VLAN-IP mask
```

The following is a summary of important commands that you should be aware of, at a minimum, regarding the Layer 3 filtering:

- Layer 3 and 4 filtering and RFC filtering:

    — **access-list command**

    — **access-group command**

- Trust exploitation:

    — **set vlan command** (configures private VLANs, if practical)

- CAM table overflow and ARP spoofing attacks:

    — **set port security command**

    — **show port command**

Access Filtering

Access filtering within the Campus module takes place on the corporate servers and corporate users VLANs and the management VLAN in the configuration example that follows. This filtering is applied to the appropriate VLAN interface by using the **ip access-group** command.

Apply RFC 2827 filtering to the corporate servers VLAN:

```
interface Vlan11
 ip access-group 110 in
!
access-list 110 permit ip corporate-servers-network any
access-list 110 deny ip any any log
```

Apply RFC 2827 filtering to the corporate users VLAN:

```
interface Vlan12
 ip access-group 111 in
!
access-list 111 permit ip corporate-users-network any
access-list 111 deny ip any any log
```

Restrict access to the management VLAN:

```
interface Vlan20
 ip access-group 120 out
!
access-list 120 permit tcp host corporate-server-IP eq service host
  management-server-IP
access-list 120 permit udp host corporate-server-IP eq service host
  management-server-IP
!
access-list 120 permit ip host PIX-inside-IP host management-server-IP eq service
access-list 120 permit ip host PIX-inside-IP host management-server-IP eq service
!
access-list 120 deny ip any any log
```

Foundation Summary

The "Foundation Summary" section of each chapter lists the most important facts from the chapter. Although this section does not list every fact from the chapter that will be on your CSI exam, a well-prepared CSI candidate should at a minimum know all the details in each "Foundation Summary" section before taking the exam.

The SAFE medium-sized network implementation has specific configuration requirements for the following components:

- ISP router

- Edge router

- Cisco IOS Firewall router

- PIX Firewall

- NIDS

- HIDS

- VPN concentrator

- Layer 3 switch

The primary purpose of the ISP router is to do the following:

- Provide connectivity from the medium-sized network to a provider's network

- Mitigate against DDoS and IP address spoofing attacks

The edge router within the medium-sized network model does the following:

- Provides a demarcation point between the ISP and the network

- Provides coarse IP filtering of expected traffic

- Reinforces the filtering provided by the ISP

If required, you can adopt a defense-in-depth approach within the medium-sized network design. This alternative design incorporates the functionality of the Cisco IOS Firewall and the functionality of the edge router in a single device.

The PIX Firewall in the medium-sized network model uses four interfaces:

- An inside interface

- An outside interface

- A remote-access segment interface

- A public services segment interface

Within the medium-sized network design:

- NIDS appliances are used within the following:

  — Public services segment

  — Inside PIX Firewall segment

  — Layer 3 core switch

- A HIDS is implemented on all servers.

- The VPN concentrator is implemented on a transit VLAN off the PIX Firewall. This configuration allows for the granular control of remote-user traffic that is accessing the medium-sized network.

The Layer 3 core switch that is found in the Campus module of the medium-sized network design provides the following functionality:

- VLAN segregation

- Access filtering

Q&A

As mentioned in the introduction, "All About the Cisco Certified Security Professional Certification," you have two choices for review questions. The questions that follow next give you a bigger challenge than the exam itself by using an open-ended question format. By reviewing now with this more difficult question format, you can exercise your memory better and prove your conceptual and factual knowledge of this chapter. The answers to these questions are found in Appendix A.

For more practice with exam-like question formats, including questions using a router simulator and multiple choice questions, use the exam engine on the CD-ROM.

1. What are the four segments used on the PIX Firewall in the medium-sized network design?

2. Name the main components within the medium-sized network design?

3. What mitigation is performed by the ISP router?

4. How can the Cisco IOS Firewall be used within the medium-sized network design?

5. How do you implement RFC 1918 filtering?

6. Where is a NIDS implemented in the medium-sized network design?

7. What functionality does the Layer 3 switch provide within the medium-sized network?

8. Where is RFC 1918 filtering performed within the medium-sized network?

This chapter covers the following topics:

- Configuration Options for Remote-User Network Design

- Key Devices

- Threat Mitigation

- Design Guidelines

CHAPTER 17

Designing Remote SAFE Networks

As mentioned in Chapter 13, "Designing Small SAFE Networks," and Chapter 15, "Designing Medium-Sized SAFE Networks," the principle goal of the Cisco SAFE blueprints is to provide to interested parties best-practice information on how to design and implement secure networks. SAFE serves as a guide to network architects who are examining the security requirements of their networks. SAFE combats security threats on a modular basis, which enables network architects to create scalable, corporate-wide security solutions.

In this chapter, the third of three chapters covering the design requirements of the "SAFE: Extending the Security Blueprint to Small, Midsize, and Remote-User Networks" (SAFE SMR) design model, you examine the specific security design requirements of the SAFE remote-user network.

> **NOTE**   Readers should be aware that the implementation requirements for the remote-user network are not covered in a specific chapter within this book because remote network implementation is currently not a specific exam objective. However, readers should be aware of the generalized deployment of the components within the remote-user network.

"Do I Know This Already?" Quiz

The purpose of the "Do I Know This Already?" quiz is to help you decide if you really need to read the entire chapter. If you already intend to read the entire chapter, you do not necessarily need to answer these questions now.

The 10-question quiz, derived from the major sections in the "Foundation Topics" portion of the chapter, helps you determine how to spend your limited study time.

Table 17-1 outlines the major topics discussed in this chapter and the "Do I Know This Already?" quiz questions that correspond to those topics.

Table 17-1 *"Do I Know This Already?" Foundation Topics Section-to-Question Mapping*

Foundation Topics Section	Questions Covered in This Section
Configuration Options for Remote-User Network Design	1–2
Key Devices for Remote-User Networks	3
Mitigating Threats in Remote-User Networks	4–5
Design Guidelines for Remote-User Networks	6–10

CAUTION The goal of self-assessment is to gauge your mastery of the topics in this chapter. If you do not know the answer to a question or are only partially sure of the answer, you should mark this question wrong for purposes of the self-assessment. Giving yourself credit for an answer you correctly guess skews your self-assessment results and might provide you with a false sense of security.

1. Within the remote-user network design model, how many design options are there?

   a. One

   b. Two

   c. Three

   d. Four

   e. Five

2. Which remote-user design options provide a stateful firewall?

   a. Cisco VPN hardware client option

   b. Remote-site router option

   c. Cisco VPN Client option

   d. Remote-site firewall option

3. Which of the following are key devices within the remote-user design model?

   a. VPN concentrator

   b. VPN hardware client

   c. VPN firewall router

   d. Wireless access point

   e. VPN firewall

4. In remote-user network design, IP spoofing attacks are mitigated by which of the following?

    a. RFC 1918 filtering

    b. Encrypting traffic

    c. RFC 2827 filtering

    d. Virus-scanning software

5. Which of the following are anticipated threats to the remote-user network?

    a. Application layer attacks

    b. Man-in-the-middle attacks

    c. Network reconnaissance

    d. Virus and Trojan-horse attacks

    e. Port redirection

6. Is virus-scanning software recommended only in the Cisco VPN Client option?

    a. Yes

    b. No

7. The VPN hardware client can operate in how many modes?

    a. One

    b. Two

    c. Three

    d. Four

    e. Five

8. Remote management of the VPN hardware client uses what type of connection?

    a. Telnet

    b. SSL

    c. Console

    d. SNMP

    e. SSH

9. User authentication occurs in the remote router design option.

   a. True

   b. False

10. The remote-user design model assumes what medium is generally used to provide connectivity?

    a. ISDN

    b. Ethernet

    c. Internet

    d. Wireless

    e. PSTN

The answers to the "Do I Know This Already?" quiz are found in Appendix A, "Answers to the 'Do I Know This Already?' Quizzes and Q&A Sections." The suggested choices for your next step are as follows:

- **8 or less overall score**—Read the entire chapter. This includes the "Foundation Topics" and "Foundation Summary" sections, and the "Q&A" section.

- **9 or more overall score**—If you want more review on these topics, skip to the "Foundation Summary" section and then go to the "Q&A" section. Otherwise, move to the next chapter.

Foundation Topics

The implementation decisions that are recommended in the SAFE SMR white paper are based on numerous factors, including required network functionality and certain design objectives, which are discussed in Chapter 2, "SAFE Design Fundamentals."

The remote-user network design considers the requirements of both mobile and home-office workers. The primary design focus is on providing secure connectivity between the remote user or remote site and the corporate headend, using the Internet as the means of connectivity. Other forms of connectivity can be used with this design, but this might lead to certain components within the design becoming superfluous. For example, if ISDN is used to provide connectivity, the use of an encrypted VPN to secure connectivity might no longer be deemed necessary.

Finally, remember that when using any of the remote-user network design model recommendations, the security perimeter of your organization is extended to include those remote sites.

Configuration Options for Remote-User Network Design

Within the SAFE SMR model, the remote-user network design consists of four possible module options:

- Remote-site firewall

- Remote-site router

- VPN hardware client

- Cisco VPN Client

Table 17-2 describes each of the preceding options.

Table 17-2 *Remote-User Network Design Options*

Option	Description
Remote-site firewall	The remote site is protected by a dedicated firewall, which is IPSec-VPN enabled. WAN connectivity is provided by a broadband access device supplied by an ISP.
Remote-site router	The remote site uses a router that has both firewall and IPSec-VPN functionality. The router normally terminates the WAN connectivity, but it can also be used to terminate to an ISP-supplied broadband access device.

continues

Table 17-2 *Remote-User Network Design Options (Continued)*

Option	Description
VPN hardware client	The remote site uses a dedicated VPN hardware client that provides IPSec-VPN connectivity. WAN connectivity is provided by a broadband access device supplied by an ISP.
Cisco VPN Client	A remote user uses a Cisco VPN Client and personal firewall software on a PC.

The functionality of each of these four design options is discussed in subsequent sections of this chapter.

Key Devices for Remote-User Networks

Each of the options presented in Table 17-2 can use a variety of key devices within each model of the remote-user network design. These devices are described in Table 17-3.

Table 17-3 *Remote-User Key Devices*

Device	Description
Broadband access device	Provides connectivity to the broadband network.
Layer 2 hub	Provides connectivity between local network devices. This can be a standalone device or integrated within the VPN hardware device.
VPN firewall	Provides local network protection through stateful filtering of traffic. Provides secure VPNs via IPSec tunnels between the headend and local site.
Personal firewall software	Provides individual PCs with protection.
VPN firewall router	Provides local network protection through stateful filtering of traffic. Provides secure VPNs through IPSec tunnels between the headend and local site.
Remote-access VPN client	Provides secure VPNs via IPSec tunnels between the headend and individual PCs by using a software client.
VPN hardware client	Provides secure VPN via IPSec tunnels between the headend and the local site by using a dedicated hardware device.

Figure 17-1 illustrates the four options that are available in the remote-user network design model.

Mitigating Threats in Remote-User Networks

Table 17-4 presents the threats that can be anticipated for the remote-user network design model and summarizes the mitigation techniques for each anticipated threat.

Figure 17-1 *Remote-User Design Model*

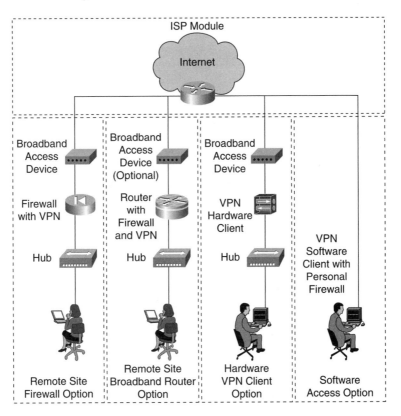

Table 17-4 *Remote-User Network Threats and Threat Mitigation*

Threat	Threat Mitigation
IP spoofing	Mitigated by using RFC 1918 and RFC 2827 filtering at the ISP edge and remote-site connectivity device
Man-in-the-middle attacks	Mitigated by encrypting traffic
Network reconnaissance	Mitigated by filtering protocols at the remote site
Unauthorized access	Mitigated by filtering and stateful inspection of sessions by the firewall or router at the remote site or by using the personal firewall on standalone devices
Virus and Trojan-horse attacks	Mitigated by using virus-scanning software at the host level

Figure 17-2 illustrates the remote-user threats and threat mitigations that can be expected within the various options available in the remote-user network design model.

Figure 17-2 *Remote-User Design Model*

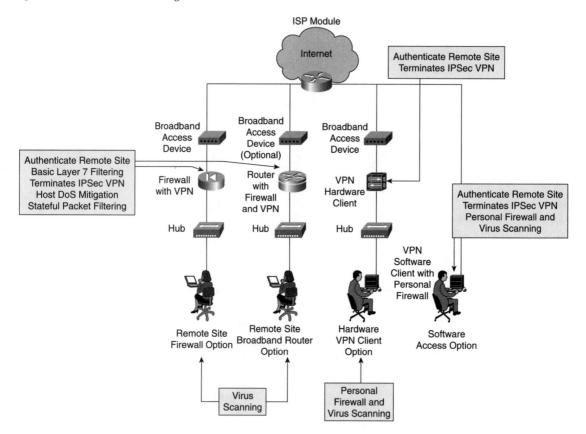

Design Guidelines for Remote-User Networks

The four design options that are available within the remote-user network design model are discussed in depth in this section. For all four options, virus-scanning software is recommended to mitigate the threat of viruses and Trojan-horse programs being able to infect the user's PC.

Remote-Site Firewall

In the remote-site firewall option, the design emphasis is on the home-office worker or a small branch office. It is assumed that Internet connectivity is provided via an ISP-supplied broadband access device, such as an xDSL or cable modem, and that the VPN firewall is located behind this ISP device.

Apart from providing connection-state enforcement and detailed filtering for sessions that are initiated through the firewall, the firewall also provides secure IPSec connectivity between the firewall device itself and the VPN-enabled headend device. This site-to-site IPSec VPN enables PCs that are located on the remote-site network to access corporate resources without the need of individual VPN software clients. (The Cisco VPN Client is discussed in depth in the section "Cisco VPN Client," later in the chapter.)

With a stateful firewall present in the model, it is possible for a remote site to have direct Internet access rather than having to rely on the corporate headend for access. If this option is used, the firewall requires a public IP address and the use of Network Address Translation (NAT) to allow multiple hosts behind the firewall to access the Internet. Also, because this firewall protects the LAN from the Internet, the use of a personal firewall on individual PCs may be deemed unnecessary. However, personal firewalls may be necessary for mobile users for whom additional protection is advantageous.

Regarding the IP addressing of the remote sites, if NAT is not used to communicate with the headend site, a hierarchal addressing scheme must be adopted to ensure that each remote site uses a unique network address range that is routable across the WAN. This hierarchal design also facilitates address summarization and permits remote-site intercommunications.

Control of access to the corporate network and the Internet is performed within the configuration of both the remote-site firewall and the VPN headend device at corporate headquarters. This mechanism is transparent to the remote-site users, and after these devices authenticate and the LAN-to-LAN VPN is established, individual users do not need to perform any form of user authentication to access the corporate network.

Finally, the management of the remote-site firewall can be administered either locally, if the skills are present and the security policy permits, or, more likely, remotely through the use of a dedicated IPSec VPN. This VPN connection terminates directly onto the public interface of the firewall and then back to the corporate headquarters and permits a centralized control of the remote firewall. The VPN connection also ensures that remote users are unable to alter the remote-site firewall's configuration.

Remote-Site Router

The remote-site router option is very similar to the remote-site firewall option discussed in the previous section, with two notable differences.

First, because the router is a full-featured VPN router, advanced applications, such as QoS and stateful firewall, can be supported. Second, if permitted by the ISP, the option is available to integrate the functionality of both the VPN firewall and broadband access devices into a single device.

VPN Hardware Client

The VPN hardware client option is also nearly identical to the remote-site firewall option previously discussed, with the exception that the VPN hardware client does not have a resident stateful firewall. Consequently, this option requires the use of a personal firewall on each individual host that is located behind the VPN hardware client. The use of a personal firewall is even more paramount if split tunneling is enabled, because without the use of a personal firewall, the individual hosts behind the VPN hardware client are protected only by NAT. If split tunneling is not used, a personal firewall may not be necessary on the individual hosts.

Access to the corporate network and the Internet is controlled centrally from the headquarters location. The VPN hardware client undergoes device authentication with the VPN headend device using a predetermined authentication mechanism. After being authenticated, a security policy is "pushed" to the VPN hardware client from the headend VPN device. This policy defines the operational characteristics of the client. The VPN hardware client is capable of operating in one of two modes:

- **Client mode**—All users behind the hardware client appear as a single user on the corporate intranet via the use of NAT overload or what is also commonly called Port Address Translation (PAT).

- **Network extension mode**—All devices access the corporate intranet as if they were directly connected to it, and hosts in the intranet may initiate connections to the hosts behind the hardware client after the tunnel is established.

From a management aspect, client mode is simpler to manage and, hence, is more scalable than network extension mode. However, network extension mode provides more versatility. The modes are equally secure.

Finally, the management of the VPN hardware client device itself can be administered either locally, if the skills are present and the security policy permits, or, more likely, centrally from the corporate headquarters using a Secure Sockets Layer (SSL) connection.

Cisco VPN Client

In the Cisco VPN Client option, the design emphasis is on the mobile or home-office worker. In this model, it is assumed that the user has the Cisco VPN Client installed on his PC, and Internet connectivity is provided from either an ISP dial-up connection or via the LAN.

The Cisco VPN Client provides the means to establish a secure, encrypted IPSec tunnel from the client's PC to the VPN headend device located at corporate headquarters. Access and authorization to the corporate network is controlled centrally from the headquarters location. The Cisco VPN Client first undergoes a group authentication followed by a user authentication with the VPN headend device. Once authenticated, various parameters are pushed down to the client. These include an allocated IP address for use by the client and can include other IP parameters, such as DNS and WIN server addresses. It is even possible to push down a local firewall policy that the client must use while connected over the VPN. At the headend, access to corporate resources is controlled by the corporate firewall, where filtering of the remote users can take place.

By default, the Cisco VPN Client uses the tunneling mode tunnel-everything, as opposed to split-tunneling mode. This mode of operation is determined by the headend device and is one of the parameters pushed to the client. With tunnel-everything mode, Internet access is via the corporate headquarters when a VPN tunnel is established. However, in circumstances where the user is required to use split-tunneling mode, the use of a personal firewall is required to mitigate against threats such as unauthorized access to the PC.

Foundation Summary

The "Foundation Summary" section of each chapter lists the most important facts from the chapter. Although this section does not list every fact from the chapter that will be on your CSI exam, a well-prepared CSI candidate should at a minimum know all the details in each "Foundation Summary" section before taking the exam.

Table 17-5 describes the design options for a remote-user network.

Table 17-5 *Remote-User Design Options*

Option	Description
Remote-site firewall	The remote site is protected by a dedicated firewall, which is IPSec-VPN enabled. WAN connectivity is provided by a broadband access device supplied by an ISP.
Remote-site router	The remote site uses a router that has both firewall and IPSec-VPN functionality. The router normally terminates the WAN connectivity, but it can also be used to terminate to an ISP-supplied broadband access device.
VPN hardware client	The remote site uses a dedicated VPN hardware client that provides IPSec-VPN connectivity. WAN connectivity is provided by a broadband access device supplied by an ISP.
Cisco VPN Client	A remote user uses a Cisco VPN Client and personal firewall software on a PC.

Table 17-6 describes the key devices used in a remote-user network.

Table 17-6 *Remote-User Key Devices*

Device	Description
Broadband access device	Provides connectivity to the broadband network.
Layer 2 hub	Provides connectivity between local network devices. This can be a standalone device or integrated within the VPN hardware device.
VPN firewall	Provides local network protection through stateful filtering of traffic. Provides secure VPNs via IPSec tunnels between the headend and local site.
Personal firewall software	Provides individual PCs with protection.

continues

Table 17-6 *Remote-User Key Devices (Continued)*

Device	Description
VPN firewall router	Provides local network protection through stateful filtering of traffic. Provides secure VPNs through IPSec tunnels between the headend and local site.
Remote-access VPN client	Provides secure VPNs via IPSec tunnels between the headend and individual PCs by using a software client.
VPN hardware client	Provides secure VPN via IPSec tunnels between the headend and the local site by using a dedicated hardware device.

Table 17-7 explains the threats you should anticipate in a remote-user network and the techniques to mitigate them.

Table 17-7 *Remote-User Network Threats and Threat Mitigation*

Threat	Threat Mitigation
IP spoofing	Mitigated by using RFC 1918 and RFC 2827 filtering at the ISP edge and remote-site connectivity device
Man-in-the-middle attacks	Mitigated by encrypting traffic
Network reconnaissance	Mitigated by filtering protocols at the remote site
Unauthorized access	Mitigated by filtering and stateful inspection of sessions by the firewall or router at the remote site or by using the personal firewall on standalone devices
Virus and Trojan-horse attacks	Mitigated by using virus-scanning software at the host level

Q&A

As mentioned in the introduction, "All About the Cisco Certified Security Professional Certification," you have two choices for review questions. The questions that follow next give you a bigger challenge than the exam itself by using an open-ended question format. By reviewing now with this more difficult question format, you can exercise your memory better and prove your conceptual and factual knowledge of this chapter. The answers to these questions are found in Appendix A.

For more practice with exam-like question formats, including questions using a router simulator and multiple choice questions, use the exam engine on the CD-ROM.

1. What workers are considered within the remote-user design model?

2. What are the four design options available within the remote-user design model?

3. What modes can the VPN hardware client operate in?

4. The Cisco VPN Client uses _____ and ____ types of authentication.

5. What are the additional benefits that the remote-site router provides compared to the remote-site firewall option?

6. What type of filter is used to prevent IP spoofing attacks?

7. What happens to the security perimeter of an organization when it is using the remote-user design model?

8. What is the difference between the VPN tunnel types: tunnel-everything and split tunnel?

9. How is the remote-site firewall design option remotely managed?

Reference

Convery, Sean, and Roland Saville. "SAFE: Extending the Security Blueprint to Small, Midsize, and Remote-User Networks." Cisco Systems, Inc., 2001.

Part V: Scenarios

Chapter 18   Scenarios for Final Preparation

Scenarios for Final Preparation

This chapter presents six scenarios that you can use to review most of the concepts contained in this book. The scenarios are designed to assist you in the final preparation for the CSI exam. Each of the scenarios is followed by a list of tasks to complete or questions to answer, all of which are designed to help you review for the exam. The second half of the chapter provides the solutions to the tasks and the answers to the questions.

This chapter emphasizes an overall understanding of the SAFE design philosophy, associated security threats, threat mitigation, the Cisco Secure product portfolio, and the implementation of these products in the small, medium-sized, and remote-user network designs.

Scenario 18-1

This scenario, depicted in Figure 18-1, involves a typical small network design model in a standalone configuration.

Figure 18-1 *Small Network Design*

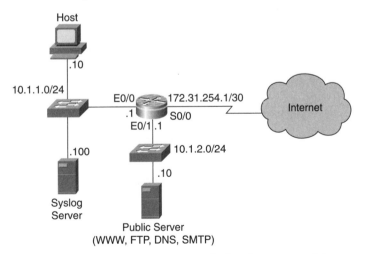

Assume that basic security has already been applied to the router and that you are connected to the console port and able to access exec mode. Given this network scenario, perform the following tasks:

1. Configure the router so that it reports to the syslog server.

2. Apply the Cisco IOS Firewall to the inside and outside interfaces using the name "FIREWALL" and only allow inspection for TCP, UDP, FTP, and SMTP services. Enable the logging of session information.

3. Allow only legitimate traffic from the inside network and, at the same time, prevent IP address spoofing.

4. Deny all outbound traffic from the inside network. (Remember that the inspection list allows openings in the ACL.)

5. Allow only legitimate traffic from the DMZ segment and, at the same time, prevent IP address spoofing.

6. Prevent all traffic on to the DMZ apart from those services that are available from the public server.

7. Apply RFC 1918 filtering to the outside interface.

Scenario 18-2

This scenario, depicted in Figure 18-2, involves a typical Corporate Internet module from the medium-sized network design model.

Figure 18-2 *Medium-Sized Network Design with Corporate Internet Module*

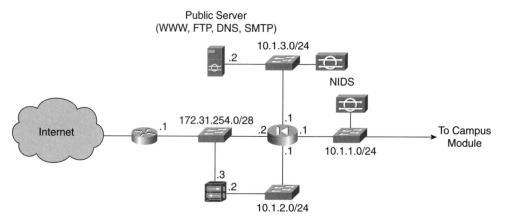

Assume that basic security has already been applied to all the devices and that you are connected to the console port and able to access exec mode. Given this network scenario, perform the following tasks:

1. On the public interface of the edge router, allow IPSec traffic from the remote-site peers 10.10.1.1 and 10.10.2.1 (not shown). Also allow remote-access VPN traffic.

2. On the PIX Firewall, permit outside users access to the public services. Note that the public server, 10.1.3.2, appears publicly as 172.31.254.4 via static NAT on the PIX Firewall.

3. Allow only legitimate traffic from remote-access users to the public services segment. Note that the VPN concentrator is configured with a remote-access address pool of 192.168.1.1 to 192.168.1.254.

4. Allow remote-access user traffic to the Internet and internal network.

Scenario 18-3

This scenario, depicted in Figure 18-3, involves a typical Campus module from the medium-sized network design model.

Figure 18-3 *Medium-Sized Network Design with Campus Module*

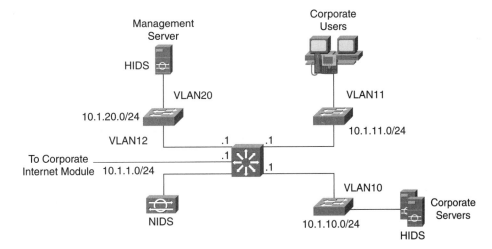

Assume that basic security has already been applied to all the devices and that you are connected to the console port and able to access exec mode. Given this network scenario, perform the following tasks:

1. On the core switch, configure the four VLANs that are shown, including their IP addressing.

2. Apply RFC 2827 filtering to VLAN10, VLAN11, and VLAN20.

Scenario 18-4

A small company, Company XYZ, is a supplier of printer consumables through a locally hosted website. It is located in a single premises with two floors. There are about 20 users located on each of these floors. All users require access to the Internet and to local services such as the corporate intranet. Internet connectivity is provided by a local ISP router. Public services consist of domain name, file, e-mail, and web services.

Recently, concerns have been raised about the network's lack of security, particularly the vulnerability of the publicly accessible servers. Taking these concerns into consideration, the company has decided to implement a firewall solution using a DMZ to secure the public services and the network as a whole.

The tasks for this scenario are as follows:

1. Sketch out a network design for this company based on the information provided.

2. Company XYZ has 10 salespeople on staff who require network access to company resources from time to time while in the field. How can this be best achieved?

3. The network administrator at Company XYZ is concerned about the integrity of the corporate servers from potential attacks. How best can he alleviate his concerns?

Scenario 18-5

Company ABC is an engineering firm with over 500 staff located in three premises: a main office and two branches. The main office has 400 staff distributed over four floors, and each branch accommodates 50 staff.

The company has decided that the existing network infrastructure needs to be modernized and that the new network should support the staff and office locations specified and should include the following requirements:

■ A corporate WAN that uses IPSec VPNs

■ Centralized corporate resources

■ The availability of public services via the Internet

■ A security-centric design

■ Remote access via the Internet for mobile workers

■ Centralized management and support

For this scenario, sketch out the network design for this company based on the information provided.

Scenario 18-6

A typical medium-sized company is shown in Figure 18-4.

The questions for this scenario are as follows:

1. With reference to Figure 18-4, where would you deploy a NIDS and HIDS?

2. In the edge router (ER), what type of mitigation can you apply to the public interface of the router? What are the commands to implement this action?

Figure 18-4   *Typical Medium-Sized Company Network Topology*

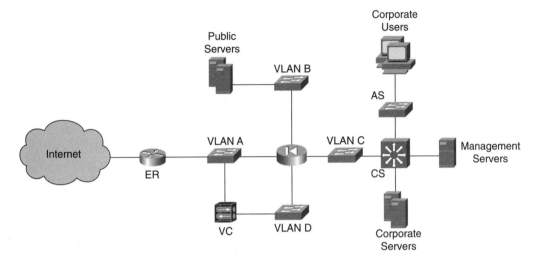

3. The VPN concentrator (VC) performs what role within the network?

4. The PIX Firewall mitigates what kind of attacks?

5. Where would you implement the use of private VLANs and for what purpose?

6. What is the purpose of RFC 2827 filtering on the core switch (CS)?

Answers to Scenario 18-1

1. *Configure the router so that it reports to the syslog server.*

    Syslog report is configured as follows:

    ```
    FW(config)#logging 10.1.1.100
    ```

2. *Apply the Cisco IOS Firewall to the inside and outside interfaces using the name "FIREWALL" and only allow inspection for TCP, UDP, FTP, and SMTP services. Enable the logging of session information.*

    The correct configuration of the Cisco IOS Firewall is as follows:

    ```
    FW(config)#ip inspect audit-trail

    FW(config)#ip inspect name FIREWALL tcp
    FW(config)#ip inspect name FIREWALL udp
    FW(config)#ip inspect name FIREWALL ftp
    FW(config)#ip inspect name FIREWALL smtp

    FW(config)#interface e0/0
    FW(config-if)#ip inspect FIREWALL in
    ```

```
FW(config)#interface s0/0
FW(config-if)#ip inspect FIREWALL in
```

3. *Allow only legitimate traffic from the inside network and, at the same time, prevent IP address spoofing.*

    The correct configuration is as follows:

    ```
    FW(config)#access-list 111 permit ip 10.1.1.0 0.0.0.255 any
    FW(config)#access-list 111 deny ip any any

    FW(config)#interface e0/0
    FW(config-if)#ip access-group 111 in
    ```

4. *Deny all outbound traffic from the inside network. (Remember that the inspection list allows openings in this ACL.)*

    The correct configuration is as follows:

    ```
    FW(config)#access-list 112 deny ip any any

    FW(config)#interface e0/0
    FW(config-if)#ip access-group 112 out
    ```

5. *Allow only legitimate traffic from the DMZ segment and, at the same time, prevent IP address spoofing.*

    The correct configuration is as follows:

    ```
    FW(config)#access-list 121 permit ip 10.1.2.0 0.0.0.255 any
    FW(config)#access-list 121 deny ip any any

    FW(config)#interface e0/1
    FW(config-if)#ip access-group 121 in
    ```

6. *Prevent all traffic on to the DMZ apart from those services that are available from the public server.*

    The correct configuration is as follows:

    ```
    FW(config)#access-list 122 tcp any host 10.1.2.10 eq www
    FW(config)#access-list 122 tcp any host 10.1.2.10 eq ftp
    FW(config)#access-list 122 udp any host 10.1.2.10 eq domain
    FW(config)#access-list 122 tcp any host 10.1.2.10 eq smtp

    FW(config)#interface e0/1
    FW(config-if)#ip access-group 122 out
    ```

7. *Apply RFC 1918 filtering to the outside interface.*

    The correct configuration is as follows:

    ```
    FW(config)#access-list 131 deny ip 10.0.0.0 0.255.255.255 any
    FW(config)#access-list 131 permit ip 172.31.254.0 0.0.0.3  any
    ```

```
FW(config)#access-list 131 deny ip 172.16.0.0 0.15.255.255 any
FW(config)#access-list 131 deny ip 192.168.0.0 0.0.0.255 any
FW(config)#access-list 131 permit ip any any

FW(config)#interface s0/0
FW(config-if)#ip access-group 131 in
```

Answers to Scenario 18-2

1. *On the public interface of the edge router, allow IPSec traffic from the remote-site peers 10.10.1.1 and 10.10.2.1 (not shown). Also allow remote-access VPN traffic.*

The edge router's public interface filtering is configured as follows:

```
edge_rtr(config)#access-list 100 permit udp host 10.10.1.1 host 172.31.254.2
eq isakmp
edge_rtr(config)#access-list 100 permit udp host 10.10.2.1 host 172.31.254.2
eq isakmp
edge_rtr(config)#access-list 100 permit esp host 10.10.1.1 host 172.31.254.2
edge_rtr(config)#access-list 100 permit esp host 10.10.1.1 host 172.31.254.2

edge_rtr(config)#access-list 100 permit udp any host 172.31.254.3 eq isakmp
edge_rtr(config)#access-list 100 permit esp any host 172.31.254.3

edge_rtr(config)#interface s0/0
edge_rtr(config-if)#ip access-group 100 in
```

2. *On the PIX Firewall, permit outside users access to the public services. Note that the public server, 10.1.3.2, appears publicly as 172.31.254.4 via static NAT on the PIX Firewall.*

The correct configuration is as follows:

```
PIX_FW(config)#access-list outside_access_in permit tcp any host
172.31.254.4 eq ftp
PIX_FW(config)#access-list outside_access_in permit tcp any host
172.31.254.4 eq www
PIX_FW(config)#access-list outside_access_in permit tcp any host
172.31.254.4 eq smtp
PIX_FW(config)#access-list outside_access_in permit udp any host
172.31.254.4 eq domain
```

3. *Allow only legitimate traffic from remote-access users to the public services segment. Note that the VPN concentrator is configured with a remote-access address pool of 192.168.1.1 to 192.168.1.254.*

The correct configuration is as follows:

```
PIX_FW(config)#access-list remote_access_in permit tcp 192.168.1.0
255.255.255.0 host 172.31.254.4 eq ftp
PIX_FW(config)#access-list remote_access_in permit tcp 192.168.1.0
255.255.255.0 host 172.31.254.4 eq www
```

```
PIX_FW(config)#access-list remote_access_in permit tcp 192.168.1.0
255.255.255.0 host 172.31.254.4 eq smtp
PIX_FW(config)#access-list remote_access_in permit udp 192.168.1.0
255.255.255.0 host 172.31.254.4 eq domain
```

4. *Allow remote-access user traffic to the Internet and internal network.*

The correct configuration is as follows:

```
PIX_FW(config)#access-list remote_access_in permit ip 192.168.1.0
255.255.255.0 any
```

Answers to Scenario 18-3

1. *On the core switch, configure the four VLANs that are shown, including their IP addressing.*

The correct configuration is as follows:

```
core_sw(config)#interface vlan10
core_sw(config-if)#ip address 10.1.10.1 255.255.255.0

core_sw(config)#interface vlan11
core_sw(config-if)#ip address 10.1.11.1 255.255.255.0

core_sw(config)#interface vlan12
core_sw(config-if)#ip address 10.1.1.1 255.255.255.0

core_sw(config)#interface vlan20
core_sw(config-if)#ip address 10.1.20.1 255.255.255.0
```

2. *Apply RFC 2827 filtering to VLAN10, VLAN11, and VLAN20.*

The correct configuration is as follows:

```
core_sw(config)#access-list 110 permit ip 10.1.10.0 0.0.0.255 any
core_sw(config)#interface vlan10
core_sw(config-if)#ip access-group 110 in

core_sw(config)#access-list 111 permit ip 10.1.11.0 0.0.0.255 any
core_sw(config)#interface vlan11
core_sw(config-if)#ip access-group 111 in

core_sw(config)#access-list 120 permit ip 10.1.20.0 0.0.0.255 any
core_sw(config)#interface vlan20
core_sw(config-if)#ip access-group 120 in
```

Answers to Scenario 18-4

   1.   *Sketch out a network design for this company based on the information provided.*

   See Figure 18-5 for a network drawing.

Figure 18-5   *Company XYZ Network Topology*

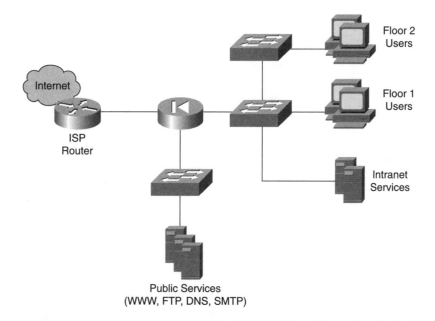

Public Services
(WWW, FTP, DNS, SMTP)

> **NOTE**   An alternative to the solution shown in Figure 18-5 is to replace the PIX Firewall with a Cisco IOS Firewall router.

   2.   *Company XYZ has 10 salespeople on staff who require network access to company resources from time to time while in the field. How can this be best achieved?*

   Because the PIX Firewall is capable of supporting remote-access IPSec VPNs enabling this form of connectivity on the PIX Firewall is the easiest way to accommodate the remote-access requirements of the salespeople. Sales staff would then require only the installation of the Cisco Secure VPN software client on their PCs and Internet connectivity to establish a secure link to the corporate resources.

   3.   *The network administrator at Company XYZ is concerned about the integrity of the corporate servers from potential attacks. How best can he alleviate his concerns?*

   By the use of a HIDS, the network administrator can monitor and protect the corporate servers from attack. Additionally, all servers would still need to be kept up to date with all relevant software patches and antivirus software.

Answers to Scenario 18-5

1. *Sketch out a network design based on the information provided.*

   See Figure 18-6 for a network drawing.

Figure 18-6   *Company ABC Network Topology*

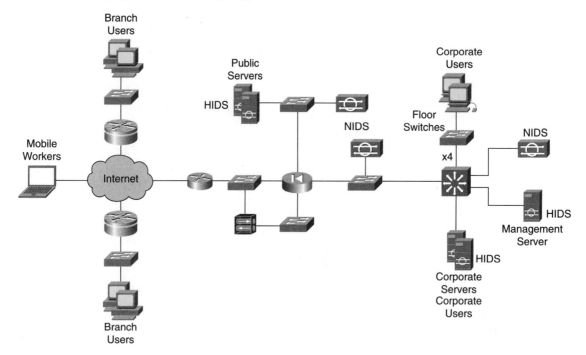

Answers to Scenario 18-6

1. *With reference to Figure 18-4, where would you deploy a NIDS and HIDS?*

   NIDS sensors are normally deployed on VLAN B and VLAN C of the PIX Firewall. A NIDS sensor deployed off a SPAN port on the core switch is also commonly performed.

2. *In the edge router (ER), what type of mitigation can you apply to the public interface of the router? What are the commands to implement this action?*

   It is normal practice to provide IP addressing spoofing mitigation and basic filtering on the public interface of the edge router.

   RFC 1918 filtering is achieved by using the following commands:

   ```
   access-list number deny ip 10.0.0.0 0.255.255.255 any
   access-list number deny ip 172.16.0.0 0.15.255.255 any
   ```

```
access-list number deny ip 192.168.0.0 0.0.255.255 any
access-list number permit any any
```

RFC 2827 filtering only permits a source address that is valid from the organization's public address range. This type of filtering is applied using an access list.

Finally, in addition to RFC 1918 and RFC 2827 filters, basic filtering is applied to the remaining traffic flow to permit only that traffic that is specifically required to transit the interface.

3. *The VPN concentrator (VC) performs what role within the network?*

The VPN concentrator provides the facility to terminate remote-access IPSec VPNs.

Remote users are allocated to groups that have configurable parameters such as IP address pool and other IP service parameters.

Connection to the VPN concentrator in the remote-access scenario is achieved through the use of a VPN software client that resides on the remote user's PC and is configured with the VPN connection parameters.

4. *The PIX Firewall performs what mitigation roles?*

The PIX Firewall performs the following mitigation roles:

- Provides remote-site authentication

- Provides basic Layer 7 filtering

- Provides host DoS mitigation

- Provides stateful packet filtering

- Terminates remote-site IPSec VPNs

5. *Where would you implement the use of private VLANs and for what purpose?*

Private VLANs are deployed on all switches that are capable of supporting this feature and where there are concerns about trust exploitations. Typically, all switch ports on the public services segment would be enabled for private VLANs. This prevents a compromised host on the VLAN from being used to attack another host on the same VLAN.

6. *What is the purpose of RFC 2827 filtering on the core switch (CS)?*

RFC 2827 filtering on the core switch ensures that only traffic with a valid source address for a specific VLAN is allowed to exit from that VLAN.

Part VI: Appendixes

Answers to the "Do I Know This Already?" Quizzes and Q&A Sections

Chapter 2

"Do I Know This Already?" Quiz

1. c
2. d
3. a
4. d
5. b
6. b, e
7. b, d
8. c
9. d
10. c
11. e
12. c

Q&A

1. *What does a good network security policy allow?*

   A good network security policy allows the network administrators or security personnel to deploy security systems and software throughout the infrastructure, which includes providing to the administrative personnel the capacity to deploy IDSs, antivirus software, and other technologies in order to mitigate both existing threats and potential threats.

2. *What does the network security policy define?*

   The security policy defines the procedures that are used and the suggested guidelines to be implemented by security personnel and network administrators.

3. *How does a "defense-in-depth" approach work in network security?*

A "defense-in-depth" approach involves the deployment of security as several layers within the network. If an attacker bypasses one layer, she still faces additional layers before she reaches critical network resources. This layered defense approach maximizes the security around critical resources.

4. *What is an OOB network used for in SAFE?*

An OOB network is a network that carries only management traffic on it. It is completely separate from the network that carries the normal enterprise traffic.

5. *What can be used in place of an OOB network?*

Encrypted communication can be used in place of an OOB network as long as both endpoints of the communication channel are secure.

6. *What is authentication?*

Authentication is the determination that a user or administrator has the necessary credentials to access a device or system.

7. *What is authorization?*

Authorization is the determination that a user or administrator has sufficient privileges to execute a command or a process.

8. *How does a NIDS work?*

A NIDS works by monitoring network traffic for patterns of attack. Once an attack has been detected, the NIDS may simply raise an alarm on a management console, execute a block by inserting a new rule into a router's or firewall's ACL, or execute a TCP reset (for TCP connections only).

9. *How does a HIDS work?*

A HIDS works by monitoring the host and attempting to detect illegal actions such as the replacement of a critical file or the execution of an illegal instruction in computer memory.

10. *Why is deployment critical to the success of the IDS?*

As networks have grown tremendously over the past few years, the amount of traffic traversing the network wire has also increased. This results in the need to properly place the IDS at strategic locations throughout the network to maximize its effectiveness.

11. *How is SAFE able to accommodate emerging network applications?*

SAFE accommodates emerging applications through the flexibility of the blueprint design. The deployment of new applications does not require a significant re-engineering of the network security state; rather, minor modifications can be made to provide access to these applications.

12. *What are the four types of threats faced by a network?*

Internal threats, external threats, structured threats, and unstructured threats

13. *What are internal threats?*

Internal threats are structured or unstructured threats from within the network, such as attacks initiated by disgruntled former or current employees.

14. *What are external threats?*

External threats are structured or unstructured threats from outside the enterprise network, such as attacks initiated by "script kiddies."

15. *What are structured threats?*

Structured threats are created by a lone attacker or a small group of attackers who are highly motivated and technically competent. Such threats typically involve sophisticated hacking techniques to bypass all security measures in order to penetrate the network.

16. *What are unstructured threats?*

Unstructured threats primarily consist of random attackers using various common tools, such as malicious shell scripts, password crackers, credit card number generators, and dialer daemons.

Chapter 3

"Do I Know This Already?" Quiz

1. c

2. c

3. d

4. e

5. a, d

6. **b, e**

7. **a, d**

8. **c**

9. **c**

10. **b, c**

Q&A

1. *What are some of the benefits of using a dedicated appliance for security rather than the same integrated functionality in another device?*

    Some of the benefits of using a dedicated appliance for security are that appliances tend to provide greater depth of functionality as well as provide for a hardened system. Although the cost is greater, the flexibility achieved through dedicated appliances is also significantly greater.

2. *What are the two significant advantages to SAFE's use of modules in the blueprint?*

    The SAFE design philosophy is achieved through the use of modules. This approach has two significant advantages:

    - The security relationship between the modules can be addressed.

    - Modularity permits the designers to phase in security on a per-module basis rather than attempt to implement security throughout the entire network architecture in a single phase.

3. *What is the primary method that a DDoS attack uses to achieve its effects?*

    The goal of a DDoS attack is to shut down an entire network rather than one particular host, and the primary method that is used to achieve this is to consume all the bandwidth going to and from the network. One possible side effect of a DDoS attack is that a target system on the network crashes.

4. *Why do hosts represent the greatest risk on a network?*

    Hosts represent the greatest risk on a network because of the large number of different hardware platforms, operating systems, and applications—each with its own set of patches and updates— and their high visibility. Hosts represent the lowest-hanging fruit on a network and are the target of choice for an attacker.

5. *Is it important to lock down Telnet, web, or SNMP access to devices, and if so, why?*

    It is important to lock down all access to devices. Attackers can use Telnet access to gain access to the CLI of devices and possibly to privileged EXEC mode. The username and password of a Telnet session is passed in the clear on a network, exposing it to anyone who may be sniffing the network. If an attacker gains access to the privileged EXEC mode on devices, they can make configuration changes. Web and SNMP access should also be locked down for the same reason.

6. *What is the role of VTP in a network? What could an attacker do with VTP? How can attacks using VTP be made less likely to succeed?*

VTP is used to communicate VLAN information from a VTP server to clients. The information transmitted relates to the configured VLANs on the network. If attackers can spoof or forge VTP advertisements, they may be able to do a variety of things, such as delete VLAN information or even create new VLANs. To make such an attack less likely to succeed, the administrator needs to use VTP password authentication to authenticate VTP advertisements.

7. *What is 802.1x? How can it be used to improve the security of a network?*

The IEEE standard 802.1x was developed originally for switches on wired networks but has been more widely deployed in conjunction with wireless networks. In brief, 802.1x requires authentication of a client to a network. If the authentication succeeds, the access point or switch then allows traffic to pass through. Otherwise, the user cannot connect to network resources, such as DHCP and DNS, or any other services.

8. *What are the four factors a software audit should consider when determining the security of an application?*

Software audits should analyze several areas when determining the security of an application:

- The calls the application makes to other applications and to the operating system itself
- The application privilege level
- The application level of trust for the surrounding systems
- The method of transport the application uses to transmit data across the network

Chapter 4

"Do I Know This Already?" Quiz

1. a, e

2. d

3. c

4. d

5. b, c

6. d

7. b

8. b, c, d

9. a, c

10. c, d, e

11. a, d

Q&A

1. *What is the purpose of the ISP router in the SAFE medium-sized network blueprint? What features does this device provide for traffic control?*

   This router's primary purpose is to provide connectivity to a provider network. For traffic control, ACLs provide for address filtering in accordance with RFC 1918 and RFC 2827 in both directions of traffic.

2. *What management devices are found in the Campus module of the SAFE medium-sized network blueprint?*

   The following management devices are found in the Campus module of the SAFE medium-sized network blueprint:

Management hosts	Provide management for network devices; typically use SNMP
Syslog host	Aggregates firewall, router, and NIDS logs
Access control server	Provides authentication services to network devices such as network access servers
OTP server	Provides for authorization of one-time password authentication relayed from the access control server
Sysadmin host	Provides for configuration, software, and content changes on network devices

3. *What are the functions provided by the Layer 3 switch in the medium-sized network Campus module?*

   The functions provided by the Layer 3 switch in the medium-sized network Campus module are as follows:

   • Routing and switching of production and management traffic

   • Distribution layer services such as routing, QoS, and access control

- Connectivity for the corporate and management servers

- Traffic filtering between subnets

4. *What is the primary function of the Layer 2 switches in the Campus and Corporate Internet modules of the SAFE design?*

The primary purpose of the Layer 2 switches is to provide connectivity for end-user workstations. Additionally, these switches are configured with private VLANs to reduce the potential of device compromise through trust exploitation.

5. *What is the function of the internal router in the Corporate Internet module of the SAFE medium-sized network blueprint?*

The primary function of the internal router is to provide for Layer 3 separation and routing between the Campus and Corporate Internet modules. The device functions solely as a router without any filtering capabilities and provides a final point of demarcation between the routed intranet and the external network.

6. *Where are the NIDS appliances located in the Corporate Internet module of the SAFE medium-sized network blueprint?*

The NIDS appliances are deployed in two locations: in the public services segment and in the internal segment between the firewall's private interface and the internal router. This allows for traffic inspection and analysis in two critical junctions of the blueprint.

7. *What are the key network devices in the Corporate Internet module of the SAFE small network blueprint and what are their functions?*

The key network devices in this module are the firewall and the Layer 2 switch in the public services segment. The firewall provides filtering capabilities and one additional DMZ. The Layer 2 switch provides connectivity and the configuration of private VLANs in the DMZ of the firewall.

8. *The firewall in the SAFE medium-sized network blueprint divides the Corporate Internet module into four segments. What are they?*

The four segments are

- External segment

- Public services segment

- VPN/dial-in segment

- Internal segment

9. *What are some of the precautions to take when placing a NIDS appliance outside of the firewall in the Corporate Internet module of the SAFE medium-sized network blueprint?*

   Configure the NIDS to alarm at a lower severity than alarms generated by the NIDS behind the firewall's private interface, and configure the NIDS' alarms to log to a separate management server so that the legitimate alarms receive the appropriate attention.

10. *What authentication protocol is recommended at the NAS of the Corporate Internet module in the SAFE medium-sized network blueprint?*

    Authentication using the three-way CHAP is recommended.

Chapter 5

"Do I Know This Already?" Quiz

1. f
2. e
3. d
4. b
5. a
6. a
7. b, d
8. e
9. e
10. a
11. a, b, c, d

Q&A

1. *What are the three elements of a good security policy?*

   The three elements of a good security policy are that the policy must be capable of being implemented; must clearly define the areas of responsibility and the roles of users, administrators, and managers; and must be enforceable and applicable to everyone.

2. *What are some of the more common threats described in RFC 2196?*

RFC 2196 describes three common threats to a network:

- The unauthorized access to resources or information
- The unintentional and unauthorized disclosure of information
- Denial of service

3. *What are the key trade-offs that define the corporate security goals?*

The key trade-offs that define the corporate security goals are as follows:

- Services offered versus the security provided
- Ease of use versus security
- Cost of security versus risk of loss

4. *Within the field of network security, what does CIA stand for?*

Confidentiality, integrity, and availability

5. *What are some of the physical assets of a network?*

Physical assets of a network include hardware items, such as computers, switches, firewalls, routers, and other devices, that physically exist on a network.

6. *What is a privacy policy?*

A privacy policy defines reasonable expectations for privacy regarding such issues as monitoring of e-mail, logging of keystrokes, and access to users' files.

7. *What is an acceptable-use policy?*

An acceptable-use policy defines the boundaries of acceptable use of corporate resources (whether they be physical equipment or network services) as well as the responsibilities of the user in protecting corporate assets and equipment.

8. *Describe the four phases of the security wheel.*

The four phases of the security wheel are

1. Securing the network. Includes the deployment of systems to stop or prevent unauthorized access or activities.

2. Monitoring the network. Involves validating the security implementation conducted in the first stage by detecting violations of the security policy.

3. Testing the security of the network. Involves validating the effectiveness of the security policy implementation through system auditing and vulnerability scanning.

4. Improving the security of the network. Involves using the information gathered during the monitoring and testing phases to improve the security implementation of the network.

Chapter 6

"Do I Know This Already?" Quiz

1. c

2. e

3. b, c

4. d

5. e

6. c

7. a, e

8. c

9. c, d

10. a

Q&A

1. *What are some of the benefits and drawbacks of ICMP scanning?*

   ICMP is one of the most commonly used network protocols on the Internet. It allows for diagnostic determination of connectivity between hosts and networks. ICMP scans can be used by attackers to identify active IP addresses on a target network. The biggest limitation to ICMP scanning is that if the target network is blocking ICMP at the edge router, these scans do not work. Also, if the target network is logging any ICMP activity that is typically used in network scans, an ICMP scan is easily seen and the activity noted.

2. *What is the order of events of an attack on a target network?*

   Reconnaissance, target identification and enumeration, and access attack

3. *What are trust exploitation attacks?*

   Trust exploitation attacks occur when an attacker is able to access one system from another without authenticating because of a trust relationship between the two systems. Trust exploitation attacks can also be executed by one system on a subnet against another because of the lack of filtering within the subnet traffic.

4. *Name some DDoS attacks?*

   stacheldracht, trin00, Tribe Flood Network (TFN), TFN2K, mstream, and shaft

5. *What are buffer overflows?*

   Buffer overflows are attacks that are made possible by improper bounds checking of input data in a program. By sending properly crafted data to the program, the attacker is able to redirect the program to execute code of the attacker's choice. This typically results in the creation of a shell within which the attacker gains access to the system.

6. *What type of attacks are buffer overflows and format string attacks?*

   Application layer attacks

7. *How does the TCP SYN flood attack work?*

   The TCP SYN flood attack is a DoS attack that is used to open a large number of half-open TCP connections to the target. TCP SYN packets are sent to the target system who then responds with SYN-ACK packets. The attacker does not send back the necessary ACK packets to the target but keeps sending new SYN packets until the TCP SYN queue on the host becomes filled. Once filled, the target can no longer accept any more TCP connections until some of the TCP SYN connections in the queue age out.

8. *What is a blind-TCP scan?*

   In a blind-TCP scan, the attacker scans a network range using TCP instead of ICMP. This scan can search for common services such as web, e-mail, and FTP services. Although this may not provide a complete picture of all possible hosts that are reachable across the Internet, it does provide a sufficient list of publicly available servers. The scan is also virtually hidden from network administrators because it searches only a set of ports that are likely to be open.

9. *If a TCP ACK packet is sent to a port where a service is not listening, what is the response defined in RFC 793?*

   No response. The TCP packet is silently discarded.

10. *If a TCP ACK packet is sent to a port where a service is listening, what is the response defined in RFC 793?*

    A TCP RST packet is sent back.

11. *What are the two types of systems that are used in a DDoS attack?*

Handlers and agents. Handlers are systems that are initially exploited by an attacker, who then sets up the DDoS software on them. Handlers are then used to scan other hosts that may have a vulnerability that can be exploited to gain access. Once those hosts have been compromised, the agents can be installed and the hosts are ready for use in a DDoS attack. One handler host can control multiple agent hosts.

Chapter 7

"Do I Know This Already?" Quiz

1. b, d
2. b
3. a
4. e
5. a, d, e
6. b
7. e
8. b
9. a, c
10. a

Q&A

1. *What is an IP spoofing attack?*

In an IP spoofing attack, an attacker attempts to gain access to a restricted resource by disguising the IP address of her system. The system being spoofed by the attacker has access to the restricted resource, and that restriction is based solely on the source IP address of the communication.

2. *How can an attacker receive packets if he is spoofing the IP address of his system to attack the target?*

To receive packets at the spoofing computer, the attacker must control the routing tables on the target network and set static routes in the routing tables to redirect the packets for the spoofed IP address to the attacker's system.

3. *How do packet sniffers work?*

A packet sniffer is a software application that works by placing a network adapter card in promiscuous mode. In promiscuous mode, the network card is able to receive all packets on the physical network wire and pass those packets up to an application.

4. *What kind of information can packet sniffers capture?*

Packet sniffers can be used to capture sensitive information such as usernames and passwords as they are transmitted in clear text over such applications as SNMP, Telnet, FTP, and HTTP between the client and the server. Additionally, packet sniffers can capture potentially sensitive data in unencrypted e-mail.

5. *What is a brute-force password attack?*

A brute-force password attack is a low-tech attack in which the attacker connects to the system and tries various account names and common default passwords for that account.

6. *Once attackers have cracked an account through password attacks, what can they do?*

Once attackers have cracked an account through password attacks, they can then access the system with the same privilege level as the compromised user. If the account has administrative privileges, the attacker can create back doors for future access to the system.

7. *What is a man-in-the-middle attack?*

In a man-in-the-middle attack, the attacker is able to intercept packets crossing a network, modify or falsify the information in those packets, and reinject the modified packets into the network.

8. *What is a port redirection attack?*

In a port redirection attack, an attacker uses a compromised host to relay traffic passed through an open port on a firewall or in a router's ACLs that would normally be denied. The attacker tunnels the traffic through the compromised host.

9. *What are two software packages that an attacker can use to execute a port redirection attack?*

Netcat and httptunnel

10. *What is a virus?*

Viruses are small pieces of mobile code that attach to other programs or documents and can infect a computer when the program is executed or the document is opened.

11. *What is a Trojan-horse application?*

   Trojan horses are applications that appear to be benign but contain potentially malicious code that can be used to attack the system it is run on.

Chapter 8

"Do I Know This Already?" Quiz

1. e
2. d
3. a
4. b
5. d
6. b, d
7. e
8. a
9. b
10. d

Q&A

1. *What are the two basic methods of mitigating reconnaissance attacks?*

   Reducing network posture visibility and application hardening

2. *What is network posture visibility reduction?*

   Network posture visibility reduction is an effort to reduce to a minimum the number of services in the public-facing segment of the network. Only those services that are essential for network operation are accessible from the Internet, such as SMTP, HTTP, and DNS.

3. *What steps should be taken to harden an application against attack?*

   Application hardening involves staying current on patches for all applications and reducing any information the applications may provide through service banners.

4. *DoS and DDoS attacks focus on what part of the network architecture?*

DoS attacks and DDoS attacks focus on the weak points in the network architecture where these attacks may have an advantage. Typically, this is at the edge router of the network.

5. *What are the three primary methods of mitigating DoS and DDoS attacks?*

Implementing antispoofing techniques such as RFC 2827 filtering, applying anti-DoS features in the edge router and firewalls, and applying traffic-rate limitations to nonessential traffic.

6. *What is RFC 2827 filtering and who does it?*

RFC 2827 calls for filtering at the edge of the ISP network where customer networks connect. Traffic should be filtered at the edge by restricting traffic to only those prefixes assigned that are to the customer. Typically, the ISP implements RFC 2827 filtering at the edge but enterprise networks can also make good use of RFC 2827 filtering because filtering prevents any spoofed traffic from originating in the enterprise network.

7. *In addition to traffic-rate limiting, what can be done to mitigate DoS attacks?*

QoS can also be implemented in addition to traffic-rate limiting. QoS enables an organization to identify permitted traffic and ensure that it is handled quickly while other, potentially unauthorized traffic is relegated to slower handling.

8. *Why is it easy to mitigate unauthorized access attacks?*

Mitigation of unauthorized access attacks simply relies on denying access to ports that an attacker should not be able to connect to. This can be done by implementing tight ACLs both on routers and on firewalls.

9. *Why are application layer attacks always a security risk?*

Application layer attacks can never be completely eliminated because new vulnerabilities are being constantly discovered in applications across every platform and operating system. Additionally, as software becomes increasingly complex, the likelihood of a catastrophic vulnerability increases dramatically.

10. *How can application layer attacks best be mitigated?*

Application layer attacks can best be mitigated by implementing system administration BCPs, by keeping current on all software patches, by subscribing to mailing lists, such as *bugtraq* and the *CERT* mailing lists, and by reading the operating system and network logs and using available log-analysis tools to identify trends that may indicate a potential attack.

11. *How do NIDSs help to mitigate application layer attacks?*

   A NIDS detects a potential attack and can then instruct a router or firewall to terminate the session.

12. *How can HIDSs help to mitigate application layer attacks?*

   A HIDS can protect a host by detecting unauthorized activity or file modifications through a process on the host and then respond to that activity by denying it and raising an alarm on the HIDS console.

13. *How can trust exploitation attacks be mitigated?*

   Trust exploitation attacks can be mitigated through tight network access control and tight constraints on trust levels within a network.

Chapter 9

"Do I Know This Already?" Quiz

1. d

2. a, c

3. e

4. c, e

5. a, c

6. b, d

7. b, d, e

8. b, c

9. d

10. b

11. e

Q&A

1. *Describe the characteristics of a strong password.*

   Strong passwords have the following characteristics: a minimum length of at *least* eight characters; upper- and lowercase characters; both alphanumeric and nonalphanumeric characters such as #,@,%, and $. Ideally passwords are randomly generated.

2. *What is two-factor authentication?*

A two-factor authentication system is one that requires two items of information to complete the authentication. Typically, these items are something that a person has (such as an ATM card or a token card) and something that a person knows (a PIN number or a password).

3. *How can cryptography mitigate packet sniffers?*

Cryptography renders packet sniffers irrelevant. A packet sniffer that is monitoring a cryptographic channel sees data that appears to be only a random string of bits. The original message is not readable as it traverses the network.

4. *How can an attacker insert himself between two systems using cryptography in a man-in-the-middle attack?*

A man-in-the-middle attack against an encrypted session can succeed only if the attacker can insert himself into the key-exchange process such that the attacker negotiates a separate session key with both parties and relays the communication sufficiently fast enough to keep up with the other two machines.

5. *How can Trojan-horse applications be mitigated?*

Through the use of antivirus or HIDS software.

6. *RFC 2827 describes filtering by service providers at their edge devices. How can an enterprise network that is connecting through a service provider also benefit from RFC 2827 filtering?*

Service provider customers can implement egress filters according to the RFC 2827 guidelines as an additional filter to prevent their networks from becoming a source of DoS attacks.

7. *Port redirection is effective when there is a poor or weak trust model between systems. How can an attacker use such an attack to gain access to the internal host through the DMZ web server shown earlier in Figure 9-3?*

By identifying a vulnerability in the web server software that provides access to the server, the attacker can then access the server. Once on the server, the attacker can set up the port redirection software (such as HTTPtunnel), have the software listen on the web port of the server, and point to the other end of the tunnel at a port, such as the Telnet port, on the internal system.

8. *How do switched infrastructures affect packet sniffers?*

Switches do not direct all traffic within a network segment to a switch port. Because of this, switched infrastructures present a significant hurdle to packet sniffers by reducing the amount of traffic seen by the host that is doing the sniffing. The attacker has access only to the traffic that is destined for the specific port that the compromised host connects to.

9. *What are two methods that antisniffer tools use to detect the possible presence of a sniffer?*

   Antisniffer tools can detect changes in the response time of hosts to determine whether the hosts are processing more traffic than their own. Other software can run on the host and detect whether the network interface has entered promiscuous mode, which is necessary to facilitate sniffing activities.

10. *How do password-testing tools work?*

    Password-testing programs such as LC4, Crack, and John the Ripper can take a list of known passwords and try various case changes and the addition of nonalphanumeric characters. They then encrypt these passwords and compare them against the stored hashes in the password file. If they match, then the password has been "cracked."

Chapter 10

"Do I Know This Already?" Quiz

1. b, e
2. e
3. b
4. b
5. d, e
6. b
7. c
8. e
9. c
10. d
11. a, d
12. b, d

Q&A

1. *The flow of network management traffic that follows the same path as normal data is referred to as a(n) ___-band traffic flow.*

   In

2. *Of the three remote-access protocols discussed in this chapter, which is the least secure and why?*

Telnet. Data, including usernames and passwords, is sent in clear text.

3. *What is the primary goal of SAFE in reference to network management?*

The secure management of all devices and hosts within a network.

4. *Give the reason for using tunneling protocols with management protocols.*

The main reason for tunneling a management protocol is to secure a normally insecure protocol. An example would be the tunneling of TFTP data. Without tunneling, this data is sent in clear text and is vulnerable to various attacks.

Additionally, the remote management of a device that is outside of your management domain benefits from the use of a tunneling protocol such as IPSec.

5. *Out-of-band management normally uses a(n) _____ network for management traffic.*

Parallel

6. *Name two usage categories that network management protocols provide?*

Network management protocols provide the following usage categories:

- Remote access
- Reporting and logging
- Network monitoring and control
- File management
- Time synchronization

7. *A network administrator should always be aware of the level of _____ a management protocol provides.*

Security

8. *What ports does SNMP use and what is the function of each port?*

UDP 161—Agents listen on this port

UDP 162—Used for trap reporting to the manager

9. *SSH is a secure shell program and provides protection from _____, _____, and _____ attacks.*

DNS, IP spoofing, IP source-routing

10. *What public-key cryptosystem does SSL use during the initial exchange or handshake process?*

RSA

11. *What version of SNMP should you use if you want to ensure that SNMP traffic is encrypted?*

SNMP version 3

12. _____ *management protocols should always be used in preference to _____ protocols.*

Secure, insecure

13. *NTP version 3 supports cryptographic authentication between peers. Why is this useful?*

Without this authentication, it is possible for an attacker to send bogus NTP data and, hence, affect time-sensitive services such as digital certificates, which can lead to a potential DoS.

14. *SSH can use what ciphers?*

RC2, RC4, IDEA, DES, and 3DES.

15. *If you cannot secure management data for whatever reason, you should always be aware of the potential for what?*

Data interception and falsification

Chapter 11

"Do I Know This Already?" Quiz

1. **b, d**
2. **b, c**
3. **c, e**
4. **e**
5. **c**
6. **c, e**
7. **b**
8. **b, c**
9. **a, b, d**
10. **b, d**

11. d

12. b

Q&A

1. *Define IDS.*

   IDS is a system that monitors all inbound and outbound network activity on selected segments within a network and looks for predetermined patterns or signatures of traffic flow that may indicate a network or system attack from someone attempting to break into or compromise a system.

2. *What protocol do Cisco Secure IDS devices use to communicate with each other?*

   Post Office Protocol

3. *Traditionally, what devices provided perimeter security?*

   Firewalls

4. *What are the three types of responses that a sensor can perform in reply to an attack?*

   TCP reset

   IP blocking or shunning

   IP logging

5. *What are the perimeter security features provided by a Cisco router?*

   Control of TCP/IP services

   Extensive ACL functionality

   Network Address Translation

   IPSec support

6. *Define a perimeter.*

   A perimeter usually exists where a private network meets a public network. It can also be found internally in a private network where sensitive data may need to be protected from unauthorized access. However, more commonly, it is just thought of as the entry point into a network for connections that are not to be trusted.

7. *Network sensing, attack response, and device management are functions of what device?*

   Cisco Secure IDS sensor

8. *What is the Cisco Secure Scanner?*

   The Cisco Secure Scanner is a software application that offers a complete suite of network scanning tools and is designed to run on either the Windows or Solaris operating systems.

9. *Define stateful packet filtering.*

   Stateful packet filtering limits information into a network based not only on the destination and source address but also on the packet data content.

10. *Describe the two versions of Cisco Secure HIDS that are available.*

    Cisco Secure HIDS is available in the Standard Edition Agent and Server Edition Agent version.

    The Standard Edition Agent is for general host use and protects by evaluating requests to the operating system before they are processed.

    The Server Edition Agent protects as defined in the Standard Edition Agent but also protects the web server application and the web server API.

Chapter 12

"Do I Know This Already?" Quiz

1. c
2. a, c, d
3. b
4. d
5. a, d
6. b, c, e
7. b
8. a, e
9. a, c, d
10. d
11. a, d, e
12. b, d, e

13.   b, c, e

14.   b, c, d, e

Q&A

1.   *What does AVVID stand for?*

Architecture for Voice, Video, and Integrated Data

2.   *Which two authentication protocols does Cisco Secure ACS use?*

RADIUS

TACACS+

3.   *Currently, what models are available for the Cisco 3000 Series Concentrator?*

3005, 3015, 3030, 3060, and 3080

4.   *The Cisco _____ and the Cisco ___ Series routers are entry-level VPN-enabled routers.*

SOHO

800

5.   *What two operating modes are available to the Cisco VPN 3000 Hardware Client?*

Client mode

Network extension mode

6.   *What does AAA stand for?*

Authentication, authorization, and accounting

7.   *Cisco ___ and _____ are two security management solutions available from Cisco.*

VMS, CSPM

8.   *Name the principle building blocks of the AVVID design.*

Network infrastructure

Service control

Communications services

9.   *Identity management can be achieved by using what Cisco product?*

Cisco Secure Access Control Server

10. *What two types of VPNs are supported by the PIX Firewall?*

Site-to-site

Client-to-site

11. *The capability of a Cisco router to support VPN connectivity is determined by what?*

Cisco router VPN capability is determined by the version of Cisco IOS software it is running.

12. *What is the Cisco VPN 3000 Series Concentrator?*

The Cisco VPN 3000 Series Concentrator is a range of purpose-built, remote-access VPN devices that provide high performance, high availability, and scalability while utilizing the most advanced state-of-the-art encryption and authentication techniques that are currently available within the industry.

Chapter 13

"Do I Know This Already?" Quiz

1. **b, d**

2. **a, e**

3. **a**

4. **d**

5. **b**

6. **b, d**

7. **b, c, e**

8. **a**

9. **b, e**

Q&A

1. *What modules are found within the small network design?*

Corporate Internet module

Campus module

2. *Where are private VLANs used in the small network design?*

    On the public services segment

    Optionally within the Campus module

3. *What two security devices can be used in the Corporate Internet module to connect to the ISP module?*

    Firewall

    Cisco IOS Firewall router

4. *Where would you use intrusion detection in the small network design?*

    A HIDS is used on servers located on the public services segment and can also be used on corporate internal servers, if required.

    It is also possible to use a limited form of an NIDS with the PIX Firewall or Cisco IOS Firewall router.

5. *VPN functionality is provided by what devices in the small network design?*

    Firewall

    Cisco IOS Firewall router

    It is also possible to place a dedicated VPN device, such as the Cisco VPN 3000 Series Concentrator, if desired.

6. *The Corporate Internet module connects to which modules?*

    ISP module

    Campus module

7. *What are the two configuration types available in the small network design?*

    Headend or standalone configuration

    Branch configuration

8. *The Campus module provides functionality to what components?*

    Corporate servers

    Corporate users

    Management server

    Layer 2 switch

9. *Because no Layer 3 services are available in the Campus module, an increased emphasis is placed on _____ and ____ security.*

Application, host

10. *What is a common design deviation in the Corporate Internet module?*

To use dedicated devices to provide the functional components of the module rather than having the functionality in a single box.

11. *The Corporate Internet module provides what services?*

Internet, corporate public servers, VPN connectivity

Chapter 14

"Do I Know This Already?" Quiz

1. c

2. b, d, e

3. b

4. a, b, d, f

5. b

6. b

7. b, c, d, e, g

8. a

9. c

10. c

Q&A

1. *What is RFC 2827 filtering?*

RFC 2827 filtering ensures that any traffic with a source address that is not part of the organization's public address space is filtered out.

2. *What public services should be available to Internet users?*

It is normal practice to allow only those specific ports that are required for a service to function. All other access should be denied. Any attempt to gain access to other public services ports should be logged.

3. *What is the command to implement a Cisco IOS Firewall rule set to an interface?*

ip inspect *name* [**in** | **out**]

4. *What technique is used to perform rate limiting within the ISP router?*

Rate limiting of traffic in the ISP router can be achieved by the use of committed access rate (CAR) filtering. This technique flags traffic to be rate limited via an ACL. Matched traffic is then rate limited according to the parameters selected in the **rate-limit** command.

5. *How do you implement RFC 1918 filtering?*

To implement RFC 1918 filtering, the following filter rules are defined on an extended IP ACL, which is then applied to the appropriate interface:

access-list 140 deny ip 10.0.0.0 0.255.255.255 any

access-list 140 deny ip 172.16.0.0 0.15.255.255 any

access-list 140 deny ip 192.168.0.0 0.0.255.255 any

6. *How should traffic that is flowing from the internal network to the public services segment be restricted?*

Only the traffic that is specifically required to flow to the public services segment should be allowed. All other traffic should be explicitly denied.

7. *How are remote users affected in the small network when the small network is used in a branch configuration?*

Under this circumstance, all remote connectivity is normally provided via the corporate headquarters. Consequently, all related configuration for remote user connectivity is removed from the design.

8. *What commands are used to implement IDS services on the PIX Firewall in the small network design?*

ip audit name IDS info action alarm

ip audit name IDS attack action alarm drop reset

ip audit interface outside IDS

ip audit interface inside IDS

ip audit interface dmz IDS

9. *What is the importance of the* **isakmp key** *command?*

The **isakmp key** command defines the preshared key to be used by the specified peer in the command.

Chapter 15

"Do I Know This Already?" Quiz

1. b, d, e

2. b

3. a, c, e

4. b, c, d

5. b, e

6. b

7. a

8. b, e, g, h

9. b, c, d

10. b

11. c

12. a

Q&A

1. *What modules are found within the medium-sized network design?*

   Corporate Internet module

   Campus module

   WAN module

2. *At what locations in the medium-sized network design are private VLANs used?*

   On the public services segment

   Within the campus module

3. *What devices in a medium-sized network design provide VPN connectivity?*

   Firewall

   VPN concentrator

4. *Where would you use intrusion detection in the medium-sized network design?*

   HIDS is used on servers that are located on the public services segment and within the campus module on the corporate intranet and management servers.

A NIDS is used on both the public services and inside segments of the firewall. It is also used on the core switch of the campus module. Optionally, a NIDS can be used on the outside of the firewall.

5. *Traditional dial-in users are terminated in which module of the medium-sized network design?*

Corporate Internet module

6. *What type of filter is used to prevent IP spoofing attacks?*

RFC 2827 filtering mitigates IP spoofing attacks

7. *In the medium-sized network design, the ACS is located in which module?*

The ACS is located within the campus module

8. *What is facilitated by the use of a Layer 3 switch within the Campus module?*

Because multiple VLANs are used within the Campus module, a Layer 3 switch provides the functionality to route between each VLAN.

9. *What services does the Campus module provide?*

End-user workstations, corporate servers, management servers, Layer 2 services, and Layer 3 services

10. *In the SAFE medium-sized network design, what are the recommended IPSec policy parameters?*

Tunnel everything, use 3DES, and use SHA/HMAC

11. *What services does the Corporate Internet module provide?*

Internet, corporate public servers, VPN, and dial-in connectivity

Chapter 16

"Do I Know This Already?" Quiz

1. b, c, d

2. a, c

3. a, e

4. c

5. a, d

6. a

7. d

8. a, d, e

9. b

10. b

11. b, d

12. b

13. d

14. d

15. b, c, e

Q&A

1. *What are the four segments used on the PIX Firewall in the medium-sized network design?*

   Inside

   Outside

   Remote access

   Public services

2. *Name the main components within the medium-sized network design?*

   ISP router

   Edge router

   Cisco IOS Firewall router

   PIX Firewall

   NIDS

   HIDS

   VPN concentrator

   Layer 3 switch

3. *What mitigation is performed by the ISP router?*

   DDoS

   IP spoofing

4. *How can the Cisco IOS Firewall be used within the medium-sized network design?*

If required, a defense-in-depth approach can be adopted within the medium-sized network design. This alternative design incorporates the functionality of the Cisco IOS Firewall and the functionality of the edge router in a single device.

5. *How do you implement RFC 1918 filtering?*

To implement RFC 1918 filtering, the following filter rules are defined on an extended IP ACL. This ACL is then applied to the appropriate interface.

access-list 140 deny ip 10.0.0.0 0.255.255.255 any

access-list 140 deny ip 172.16.0.0 0.15.255.255 any

access-list 140 deny ip 192.168.0.0 0.0.255.255 any

6. *Where is a NIDS implemented in the medium-sized network design?*

A NIDS is deployed on the following segments:

Public services segment

PIX inside segment

Layer 3 switch

Optionally, PIX outside segment

7. *What functionality does the Layer 3 switch provide within the medium-sized network?*

VLAN segregation

Access filtering

8. *Where is RFC 1918 filtering performed within the medium-sized network?*

ISP router

Edge router

PIX Firewall—outside interface

Chapter 17

"Do I Know This Already?" Quiz

1. d

2. b, d

3. b, c, e

4. a, c

5. b, c, d

6. b

7. b

8. b

9. b

10. c

Q&A

1. *What workers are considered within the remote-user design model?*

   Mobile

   Home-office

2. *What are the four design options available within the remote-user design model?*

   Remote-site firewall

   Remote-site router

   VPN hardware client

   Cisco VPN Client

3. *What modes can the VPN hardware client operate in?*

   Client mode

   Network extension mode

4. *The Cisco VPN Client uses _____ and _____ types of authentication.*

   Group, user

5. *What are the additional benefits that the remote-site router provides compared to the remote-site firewall option?*

   Advance router functionality, such as QoS, and the capability to integrate the broadband access device into a single device.

6. *What type of filter is used to prevent IP spoofing attacks?*

   RFC 2827 filtering mitigates IP spoofing attacks.

7. *What happens to the security perimeter of an organization when it is using the remote-user design model?*

When using the remote-user design model, the security of an organization is extended to include the remote site.

8. *What is the difference between the VPN tunnel types: tunnel-everything and split-tunnel?*

Tunnel-everything—Only remote-site traffic that is specifically defined will traverse the VPN tunnel; all other traffic follows the appropriate routes.

Split-tunnel—All remote-site traffic, whatever the destination, traverses the VPN tunnel.

9. *How is the remote-site firewall design option remotely managed?*

Remote management of the firewall in the remote-site firewall option uses an IPSec VPN tunnel from the central site that terminates directly onto the firewall.

General Configuration Guidelines for Cisco Router and Switch Security

This appendix highlights general recommendations that should be adopted on all Cisco routers and switches to tighten the security of these devices.

Routers

The following steps outline the generic process for strengthening security on Cisco routers:

Step 1   Shut down all unneeded servers and services.

For small services (for example, Echo, discard, chargen), issue the following commands:

```
no service tcp-small-servers
no service udp-small-servers
```

For BOOTP, Finger, HTTP, DNS, Source Routing, and CDP, issue the following commands:

```
no ip boot server
no service finger
no ip http server
no ip domain-lookup
no ip source-route
no cdp run
```

Step 2   Secure passwords and access lines. Enable AAA and restrict access to the router.

Turn password encryption on and set passwords with the following commands:

```
service password-encryption
enable secret secret-password
no enable password
```

Generate RSA keys to enable SSH access as follows. This requires the router to support encryption.

```
crypto key generate rsa
```

Enable security on the console line by issuing the following commands:

```
line con 0
exec-timeout 5 0
login authentication default
```

Enable security on the auxiliary line by issuing the following commands:

```
line aux 0
no exec
transport input none
```

Enable security on the VTY lines by issuing the following commands:

```
line vty 0 4
access-class 10 in
login authentication default
password
exec-timeout 5 0
login
transport input ssh
```

Enable AAA by issuing the following commands:

```
aaa new-model
aaa authentication login default group tacacs+ local
aaa authorization exec default group tacacs+ local
aaa accounting exec default start-stop group tacacs+
tacacs-server host tacacs-server-address
tacacs-server key key
```

Use the following commands to apply an access list to the VTY lines to permit management host access:

```
access-list 10 permit host management-host-address
access-list 10 deny any log
```

Step 3   Turn on the router's logging and SNMP capability with the following:

```
service timestamp log datetime localtime msec
logging syslog-server-address
logging buffered
```

SNMP is enabled by issuing the following command:

```
snmp-server community community-string RO 20
```

Apply an ACL to SNMP to permit management host access by using the following commands:

```
access-list 20 permit management-host-address
access-list 20 deny any log
```

Step 4   Enable and secure NTP with the following:

```
ntp authenticate
ntp authentication-key 1 md5 ntp-key
ntp trusted-key 1
ntp access-group peer 30
ntp server ntp-server-address key 1
```

NTP access control is applied by the use of the following commands:

```
access-list 30 permit host ntp-server-address
access-list 30 deny any log
```

Step 5   Enable the use of a banner message:

```
banner motd #Banner-Message-Text

#
```

Example B-1 shows a typical banner message.

Example B-1 *Sample Banner Message*

```
banner-motd #
*************************************************************************
                            NOTICE TO USERS
This system is for the use of authorized users only.

All individuals using this system may have their use of the system
monitored and recorded (including all information which they reveal
during such use) to allow the detection of unauthorised use of the
system.

If monitoring reveals evidence of unauthorized use of the system, all
records obtained from monitoring may be passed to the relevant law
enforcement authorities and used in internal investigations.

Anyone accessing this system expressly consents to such monitoring,
recording, and disclosure taking place.
#
```

NOTE   The configuration used in the Cisco IOS switches is nearly identical to that used by Cisco routers.

CatOS Switches

The generic security configuration used within Cisco CatOS switches is described in the following steps:

Step 1   Shut down all unneeded services by issuing the following commands:

```
set ip http server disable
set cdp disable
```

Step 2   Set passwords and access restrictions. Enable AAA.

To set passwords, use the following:

```
set password
set enable
```

Set access restrictions with the following commands:

```
set ip permit enable telnet
set ip permit management-host-address 255.255.255.255 telnet
```

Enable AAA with the following:

```
set tacacs server tacacs-server-address
set tacacs key key
set authentication login local enable
set authentication login tacacs enable
set authorization exec enable tacacs+ none both
aaa authorization exec default group tacacs+ local
aaa accounting exec enable start-stop tacacs+
```

Step 3   Turn on logging and SNMP capability.

To enable Syslog, use the following commands:

```
set logging syslog_server_address
set logging timestamp enable
```

To enable SNMP, use the following commands:

```
set snmp community read-only community-string
set ip permit enable snmp
set ip permit management-host-address snmp
```

Step 4   Enable and secure NTP with these commands:

```
set ntp authentication enable
set ntp key 1 trusted md5 ntp-key
set ntp trusted-key 1
set ntp server ntp-server-address key 1
set ntp client enable
```

Step 5   Enable the use of a banner message with the following:

```
set banner motd #

Banner Message Text

#
```

Refer to Example B-1 to see a typical banner text message.

NOTE   Remember that the commands and configurations that are shown in this appendix are just examples of the generic hardening of security on Cisco routers and switches and by no means define the limits to which these devices can be secured. Other best practices such as RFC 1918 and RFC 2827 filtering should also be adopted as well as those detailed in the various SAFE white papers, which you can review at Cisco.com by searching for "SAFE."

GLOSSARY AND ABBREVIATIONS

3DES   Triple DES. *See* DES.

AAA   Authentication, authorization, and accounting (pronounced "triple a").

ACK   Acknowledgement bit in a TCP frame.

ACL   Access control list. A set of data associated with a file, directory, or other resource that defines the access permissions for users, groups, processes, or devices.

ACS   Access Control Server.

APNIC   Asia Pacific Network Information Center. A nonprofit Internet registry organization for the Asia Pacific region.

application hardening   Staying current on patches for applications and reducing information the applications provide through service banners.

ARIN   American Registry for Internet Numbers. A nonprofit organization that dispenses IP addresses in North and South America, the Caribbean, and sub-Saharan Africa.

ATM   Asynchronous Transfer Mode. A network technology for both LANs and WANs that supports real-time voice and video as well as data.

authentication   Process by which a user or administrator demonstrates knowledge of possession of an item that verifies their identity to a system.

authorization   Process by which a user or administrator demonstrates that they have the authority to execute an action on a device.

BCP   Best common practices.

BIND   Berkeley Internet Name Domain. The most commonly used DNS software.

BPDU Bridge protocol data unit. A Spanning Tree Protocol (STP) message unit that describes the attributes of a switch port, such as its MAC address, priority, and cost to reach.

buffer overflow An application layer attack made possible by the improper bounds checking of input data in a program. By sending properly crafted data to the program, the attacker redirects the program to execute code of the attacker's choice.

Campus module One of the SAFE modules; provides end-user workstations, corporate intranet servers, management servers, and the associated Layer 2 functionality.

CCDA Cisco Certified Design Associate.

CCDP Cisco Certified Design Professional.

CCIE Cisco Certified Internetwork Expert.

CCIP Cisco Certified Internetwork Professional.

CCNA Cisco Certified Network Associate.

CCNP Cisco Certified Network Professional.

CCSP Cisco Certified Security Professional.

CDP Cisco Discovery Protocol. Media- and protocol-independent device-discovery protocol that runs on all Cisco-manufactured equipment, including routers, access servers, bridges, and switches.

CERT Computer Emergency Response Team. A group of people in a specific organization who coordinate their responses to breaches of security or other computer emergencies, such as breakdowns and disasters.

CHAP Challenge Handshake Authentication Protocol. An access control protocol that dynamically encrypts the user's ID and password.

CIA Confidentiality, integrity, and availability. In the field of information security, describes the desired characteristics of protected data.

CIM *See* Corporate Internet module.

cipher text Data that has been coded (enciphered, encrypted, encoded) for security purposes.

Cisco AVVID Architecture for Voice, Video, and Integrated Data.

Cisco IOS Firewall   A software option available for most Cisco routers that provides a stateful packet-filter firewall.

Cisco Secure ACS   A complete access control server that supports the industry-standard RADIUS protocol and the Cisco-proprietary TACACS+ protocol.

Cisco VMS   CiscoWorks VPN/Security Management Solution. An integrated security management solution that is part of the SAFE blueprint for network security. VMS enables customers to deploy security infrastructures from small networks to large, complex, and widely distributed environments.

Cisco VPN 3000 Series Concentrator   A purpose-built, remote-access VPN device.

clear text   Normal text that has not been encrypted and is readable by text editors and word processors.

CLI   Command-line interface.

client mode   Mode in which all users behind the hardware client appear as a single user on the corporate intranet through the use of Network Address Translation (NAT) overload or what is also commonly called Port Address Translation (PAT).

CM   *See* Campus module.

Corporate Internet module   One of the SAFE modules; provides connectivity to the Internet and terminates any VPN connectivity. Traffic for public services, such as e-mail, web, file transfer, and name lookups, is also terminated at the Corporate Internet module.

CSI   Cisco SAFE Implementation.

CSID   Cisco Secure IDS Director.

CSPM   Cisco Secure Policy Manager. A centralized, scalable, comprehensive security policy management application for the Cisco Secure security portfolio.

DDoS   Distributed denial of service. Attacks directed against a host or network where the intent is to deny access to the host or network by consuming all of the bandwidth available to the host. This attack typically involves a large number of attacking hosts controlled by one or more attackers. *See also* DoS.

DES   Data Encryption Standard. The U.S. National Bureau of Standards secret key cryptography method that uses a 56-bit key.

DHCP   Dynamic Host Configuration Protocol. Software that automatically assigns IP addresses to client stations logging on to a TCP/IP network.

DMZ   Demilitarized zone. A middle ground between an organization's trusted internal network and an untrusted, external network such as the Internet.

DNS   Domain Name System. Name resolution software that lets users locate computers on a TCP/IP network by domain name.

DoS   Denial of service. An assault on a network that floods it with so many additional requests that regular traffic is either slowed or completely interrupted. This attack typically has a single point of origin.

DSL   Digital subscriber line. A technology that dramatically increases the digital capacity of ordinary telephone lines (the local loops) into the home or office.

egress   Means "exit."

EXEC   A phrase that is commonly used to refer to the interactive command processor of Cisco IOS.

Extranet   A website for customers rather than the general public.

firewall   A device used for implementing security policies that are designed to keep a network secure from intruders.

FTP   File Transfer Protocol. A protocol used to transfer files over a TCP/IP network.

FWSM   Firewall Services Module.

HIDS   Host-based intrusion detection system. *See* IDS.

HTTP   Hypertext Transfer Protocol. The protocol used by web browsers and web servers to transfer files, such as text and graphic files.

HTTPS   Hypertext Transfer Protocol Secure. The protocol used to access a secure web server. Using https in the URL instead of http directs the message to a secure port number rather than the default web port number of 80. The session is then managed by a security protocol.

IB   In-band.

ICMP   Internet Control Message Protocol. A TCP/IP protocol used to send error and control messages.

IDEA   International Data Encryption Algorithm. A secret key cryptography method that uses a 128-bit key.

IDS   Intrusion detection system. Software that detects illegal entrance to a computer system.

IDS sensor   Monitors network traffic constantly in real time while looking for distinctive attack patterns in the traffic flow.

IEEE   Institute of Electrical and Electronic Engineers.

IETF   Internet Engineering Task Force. A nonmembership, open, voluntary standards organization dedicated to identifying problems and opportunities in IP data networks and proposing technical solutions to the Internet community.

IIS   Internet Information Services. Microsoft's web server. Runs under the server versions of Windows NT and Windows 2000, adding full HTTP capability to the Windows operating system.

IKE   Internet Key Exchange. A method for establishing a security association (SA) that authenticates users, negotiates the encryption method, and exchanges the secret key.

in-band network management   Refers to the flow of management traffic that follows the same path as normal network data. *See also* out-of-band network management.

ingress   Means "entrance."

Internet   Network of computers in more than 100 countries that covers commercial, academic, and government endeavours.

intranet   An in-house website that serves the employees of the enterprise.

IOS   Cisco operating system software that is the primary control program used in its routers.

IP   Internet Protocol. The network layer protocol in the TCP/IP communications protocol suite.

IP address spoofing   An attacker inserts the IP address of an authorized user into the transmission of an unauthorized user to gain illegal access to a computer system.

IPSec   IP Security. A security protocol from the IETF that provides authentication and encryption over the Internet.

IPT   IP Telephony.

ISP   Internet service provider.

L2   Layer 2.

L2TP   Layer 2 Tunneling Protocol. A protocol from the IETF that allows a PPP session to run over the Internet or an ATM or Frame Relay network.

Layer 2   The communications layer that contains the physical address of a client or server station.

Layer 3   The communications layer that contains the logical address of a client or server station.

LDAP   Lightweight Directory Access Protocol. A protocol used to access a directory listing.

MAC   Media Access Control. The unique serial number burned into Ethernet and Token Ring adapters that identifies that network card from all others.

man-in-the-middle attack   An attacker intercepts data packets crossing a network, modifies or falsifies the information in those packets, and reinjects the packets into the network without being detected.

MTA   Mail transport agent.

NAS   Network access server. Hardware or software that functions as a junction point between an external and internal network.

NAT   Network Address Translation. An IETF standard that allows an organization to present itself to the Internet with far fewer IP addresses than there are nodes on its internal network.

NetBIOS   The native networking protocol in DOS and Windows networks.

network extension mode   A mode in which all devices access the corporate intranet as if they were directly connected, and hosts in the intranet may initiate connections to the hosts behind the hardware client once a tunnel is established.

network management   A generic term used to describe the execution of the set of functions that help to maintain, monitor, and troubleshoot the resources of a network.

NIDS   Network intrusion detection system. *See* IDS.

NTP   Network Time Protocol. A protocol used to synchronize the real-time clock in a computer.

OBB   Out-of-band.

OSPF   Open Shortest Path First. A routing protocol that determines the best path for routing IP traffic over a TCP/IP network based on distance between nodes and several quality parameters.

OTP One-time password. A password that is generated for use one time only. Once the password has been used, the system will authenticate a user using that same password again.

out-of-band network management Refers to the flow of management traffic that does not follow the same path as normal network data.

packet sniffer Software application that uses a network adapter card in promiscuous mode to receive all packets on the physical network wire and pass those packets up to an application.

password attack Attempt to determine the valid password to an account on a system and use it to gain access to that system.

PAT Port Address Translation. *See* NAT.

perimeter router The router that provides the first line of defense to an untrusted network.

perimeter security The security policy and devices used at the edge of a network to protect the internal network. The firewall is a typical example of a perimeter security device.

PIX Packet Internet Exchange.

POP Point of presence.

POP3 Post Office Protocol version 3. A standard mail server commonly used on the Internet.

port redirection An attack used to redirect traffic from a port on one host to another port, not necessarily on the same host.

PPTP Point-to-Point Tunnelling Protocol. A protocol from Microsoft that is used to create a VPN over the Internet.

proxy server An application that breaks the connection between sender and receiver; also called a "proxy" or "application level gateway."

PSTN Public Switched Telephone Network. The global voice telephone network.

public services segment A network segment, usually the DMZ, where the Internet services servers are located.

QoS Quality of service. The ability to define a level of performance in a data communications system.

RADIUS   Remote Authentication Dial-In User Service. An access control protocol that uses a challenge/response method for authentication.

RCP   Remote Copy Protocol. A protocol that allows users to copy files to and from a file system residing on a remote host or server.

reconnaissance attack   The act of gathering information about a network in preparation for a possible attack.

RFC   Request for Comments. A document that describes the specifications for a recommended technology. RFCs are used by the IETF and other standards bodies.

RFC 1918   Describes address allocation for private internetworks. Describes the use of certain IP address ranges for private networks.

RFC 2827   Describes network ingress filtering to mitigate denial of service attacks that employ IP address spoofing.

RIP   Routing Information Protocol. A simple routing protocol that is part of the TCP/IP protocol suite.

RIPE   Réseaux IP Europénnes. Group formed to coordinate and promote TCP/IP-based networks in Europe.

risk assessment   A method used to quantify the level of risk inherent in a system.

rlogin   Remote LOGIN. A UNIX command that allows users to remotely log on to a server in the network as if they were at a terminal directly connected to that computer.

router   A device that forwards data packets from one LAN or WAN to another.

RSA   Rivest-Shamir-Adleman. A highly secure cryptography method by RSA Data Security, Inc. It uses a two-part key. The private key is kept by the owner; the public key is published.

RSH   Remote Shell. A UNIX command that enables a user to remotely log on to a server on the network and pass commands to it.

SAFE   The Cisco best-practice design blueprints for securing networks. The CSI exam focuses on the SAFE SMR blueprint.

SAFE module   A module within the SAFE design concept that describes a functional component of a network and its associated devices. The SAFE SMR blueprint includes the Corporate Internet module, the Campus module, and the WAN module.

script kiddie   An amateur that tries to illegally intrude into a system but takes the path of least resistance.

security policy   A framework definition that is used to protect the assets connected to a network.

security threat   Any action or actions against a network that are not authorized or that are in defiance of the security policy.

Security Wheel   A concept where network security is treated as a *continuous* process built around the corporate security policy.

SMB   Small and medium business.

SMR   Small, midsize, and remote-user.

SMTP   Simple Mail Transfer Protocol. The standard e-mail protocol used on the Internet.

SNMP   Simple Network Management Protocol. A widely used network monitoring and control protocol.

split-tunnel   A VPN tunnel that allows only remote-site traffic that is specifically defined to traverse it; all other traffic follows the appropriate routes.

SQL   Structured Query Language. Pronounced "SQL" or "see qwill," a language used to interrogate and process data in a relational database.

SSH   Secure Shell. Provides secure logon for Windows and UNIX clients and servers. SSH replaces Telnet, FTP, and other remote-logon utilities with an encrypted alternative.

SSL   Secure Sockets Layer. The leading security protocol on the Internet. When an SSL session is started, the server sends its public key to the browser. The browser uses this public key to send a randomly generated secret key back to the server in order to have a secret key exchange for that session.

string attack   A type of attack where an attacker relies on an improper bounds check in the format of a string to be printed by the program thus permitting the execution of arbitrary code.

syslog   System Log protocol. A transport mechanism for sending event messages across an IP network.

TACACS+   Terminal Access Controller Access Control System Plus. An access control protocol that is used to authenticate a user who is logging on to the network.

TCP   Transmission Control Protocol. The TCP part of TCP/IP.

TCP SYN   The first packet in the three-way handshake that occurs when establishing a TCP connection between two hosts. Can also be used in a DoS attack by exhausting the resources on the target host.

TCP/IP   Transmission Control Protocol/Internet Protocol. A communications protocol developed under contract from the U.S. Department of Defence to internetwork dissimilar systems.

Telnet   A terminal-emulation protocol that is commonly used on the Internet and TCP/IP-based networks.

TFN   Tribe Flood Network.

TFTP   Trivial File Transfer Protocol. A version of the TCP/IP FTP protocol that has no directory or password capability.

TLS   Transport Layer Security. A security protocol from the IETF that is a merger of SSL and other protocols.

traffic-rate limiting   A filtering technique used to limit the rate of predefined traffic on a link.

Trojan horse   A program that appears to be a normal application but, when executed, conducts covert actions on behalf of an attacker.

UDP   User Datagram Protocol. A protocol within the TCP/IP protocol suite that is used in place of TCP when a reliable delivery is not required.

URL   Uniform Resource Locator. The address that defines the route to a file on the web or any other Internet facility.

virus   Small piece of mobile code that attaches to other programs or documents and can infect a user's computer when the program is executed or the document is opened.

VLAN   Virtual LAN. A logical subgroup within a LAN that is created via software rather than manually moving cables in the wiring closet.

VMS   VPN/Security Management Solution.

VoIP   Voice over IP.

VPN   Virtual Private Network. A private network that is configured within a public network to take advantage of the economies of scale and management facilities of large networks.

VPN Hardware Client   Cisco VPN 3002 hardware client that is part of the Cisco VPN 3000 concentrator series of products and combines the ease of use and high-scalability features of the software client while providing the reliability and stability of a hardware platform.

VPN Software Client   Cisco VPN software client that establishes secure, end-to-end encrypted (IPSec) tunnels to any Cisco VPN gateways or concentrators from a wide range of operating systems, including Microsoft Windows, Linux, and Solaris.

VPN-enabled router   A Cisco VPN router that is running a version of Cisco IOS software that provides IPSec VPN capability.

VTP   VLAN Trunking Protocol.

WAN module   A SAFE module that provides WAN functionality.

WLAN   Wireless LAN.

X.25   The first international standard packet-switching network developed in the early 1970s.

Index

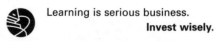